You Will Never Die

By

Irvin Mordes

This book is a work of non-fiction. Names and places have been changed to protect the privacy of all individuals. The events and situations are true.

ISBN: 1-4107-6614-4 (e-book)
ISBN: 1-4107-6613-6 (Paperback)

This book is printed on acid free paper.

1stBooks - rev. 11/12/03

Acknowledgement

I am deeply indebted to my daughter Barbara Ross, who in addition to reviewing this book and assisting me in the necessary changes encouraged me over the years to write the stories, since she was a witness to many of the happenings that took place.

Close to home, I wish to thank Adele Wurzberg, my magnificent other, who was always there for me, and who ably assisted me in correcting my grammar and punctuation. She gave me the tremendous support that I needed to complete my book.

I wish to thank my brother Herman Mordes and my niece, Marilyn Mordes, for their valuable advice and who finally pushed me into finishing the manuscript and having it published.

Many thanks to Cindy Serlo and the continuous assistance she gave me in helping to prepare the manuscript meticulously for publication.

A special thanks to Stanley Goldberg, for introducing me to the field of metaphysics and spiritualism.

I am grateful to Karen Mott for her assistance in typing the first draft of my book, and to all my friends and relatives who gave of their time to examine the book and offer their honest opinion, I say with deep sincerity, thank you.

Irvin Mordes

Table of Contents

PART I 1

CHAPTER 1 3

THE INCARNATION OF LEO VINCEY 3

CHAPTER 2 10

WHAT IS REINCARNATION? 10

CHAPTER 3 17

THE STORY OF HARRY KANTROFF 17

CHAPTER 4 30

THE LIFE OF A.G. 30

CHAPTER 5 60

INTRODUCTION TO ALVIN LEARY AND RUDOLPH
VALENTINO 60

CHAPTER 6 73

HIGHLIGHTS OF ALVIN LEARY 73

CHAPTER 7 82

THE CHILDHOOD YEARS OF PHARAOH KALLIKRATES 82

CHAPTER 8 98

ADOLESCENT PERIOD OF PHARAOH KALLIKRATES 98

CHAPTER 9 111

ADULT PERIOD OF PHARAOH KALLIKRATES 111

CHAPTER 10 124

LIFETIME OF NORAN FROM OUTER SPACE 124

CHAPTER 11 130

LIFE OF GUILLAUME, DUKE OF NORMANDY AND ALSO
ADONNA FROM ATLANTIS 130

CHAPTER 12 134

THE LIFE OF JOSEPHUS AND HIS CONNECTION WITH JESUS
.... 134

CHAPTER 13 146

WRITINGS OF ALVIN LEARY 146

PART II **171**

ABBREVIATIONS OF THE PEOPLE WHO SPOKE TO EILEEN
GARRETT AND JAMES AT THE MONTHLY RESEARCH
SESSIONS 172

5/95 174

INTRODUCTION TO EILEEN, JAMES, AND MARLENE 174

11/95 186

CROSSING TO THE "OTHER SIDE" AND QUESTIONS ON
REINCARNATION 186

2/96 204

THE PURPOSE OF LIFE 204

6/96 253

EILEEN TALKS ABOUT HERSELF 253

7/96 282

THE PHYSICAL LIFE OF EILEEN AND JAMES AS TOLD FROM THE "OTHER SIDE" 282

9/96 306

MARLENE STEWART TALKS ABOUT EILEEN GARRETT ... 306

11/96 343

EILEEN GARRETT AND JAMES 343

(MARLENE SLIPS INTO TRANCE AND JAMES COMES IN) . 343

12/96 362

CONTACT WITH MY DECEASED GIRL FRIEND AND A PICTURE OF THE FUTURE 362

EPILOGUE 383

About the Author 385

PROLOGUE

I put these facts down, because I feel it is important to document these most amazing events that have unfolded before my eyes and ears over the years. As a hypnotherapist, I have been witness to many events, demonstrations and revelations, evoked and experienced, often unexpectedly, by clients during hypnotic regression sessions; often strange and unusual events which are not easily reconciled. It is my desire that these events be judged on their own merit by an impartial audience. Frankly, I became profoundly affected by the experiences of my clients and eventually became a believer in the extraordinary phenomena with which I so intimately have become involved. As a hypnotherapist, in a career spanning approximately four decades, I have dealt with many clients infused with a sense of having lived before, of having lived somewhere else long ago, of having been, very specifically, another person - in short - *the mystery of reincarnation.*

Through the procedure of hypnotic regression, many of my clients were able to travel back through time and experienced their 'previous lives'. These events I share with the reader. This intimate and exciting whirlwind of revelations that occurred over my long and exciting career is the story I will tell. You be the judge.

INTRODUCTION

Have you ever visited a strange place and had a strong feeling that you have been there before? Have you ever met someone - knew exactly what they were going to say - and felt that you have known them your entire life? Are you inexplicably drawn to other times and other places? Have you ever had a dream that repeated itself over and over and yet did not make sense to you? If so, you may have lived in prior times and different areas or regions. Are these memories of previous lives? Therefore, if proof can be found that this is true, the probability is that we will be born again and that life as we know it can never die. There are many people who believe that we do. This is known as reincarnation or the rebirth of the soul. Half the world believes in reincarnation.

If the idea of such a possibility intrigues your imagination, you are not alone. The theory of multiple lifetimes isn't a novel one. Belief in reincarnation or transmigration of the soul, originated with primitive man. Some of the most intelligent and respected minds throughout man's long history have thought it a more acceptable explanation of life's purpose than any other doctrine.

In his book, COMING BACK, Dr. Raymond A. Moody, Jr., mentions the fact that past life regression brings on a sense of nostalgia in many regresses, as the problems from a previous life is connected to the present life. Regressees ask themselves questions as to whether they lived well in these previous lives. Were they healthy, rich, poor or someone famous? The experience of past life regression in many regressees brings on a feeling of peace and self-understanding.

FOREWORD

By

Ormond McGill, World Famous Hypnotist

Afraid of death and dying lies at the roots of humanities greatest fears. This book removes that fear for it testifies objectively to your immortality. You will never die, for you are a trinity of body, mind, and spirit. Your body can die for it is a mechanism, and mechanisms can wear out . . ., but your soul continues on and on and on dwelling in new bodies lifetime after lifetime after lifetime. And each new body in which one dwells in space and time affords adventures and opportunity to advance into ever-higher realms of consciousness. Most learn slowly and take many lifetimes, but it can happen in a Quantum Leap.

Believe it or not.

Irvin Mordes is an internationally acclaimed hypnotherapist who has spent many years investigating past-life regression hypnotherapy. The method of probing past memories and surfacing them has benefited many people. Many such memories buried in the subconscious and revealed via hypnosis tell of experiences in past lifetimes (often traumatic), which affect the client's current lifetime. A careful consideration of these ancient memories has proved excellent hypnotherapy. But are these memories fact or fantasy? Many hypnotherapists are quite content not to be concerned about this, as long as the method proved helpful to clients. But Irvin Mordes cared, and he wanted objective evidence one way or the other. He found objective evidence that such memories tucked away in the subconscious are not fantasy but are facts, when a client named Alvin Leary came into his life.

Alvin Leary is a Caucasian male born May 4, 1942. While regressed to past lifetimes, under the direction of Irvin Mordes, the man not only had past life memories, but also was able to speak and write in the language of past times, many of which were from foreign lands of which Alvin had no conscious knowledge.

The history of this man is that he never completed his schooling beyond the tenth grade, and never had any learning of languages other than English. This adds to the validity of this case, since half of the languages he wrote and spoke are languages that have not been taught for centuries. While in profound hypnosis the subject spoke in English, and the dates, people, places, etc. mentioned were checked for accuracy.

While regressed to his past lives, in the hypnotic state, the subject was able to write and speak fluently in current English, rural English, ancient English, Italian, Cherokee Indian (Tehalagic), Norman French, Idiomatic Latin, Classical Greek, Hebrew, Egyptian Hieroglyphic, Egyptian Demotic, Egyptian Hieratic, and the unknown languages of Atlantean, Lemurean, Godean and Urian.

The remarkable remembering talents of the past lives of Alvin Leary was a revelation to Irvin Mordes, and he has told of this remarkable client of hypnotic regression many times, in lectures and on radio and television. I met Irv at a hypnotherapy conference in Glendale some years back, and he told me of the case of Alvin Leary. He gave me copies of Alvin's writing during various past lifetimes, material I subsequently presented to The National Guild of Hypnotists and they published it in a booklet.

In his latest book, YOU WILL NEVER DIE, Irvin Mordes continues the further telling of past-life adventures of Alvin Leary along with fascinating details of life-beyond-death. Thrilling wonders await you.

Ormond McGill
Palo Alto, Ca.
U.S.A. 2001

The names of all living individuals have been changed to protect them from invasion of privacy.

PART I

PAST LIFE REGRESSIONS

"For if there is a sin against life, it consists perhaps not so much in despairing of life, as in hoping for another life - and eluding the implacable grandeur of this one."

Anonymous

1

CHAPTER 1

THE INCARNATION OF LEO VINCEY

I rid myself of my doubts by remembering that there is a valid reason for everything that happens. - Anonymous

It was 1971. In the center of the room, a tall man, twenty-seven and well muscled, was lying on a blue carpet, eyes closed, breathing slowly, and totally relaxed. In the near silence, a group of thirty people stared transfixed, waiting for the barest sign of ...something. Many scientists had come to verify for themselves the unusual stories that were being reported from various sources. Even the esteemed Metaphysical Research Society (Created to investigate reincarnation) had sent several of its members over to give the eyewitness confirmation to the extraordinary reports that were circulating about displays of true past regressions.

Alvin Leary, the young man on the floor, had seemed so relaxed and easy-going in the moments before we had begun tonight's session, even among a room full of strangers. It didn't seem to bother him at all. He could come out of a trance having just been a pharaoh of Egypt shouting commands to his soldiers, and upon awakening seemed unaffected by it all. Whereas, everyone else who had witnessed his transformation into Kallikrates, The Young Prince, was shaken to the core by this petulant tyrannical Egyptian ruler.

3

Alvin's breathing was heavy, and everything seemed to be going along in an orderly fashion. Soon, if all continued as normal, I knew his breathing would change abruptly and he would begin the soft steady breathing that would signal he was about to enter one of his past lives. Even after many years of regressing Alvin, I still never knew fully what to expect once he entered into one of his previous lives. During the first year of research, I had seen him display at least sixteen different former lives, but I never knew which one might appear during any specific regression.

I sincerely hoped I would not be seeing Kallikrates during this session. There was just too much riding on this particular evening, and the Pharaoh Kallikrates had many times proven too difficult to control. There was that one time he had commanded all of the women in the audience to become his slaves. And I was certainly stunned that first time, when he appeared as the boy pharaoh, shouting in some unknown tongue and demanding that I kneel by pointing his fingers towards the floor. When I tried to verbally respond to his commands he would angrily scream the word "thais." Later on, in my research about that era of Egyptian rule, I discovered that the word "thais" meant "Shut up." Oh, please don't let it be Kallikrates tonight! Although, I should add, after sometime, the young pharaoh had indeed accepted me, as his trusted servant, Nagado, his head minister, or as he called it, his "vizier."

Alvin was still breathing heavily. The onlookers were all seated, leaning forward in anticipation. I was happy to see my friend, Joe McNeil, (name changed for protection of privacy) in the crowd. He was a journalist with a major newspaper. I had met Joe at a lecture on reincarnation the year before. Joe, at that time, was a die-hard skeptic. If anything, his attendance at a past life regression was for the sole purpose of debunking such tales in his newspaper column. I was never averse to having any and all types of people involved in our research, and, I especially welcomed those that were smart and inquisitive. I have always tried to remain open to all questions. I wanted answers too. In time, Joe began to recognize the objective evidence of reincarnation. He was now one of my most ardent supporters. He looked over at me from across the room, and sensing my concern at Alvin's unresponsiveness, he gave me a big thumbs up.

I renewed my efforts and deepened the progressive relaxation of Alvin. "Deeper and deeper, going way, way down, deeper and deeper into hypnosis: limp and slack, totally relaxed." Suddenly, Alvin's lips began to quiver. Very fast. Then after a few seconds, the quivering stopped as he slipped into a profound hypnosis. His breathing now was slow and easy, and I knew that he had finally entered the theta stage of somnambulism. The regular investigators knew that this was the prelude to the moment of change.

I was never sure how I knew, but I could always tell when Alvin slipped away and another "being" was there. "What is your name?" that was my usual way of approaching this new phase. The answer came quickly "Leo." Ah, Leo. I relaxed a little. Leo was one of Alvin's most congenial incarnations, a simple man, born in Southampton, England. I was in the habit of documenting and taping every session, so I had acquired the knack of placing a microphone up close near the mouth of the subject without disturbing the hypnotic regression. During the week, I could thus review previous sessions.

I now asked a few basic questions of Leo in order to familiarize newcomers in our group with Leo's particulars. He gave his full name, "Leo Vincey," but his British accent was so thick that many of the onlookers came off their seats and crept closer. I asked, as I sometimes did, "Leo, what year is it today?" "It is 1780, in the Year of Our Lord." I continued with the simple routine I had established over the years. "When were you born, Leo?" "I was born in Southampton, May 10, 1761, in the Year of Our Lord." Leo was a pious man. "What is your mother's name?" I asked. Leo answered, "Dorothea Vincey. She died in childbirth, giving birth to me." "What is your father's name, and where is he buried?" "Charles Vincey, he died when I was six years of age. He is buried in the churchyard of the Holy Rood on the East Side of High Street next to my mother." It was curious to watch. Leo was so engaging, and spoke in a soft and gentle voice yet in a fast and clipped manner. I could almost forget that in actuality I was leaning over the closed eyes of Alvin's perfectly still body.

There was a pause as Leo grew quiet and I looked around quickly at the attendees to gauge each person's reactions. No one was moving. Everyone was concentrating on Leo.

I continued, "Leo, who has taken care of you since your father's death?" Proudly he answered, "Uncle Holly, of course! He is not my blood uncle, you know, but rather my legal guardian." After a few more exchanges, I felt confident enough to bring the audience into the interrogation. There were several reporters present. Many had been following Alvin's regressions and had prepared a barrage of questions. It was often this way, and I allowed full rein. Many of the questions were of obscure particulars, questions that might reveal some specific geographical or historical detail about that given time period. Leo's answers would provide background information that could subsequently be researched and verified.

For example, on this particular Friday evening, one of the returning journalists, who was always rather negative (although he had consistently attended the sessions off and on) asked, "Leo, are the streets lighted near where you live?" Leo responded, "Yes, they are illuminated." Everyone smiled. I interjected, "No, Leo, he means do you know what substance is used to light the streets?" "Oh, I think petroleum." One of the female attendees then spoke up, "Leo; do you ever go out to a tavern?" "I don't drink, but Uncle Holly prefers ale so I sometimes go with him to a public house, the King of George or The Vine." The woman moved closer getting more intimate with the subject. "Leo, do you sing in a church choir?" "Yes, at the Holy Rood Church." "What is your favorite hymn?" Leo looked perplexed and said he didn't really know.

Now Harry, a skeptic among the attending journalists, went on an attack. Harry, who documented everything, had written in his notes from a previous regression that Leo had clearly stated that he attended All Saints Church. Harry, getting excited that he had, at last, caught the subject in a blatant contradiction, jumped forward and heatedly asked, "Leo, can you tell me the name of the pastor of the All Saints Church?" "No, I am not familiar with him." Harry turned to me and said, "Irv, Leo clearly said last May that he was a parishioner at All Saints Church, and at the time, had given his pastor's name." Harry announced this fact as though it were a triumphant disproof of the validity of Leo from a past life. Calmly, I checked my notes and noticed that in the May session with Alvin, Leo had emerged in the year 1783.

Thinking about it, I now took control and led Alvin into a deeper hypnotic state. Still speaking directly to Leo, I said, "Leo, you have the power to move forward in time! I want you now to move forward.

7

Forward to the year 1783!" I waited a moment. "Leo, where are you now?" "I am at my tailor's shop on Coventry Street." "What is the name of your tailor?" "His name is Harry Twinny." "Leo, what year is it?" "The year, why it is 1783, in the Year of Our Lord." Not waiting, Harry quickly confronted Leo, "Leo what is the name of your pastor?" "My pastor's name is the Reverent James Frye." "What church?" Harry demanded. "Why All Saints Church, of course." Well, this really confounded Harry. "Leo, I interjected, have you always gone to this church?" "Why no, I have just recently begun to come to the Reverend Frye's sermons. The pastor at my old church, Holy Rood, passed away last year, may his soul rest in peace, and I don't much fancy the new pastor."

At this information, sighs went through the crowd breaking the tension. I could tell that most of the sighs were sighs of acceptance. As I was about to continue the questioning of Leo, a terrible change came over him. During the interrogation he had been calm and placid, but now his face grew red. He was having trouble breathing. His neck muscles tensed and his stomach began to roll. I had seen this reaction before, once when Leo had come through in the year 1788. He seemed at that time to be running from something. A man on the floor, unmoving, yet running for his life.

Out of the corner of my eye, I saw two visiting medical doctors get ready to spring into action! Leo must have jumped up to the year 1788 on his own. Immediately, I took control. "Alvin, you are now coming forward to the present! Forward! Come forward to current space and time. All organs returning too normal. Your mind is clear and normal. On the count of three you will awaken refreshed and relaxed in mind, body, and spirit. One-two-three! Wake up Alvin." Alvin opened his eyes, very relaxed. He had no remembrance of what had just taken place. He asked me for a glass of water. The onlookers were a bit shaken, but mostly amazed at what they had just witnessed.

In the following weeks, there was a great deal of communication within the community about our hypnotic regressions. Statements were verified. Alvin began writing in hieroglyphics. People were excited and word was getting out to the media. There were more requests for interviews. The past life regressions were being written up in newspapers, local and national. Radio hosts wanted me for on-the air interviews. I was requested to give more lectures. I was busy. Plus, my business at the Hypnosis Center had increased tremendously. My life was changing fast. And it was only the beginning.

CHAPTER 2

WHAT IS REINCARNATION?

*Though we travel the world over to find the beautiful,
we must carry it with us or we find it not - Ralph Waldo
Emerson*

During the time that the Pharaohs ruled Egypt, the belief was that after death, the dead came before the presence of Osirus, who made man and woman to be reborn again. They believed that the dead would follow a road, which led into a light source and to the God Osirus. By 1500 BC Hinduism and Brahmism had begun in India with the belief that reincarnation determined the status of the individual going into a higher or lower cast as animals or humans. If you lived like an animal, you would return this way, but by living a fairly good life, you will be reborn as a human being and to a station similar to your personality from a previous life.

Buddhism was founded by Gutana liddartha Buda, sometime between 480 - 560 BC who believed that you could not escape the results of your actions, and without rebirth, life has no purpose. The rebirth cycle, would continue life after life, therefore life would be everlasting. Eternal peace known as Nirvana would come when the craving for existence disappears. In the classic book, "Phaedo", written in 400 BC by Plato, he states, "If it were not for reincarnation, life would soon disappear from the universe" and he accepts reincarnation fully in his writings of the "Republic." During the time of Jesus, people believed that he was one of the old Prophets, either Elias, Jeremiah or John, the Baptist and the faith in immortality was accepted between the first and sixth century AD. Reincarnation appeared in Judaism as part of the Kaballah theology.

During the second synod of Constantinople, in the year 553 AD, all references to reincarnation were removed from the entire Bible and main events of world history. In the year 1723 a child was born in France who knew the alphabet at the age of three months; spoke French at one year and when six years old could speak Latin, Greek, Hebrew and many other languages. He died in 1728. Reincarnation was rekindled by the birth of these prodigies. People who have suddenly developed deep friendships, sweethearts who feel they have known each other from previous lives and have recalled incidents in their past lives through regression therapy, accept reincarnation as fact. Today, there are many studies being researched to verify past lives against historical occurrences through past life regression therapy and recall of information from former lives. More and more is being discovered about mankind's past existences. Some previous lives are seen as though watching their lives on a movie screen. Others relive their memories, as if they were at the age at which the past life took place, like acting out a scene on a stage. Some are calm about what they visualize, others are so frightened that they become upset and anxious. Some are astonished and surprised by their experiences.

A competent hypnotherapist/regressionist must have a professional knowledge of hypnosis, a thorough knowledge of the regression techniques, and a familiarity with false information, memories, skill, and experience in hypnotic regression therapy. It is possible in regression to remember things that did not occur. I felt that by retelling of an incident over and over, the false stories would be forgotten, and the actual BELIEVED occurrences would remain, if the narrating of the story did not change. The reliability of memory recalled during hypnosis rests not with the subject, but with the hypnotist who will determine, through investigation, if the story is fact. Improperly used, hypnosis can lead to confusion and false memories. The hypnotherapist must be aware that through subtle clues and direct questioning, the professional interviewer can guide the subject into remembering an entire invented story or the true facts in a regression. A person who channels is in an altered state of consciousness and believes that he is receiving communications from an unseen spirit or entity who answers questions or imparts wisdom. Regressees "hear" messages in their minds and think they are coming from outside sources. Some researchers have based much of their information on the regressed subject's dialogue. However, some of these messages have been verified about knowledge that the hypnotized person could not have known previously. Some researchers investigating the repeated material at different hypnotic sessions do not realize that if the story does contain unrecognized confabulation and distortion, it can enter into normal memory as "fact" and it often becomes impossible to tell what is valid and what is not. On the other hand, through repeated sessions on different occasions with a competent hypnotist, there is a greater likelihood that confabulation will be uncovered and the accurate account will be told.

Many years ago while in California I met Ormond McGill, known as the grandfather of modern hypnosis who has been practicing hypnosis since the late 1920's and has spent a lifetime examining past life regression therapy. I asked for his thoughts on reincarnation and he wrote the following:

The return of the formless into form is called "reincarnation." Some believe in it and some do not. Belief or nonbelief is irrelevant. It is the way of the Universe. Everything is patterned on birth, death, and rebirth. The very stars, vast galaxies, follow this pattern. So, if you will, accept this truth: <u>There is not a living person in the entire world that has not returned from death to live life after life after life.</u>

Here are some thoughts on reincarnation to mull over:

We have all died many deaths before we came into this immediate incarnation. What we call birth is merely the reverse side of death, like one of the two sides of a coin or like a door which we call "entrance" from the outside of a house and "exit" from the inside. The argument of a person who assumes that because they have no conscious memory of their many births and deaths proving that reincarnation is untrue is scientifically untenable. The field of human perception, as is easily demonstrated, is extremely limited. There are objects one cannot see, sounds one cannot hear, odors one cannot smell, tastes one cannot taste, and feelings one cannot feel.

With the senses of the physical body so obviously limited, it is really astonishing that anyone should question the possibility of reincarnation just because they cannot remember their previous lives, and thus conclude they have had no previous existences, for in like manner no one remembers his or her recent birth, and yet no one doubts that they were born.

It was not so very many years ago that evolution was a theory believed in by a few. Today it is accepted by the majority. What is evolution but the evolvement of the physical body, while reincarnation is the evolvement of the soul (the individual SELF). Both are concurrent and are interrelated. Body after body, or more properly expressed, life experience after life experience, must be engaged in for the growth of the soul.

In the Bible, Christ says, "Except that a man be born again, he cannot enter the Kingdom of God." That is from the English translation; and Christian doctrine has interpreted "born again" as meaning a spiritual rebirth. The original Hebrew text however has it written as "born again and again." In the Koran it is written, "God generates beings and then sends them back over and over until they return to Him."

Many of the world's great minds have credence to reincarnation. Voltaire wrote, "After all, it is no more surprising to be born twice than it is to be born once. Everything in nature is resurrection." Nietzsche states, "Live, so that thou mayest desire to live again — that is thy duty. For in any case, thou will live again."

You can unravel the matter for yourself; if you reflect upon concepts, which, at the most (currently) rarely exceeds 90 years, and then balance it against an eternity on the other side. Such beliefs paint a very unbalanced picture of Nature indeed. Likewise, the idea that one's behavior during that "minute droplet in time" in the great ocean of Eternity determines one's status in relation to God (Creator = Creation) for the remainder of each soul's existence for the eons which lie ahead is equally incongruous.

How long will the process of reincarnation continue for the soul from the formless to form and from the form to formless in repeatness? For an answer suppose we say, "For as long as there is yet much to learn, much to desire, and much to experience in the physical side of life. As long as the desire for the physical world is there, the soul will reincarnate. Yet, the process is not endless. Eventually "Enlightenment" (knowledge of its divine SELF) comes to every soul, and the cycle of rebirth is broken.

The importance of reincarnation cannot be over-emphasized if a full comprehension of soul growth is to be understood. Incarnations in the physical world are experiences in which the soul is gradually burnished to become a thing of beauty. This is Enlightenment, which is recognition of one's true SELF, e.g. one's true status in relation to Existence. It can take many lifetimes — in both the physical-world and in the mind-world — for some to reach that realization . . . that realization that some call "Nirvana" and others "Oneness with God," and yet it is possible to achieve it this very moment, as was previously mentioned. Birth and death are not phenomena which happen only once in any given human life. Such occur unintentionally. At every moment, something within us dies and something is reborn. The understanding of reincarnation is but an extension of this continuous fact.

It is of great importance that an understanding and appreciation of reincarnation is today being given more and more credence by Western cultures, for when that long awaited agreement among all people as to the truth of the matter occurs, there will no longer be doubt, no fallacious argumentation directed towards the truth of the immortal (divine) nature

15

of ourselves. Then will Occidental man awaken from the slumbers of ignorance, which have been hypnotically induced by a mistaken orthodoxy and concur with his Eastern brothers (ladies, of course, that includes you too)?

Here is the sentiment regarding reincarnation as expressed in the Hindu sacred text, <u>The Upanishads:</u> "As one's desire is, so is their destiny. For as their desire is, so is their will, and as their will is, so is their deed, and as their deed is, so is their reward, whether good or not good. For a person acts according to the desires they treasure. After death the person goes to the next world bearing in mind the subtle impressions of these deeds, and after reaping the harvest of their deeds, they return again to this world of action. Thus, one who still has the desires of the earth continues subject to rebirth. But he or she who has no earthly desires, who has no discrimination, whose mind is steady and whose heart is pure, and who does not desire to be reborn, reaches the goal, and having reached it, is form no more, and remains amongst the hosts with God."

CHAPTER 3

THE STORY OF HARRY KANTROFF

I rid myself of my doubts by remembering that there is a
valid reason for everything that happens. - Anonymous

Until the year 1962, I had been a successful photographer, a manufacturer, retailer of Venetian blinds and a home improvement salesman. All that changed when a friend loaned me a bestseller book called The Search for Bridey Murphy, by Morey Bernstein. He was a successful businessman who became interested in hypnotism. While researching the field of reincarnation he placed an American woman named Ruth Simmons into a hypnotic trance and regressed her to a past life in which it turned out that she had lived in Nineteenth Century Ireland. While in trance, speaking with an Irish brogue, she mentioned facts that only a person living at that time could have known.

Bernstein was attacked on all sides. The book was denounced by religious groups and the Psychology profession as a "hoax." Many scientists and self-ordained critics believed that Ruth Simmons as "Bridey" had not given any information that she could not have learned from her Irish grandmother. And some felt that the "Bridey Murphy" case was simply fantasy manufactured by a weak-willed, overly suggestible subject trying to please the hypnotist.

After reading Morey Bernstein's book, I said to myself, "If this story is true then we will never die!" If Bridey Murphy was actually reliving her life as Ruth Simmons, then it seemed quite probable that life never ends. Therefore, if the soul carries on from life to life, there was no longer any need to fear dying. In 1960 I wrote to Bernstein and purchased several of the phonograph records that he had made on Ruth Simmons during his regression experiments with her. The records sounded authentic to me. At this point, my life took a decided turn. I was so intrigued that I decided to become an investigator of this phenomenon of reincarnation through hypnotic past-life regression. I applied to several schools that were accredited in the teaching of hypnosis and by the end of 1962; I had completed the course work of five separate schools and had graduated as a certified hypnotherapist. Recognizing my need for objective balance, I sought to approach my subject scientifically. Also, a background in psychology seemed just the ticket to help balance and scientifically legitimize my research. In the fall of 1963, I began my first year at the University of Baltimore, majoring in psychology. I felt a little out of place at that time considering that all of the other students were eighteen or nineteen years of age, while I was on the sunny-side of forty-three.

In the winter of 1964, in one of my psychology classes I became acquainted with a nineteen-year-old student sitting next to me whose name was Harry Kantroff. He was obviously struggling with the course; his marks were dipping too close to the failure line. I was certain that I could use my skills in hypnosis to help him improve his school grades and during one of my school sessions, I said, "Harry, come to my house after school. I will place you in hypnosis, give you positive suggestions, and improve your grades." He said he was willing to try even though he felt anxious and excited.

In March of 1964, Harry Kantroff came to my home and sat in the dark brown leather reclining chair in my living room. I reclined the chair to where he was postured horizontal with the floor. In keeping with my professional discipline, I turned on my tape recorder so that I would have a record of what transpired. In a few seconds he was in a deep trance state and I gave him suggestions that would help him improve his school grades and also oriented him to retaining a more consistent state of calmness and inner relaxation. And indeed, within the following thirty days, his marks did improve tremendously. With his eyes closed, Harry rested comfortably in the recliner, the upper portion of his chest gently rising and falling in a steady relaxing manner. I tested him for depth of hypnosis and while watching Harry; I realized that he had a true affinity for the deep hypnotic state. I decided I would attempt to do what Morey Bernstein did with Ruth Simmons and regress him into a previous lifetime.

I seated myself next to Harry, placed the audio tape recorder close by, and held the microphone to his mouth. As he lay there on his back I said: "Harry, I want you to go back to the time you were in the sixth grade in school. You are sitting at your desk and in the front of the room is your sixth grade teacher." "What is the teacher's name?" Harry began to speak and a smile appeared on his face. "That is Mrs. Nichols. She is a nice teacher. I like her." Harry seemed to be enjoying this recall. He was breathing slowly and easily and his facial features had softened into a more boyish, sixth grade kind of repose. "Fine," I continued, "you are now in the fifth grade in school. Look at your teacher standing at the front of the room. What is the teacher's name?" Harry's facial features hardened and his expression changed as he exclaimed vehemently, "That is Mr. Sanders. I hate him." Harry Kantroff was speaking as though Mr. Sanders was in the room; the agitation in his voice was obvious. "You are getting younger," I continued, "You are now in the fourth grade. What is the name of your teacher?" He mentioned the teacher's name. Now go to the third, second and first grades. He continued to give me the names of all of his elementary school teachers even though in his more normally awakened state he'd only been able to remember the names of his sixth and fifth grade teachers. Later, I was able to verify that his answers were correct by making contact with his parents in Washington.

"You can now go even further back in time." I requested. "I want you to go back to the time of your birth. Where were you born?" "In Garfield Memorial Hospital in Washington." Then I led him through the veil. "You are now going back to your previous existence prior to your present time in Garfield Memorial Hospital. Pick any time you desire. Dwell upon the scene and when I speak to you again, you will be able to tell me about it." Harry was still resting easily on his back and breathing gently. I brought the microphone near to his mouth.

"Tell me, what is your name?"

Since his name was Harry Kantroff, I thought he would repeat it.

"Rov Sholem!" He exclaimed excitedly, with tremendous fright in his voice.

Suddenly and unexpectedly, he jumped out of the recliner, stood on his feet, opened his eyes, put his right hand over his left shoulder, and let out a terribly loud yell of pain as I quickly moved the microphone away from his mouth.

"Oh, my God," he exclaimed, "I have an awful pain between my shoulder blades."

I said, "Harry, there must be a pin in the chair."

I felt the recliner. There were no sharp objects as the chair was made of smooth leather. Harry had pulled himself completely out of hypnosis. After he calmed down,

I asked, "Harry, who is Rov Sholem?" He looked puzzled, "Rov Sholem! I don't know," he quizzically answered.

I questioned him further. "Maybe, you read a book by or about Rov Sholem. Perhaps you have a relative that your parents told you about whose name is Rov Sholem, or did you see a movie and the name Rov Sholem appeared?"

"I cannot place the name," he answered with an expression of inner befuddlement.

"Harry, when you go home to Washington today, mention the name Rov Sholem to your parents." The next day in class he told me that his parents did not know what he was talking about. I asked him to return to my home for another session since I conveyed my excitement about further research into his possible previous lives.

Due to school exams and studies, it was not until approximately a month later that he returned to my home for the second visit. Again, I placed him under hypnosis, turned my recorder on and regressed him back from the sixth grade through the first. He named the same teachers that he had mentioned in the first trance when he brought himself out of hypnosis. I thought that there must have been some kind of psychological block that made him jump out of the chair.

"You are in a happy situation somewhere in the past, I said. Tell me, where are you?"

He began to speak in a soft teenage voice and said, "In shul."(Jewish word for synagogue)

"What are you doing?" I asked.

"It is my bar mitzvah," he replied.

This is would be a happy occasion for a Jewish boy, for when he reaches the age of thirteen he is considered a man. I was thinking that Harry was remembering his Bar Mitzvah in Washington where he lived when he was thirteen.

"This is a happy occasion for a Jewish boy," I remarked.

"It is not all happy," he replied.

"What is wrong?"

(Speaking in an agitated state), "My people are being killed in the streets."

"Where are you?"

"I am here on the outskirts of Kiev."

"Kiev, Russia?"

"Yes, I live here on the outskirts of Kiev."

"What year is this?"

"The year is 1902." Suddenly the tone of his voice became painfully strained and his features were frozen with fear and a look of horror appeared on his face.

"Three weeks ago my mother, father and I were walking down the sidewalk and they came riding down from the north, the dirty Cossacks! One of them drew forth a saber and cut my mother's head off." Tears began rolling down his cheeks.

"What did your father do?"

"He raised his arm to protect me and they cut his arm off. I ran into a doorway and hid, then finally fell asleep. When I came out in the morning, cold and shivering, I saw that my parents were gone. I never saw them again."

I asked, "What is your name?"

He replied, "Ben Medrosh."

I was completely surprised because in the first session when I had asked his name, he had yelled the name "Rov Sholem." I now had to determine whether or not he was lying. He continued with his story.

"I went home thinking that it was all a dream, but there was no one home."

"What happened to Rov Sholem?" I inquired.

"My father made him leave the house because he did not believe in the faith." (Ben Medrosh's father was a religious man and Rov Sholem had left the home in 1900 and joined up with the Cossacks by giving them false information.)

Still under hypnosis, Harry as Ben Medrosh continued. "I spent a week in the house and finally ran out of food. I needed money and so I got a job with the Russian underground movement as a runner delivering messages. It is after nine o'clock curfew and no one is allowed on the street. I am carrying a message for the underground organization and I am standing beside a stonewall. Oh, my God! There is someone coming toward me. It is my brother Rov. He is bad. They warned me about him. I must get away, but my feet feel like lead and I can hardly move. He is coming closer. He has a knife in his hand—-!"

23

Ben Medrosh's face showed signs of anxiety and fright as the emotions within him were rising. (His face had turned a dead white, the color of snow, and you could visualize the look of terror in his facial features.) There was tremendous fear in his voice. Now I began to put the pieces together from the two trances. In this trance he had returned to the outskirts of Kiev, where his brother had stabbed him in the back and killed him. The last thought that Harry Kantroff had remembered from his previous life was the moment when his brother had stabbed him and he had yelled the name Rov Sholem in the first trance. It was an exclamation, as if to say, "Rov Sholem, my brother, why did you stab me?" It reminded me of Caesar and Brutus when Caesar remarked, "Et Tu Brute."

As Harry began to breath heavily and gasp for breath, I immediately brought him out of hypnosis. After he calmed down, I gave him a copy of the tape so that he and his parents could listen to it. The following day in class, I anxiously awaited for his parent's reaction as to what had transpired. The next day he told me that his parents were at a loss to explain any of it and he felt inwardly agitated and in the dark as to what had transpired. Even so, he had now become quite determined to get the answers as to where the information was coming from. I asked Harry to come back to my home once more. Because of final school exams, I was not able to meet him in my home again until May 5th. So it was approximately a month after the second session that I was again able to place Harry in hypnosis. I regressed him back to the year 1902 in Kiev, to the time when his father and mother were killed, since I knew this information from the previous tapes. Under a deep regressive trance I asked him to tell me more about what had happened. He again repeated the story exactly as it was recorded on the second tape. However, when he reached the scene where his brother was attacking him, just as in the previous session, he became upset, extremely agitated and began breathing heavily. I instructed him, "Leave the scene. You are getting younger and younger. You are now six years old. Where are you?" As he picked up the new scene, Harry Kantroff as Ben Medrosh calmed down, and his breathing returned to normal.

"We are having great fun," he exclaimed.

I said, "Who are we?"

My brother Rov and I. He is ten and I am six. We are playing Russian soldiers. I am on my magnificent stallion. (His father was a carpenter and had made him a wooden hobbyhorse.)

I asked, "Ben Medrosh, do you understand Russian?"

His reply was, "That is a silly question."

How do you say in Russian, "Close the door and open the window?" For a minute he spoke in Russian. Later I had the material on the tape checked by a professor of the Russian language and also several Russian teachers. They mentioned that he was speaking in one of the many dialects in Russia and his pronunciation was correct. However, after our session, when I inquired of the fully conscious Harry Kantroff whether he was familiar with the Russian language, he swore to me that he had never learned to speak Russian and that his parents did not understand the language.

Ben Medrosh, under hypnosis had mentioned that his Bar Mitzvah had occurred in 1902, which means that he was thirteen years old at the time his father and mother died. I had asked him, "In what year were you born?" He answered that he was born in the month of Adar in the year 5649, which was the Hebrew year that corresponded to the English year of

1889. Since he was confirmed in 1902 at the age of thirteen, the year 1889 was correct. He had given me the correct year based on the Hebrew calendar.

"Ben Medrosh," I asked, "I want you now to go back to the year 1889, at the time of your birth. Where were you born?"

I was born at home on the outskirts of Kiev. My Aunt Sarah was the mid-wife (Harry Kantroff does not have an Aunt Sarah living in his present life)

"Go back to the time of your birth in 1889 on the outskirts of Kiev where your Aunt Sarah is attending to you. Good, all right, you now have the power to go even farther back. You can go back as far as you want. Let yourself drift back to some previous time that attracts you. Dwell upon this scene. When I speak to you again, you will be able to answer." I waited ten seconds. You are now back, far back, far back into your past. Where are you?" He did not answer, but began to speak in a strange tongue. For approximately a minute he continued to speak in this language. I later had the tape checked by a Rabbi who said that he was speaking in Aramaic. Finally, I insisted, "Tell me, where are you?"

"Go away; let me sleep," he replied in English.

"I will let you sleep if you tell me where you are."

"We are in the hills outside of Jerusalem."

"What are you doing there?"

"The walls have been torn down. The city of Jerusalem has been sacked. We are being distributed into the hills."

"Who are we?"

"We are a band of forty."

"Who is in charge?"

"There are two Romans."

"Are they riding or walking?"

"They are riding."

"Are you walking or riding?"

"We are walking."

"What is your name?"

"I am Canaan, of the house of Cohan."

"How old are you?"

"I am of the forty-third year."

"Are you married?"

"I have not yet taken a wife."

(These are not the type of answers that one would expect from Harry Kantroff who is an American)

"What do you do for food?"

"I am a maker of horses' clothes."

I replied quizzically, "Horses' clothes?"

"I have a tamper and a knife. I tack things that go around the horse." (He probably was referring to the saddle straps)

"Do you work in a shop?" I asked.

"I work in the open on a stone."

"What are some of the seas?"

"I only know one, the Philistine." (I could not find this sea on a present day map and had to revert to a very old map to discover it)

I asked, "What are some of the countries?"

"I only know of Judea," he replied. (I was only able to find this country on a very old map.)

"What date is this that you are being distributed into the hills?"

He asked, "Do you wish this in the Roman or Hebrew year?"

I said, "give it to me in both."

"In the Roman year it is the year of King Erideas and in the Hebrew year it is 3760. (I checked this year and it corresponded to 100AD)

Harry Kantroff had been in hypnosis for over an hour. I could tell that he was tired, so I brought him back to the present, awakened him and played the tape for him. He kept shaking his head as though he could not understand what he was hearing.

I quizzed him, looking for any indication of self-projected fantasizing. "You certainly have sufficient information now to tell me whether you have read a book, perhaps your parents told you a story, or you saw a motion picture about Ben Medrosh."

Harry Kantroff looked genuinely perplexed and replied, "I cannot place it."

I said, "Go home and ask your parents about the information on this tape and tomorrow in school let me know if they come up with any answers."

The next day in class he said, "They don't know what I am talking about."

On May 20th, school classes were over and I wrote a letter to Harry's parents asking if I could interview them. The letter was returned to me and on the outside of the letter was stamped, moved no forwarding address. I was never able to find Harry Kantroff again.

The story of Harry Kantroff was the beginning of my research into reincarnation and my attempt to prove that the spiritual life never ends, but repeats itself over and over again.

My next research was based on the question: Who were the Cossacks and why did they kill Kantroff's father and mother?

The Cossacks were fierce bands of warlike horsemen who from the early 15th century roamed the steppe north of the Black Sea along the frontier of Muscovite, Russia, Lithuania, Poland and the Ottoman Empire. The name Cossack came from the Turkish Kozak, meaning adventurer or freeman living outside the existing social structure. The Cossack bands were organized into self-governing communities under elected leaders. They were conquered by Muscovite Russia. By 1700, they formed a loyal mounted military force and served as police of the Czarist government until the revolution of March 1917. They still remained independent and would raid small villages to supplement their income by taking what they wanted and killing those in the way. Until 1917, Cossack regiments acted as special police to put down peasant disturbances and later urban strikes. They were paid by the state either with money, provisions or an allotment of pastureland. Most of the Cossacks lived by the horse, gun, and sword, wandering through Russia in search of loot to plunder and extort money for the protection they offered - especially from their own ravaging brutality. To the strong they offered their mercenary services for payment; the weak they would destroy. The weapons used by the Cossacks were lances, curved sword, of the saber or scimitar type, pistolets, muskets and a few light cannons. These were the Cossacks who came storming into the village where Ben Medrosh lived on the outskirts of Kiev, killing his father and mother.

CHAPTER 4

THE LIFE OF A.G.

The really valuable method of thought to arrive at a logically coherent system is intuition - anonymous

In the fall of 1964, I continued attending classes at the University with the hope of seeing Harry Kantroff once more, but he did not return to school. I was married, had two children and needed additional income. As a certified hypnotherapist, I opened an office to help clients to control their weight, reduce stress and stop smoking through hypnosis. I also continued researching past-life regression in my office.

In June of 1969, a young, beautiful black woman, twenty years old, named A.G. (an abbreviation to protect her privacy) walked into my office and said that for many years she had dreamt the same dream. She was a tall Afro-American woman with long black hair, slim body and a well-spoken voice. She mentioned that she had a problem that had been troubling her since she was a small child. The dark skin around her brown eyes revealed a certain tension. As I listened to her story I could feel the determination and desperation in her voice. She desired a past life regression. "Since the time I was a small child I have had a repeating dream through the years that I am in a large room with a white marble floor and walls, many marble baths and hundreds of nude women who are frolicking with each other or washing themselves. I could see a woman tossing a white substance into the baths and then the dream would disappear."

While she relaxed in my office recliner, I placed her into the hypnotic state and then deepened it. When I determined that she was in a very deep state, in which a past life appears easily, I connected my tape recorder, placed the microphone to her mouth and began.

I. Mordes-"You are going back in time to a previous existence prior to your present life. Go back into your past life until your are fifteen years old and tell me what is your name? You can speak now from this lifetime. (In order that the reader may understand what a past life regression is about, I have taken the information directly off the tape.)"

I— What is your name?

AG— "Céta" (spelling of names, places, etc. may be incorrect as they are spelled by the way they sound, SAY-TAH)

I— "You are Céta. In what place do you live and what is this place called?"

AG— "I have not found out yet."

I— "Céta, what is the name of your father?"

AG— "Cënal" (SAY-NAHL)

I— "What is the name of your mother?"

AG— "Beenocht" (BEE-NOCKT)

I— "Céta, do you have any brothers or sisters?"

AG— "No"

I— "How old are you?"

AG— "Fifteen"(AG was speaking in the voice of a teenager)

I— "Do you know where you live, what country this is?"

AG— "Cënal sends me to a big house. I think I will have to soon- - - - -."

I— "What will you have to do soon?"

AG— "Beenocht didn't explain very well. It's a big house with many women."

I— "Oh, he is sending you to the big house with many women?"

AG— "I don't know what is going to happen."

I— "Your father is sending you there?"

AG— "Yes"

I— "In which city will you be? Do you know?"

AG— "I am not sure. The house is as big as a city."

I— "What does your mother say? Does she want you to go?"

AG— "No, Cënal would not let her talk to me. She was going to talk to me and tell me what would happen in the house but - - - ."

I— "She did not tell you?"

AG— "She did not have time. Cënal would not allow her to do this."

I— "Are you still at home with your father and mother?"

AG— "No, they sent me to the house." (I was able to determine from the tapes that the Sultan of Turkey had chosen Ceta during the Ottoman Empire, to live in his harem. (This was considered an honor.)

I— "How long have you been in the house?"

AG— "About three days."

I— "What have you seen in the house? What do you see there?"

AG— "It is very pretty."

I— "Whom did you meet when you went into the house?"

AG— "I have not really been presented."

I— "Do you have a room?"

AG— "No, I share a large room with many other women."

I— "Are they pretty?"

AG— (With a deep smile on her face, she answered), "Oh, yes."

I— "And are you pretty?"

AG— (Without hesitation.) "Yes"

I— "Do they tell you what you are going to do?"

AG— "I don't know yet."

I— "They haven't spoken to you?"

AG— "No, everyone has duties."

I— "This place you are in, is it in the city?"

AG— "It is set beside the ocean."

I— "What is the name of the ocean?"

AG— "I think they call it the Cimone." (Subject has difficulty with names)

I— "Cimone?"

AG— "Cimone, I am not sure. I don't know much about this place yet. I know a lot of things, but I don't know about this place yet."

I— "When Beenocht took you to the house, did she introduce you to the owner of the house?" (I deliberately gave her the wrong information to determine whether she would correct it.)

AG— (With a sense of agitation), "No, no, Beenocht is my mother."

I— "Oh! I mean your father. What is your father's name?"

AG— "Cyleel is the name he carries now." (Read the notations at the end of this chapter as to why the name may have changed. Name pronounced as SY-LEEL)

I— "Did Cyleel take you to the house?"

AG— "No, there were some troops that came with a boat and took me and many others."

I— "You had to get on a boat to arrive at the house?"

AG— "Yes"

I— "Was the house far away?"

AG— "Yes"

I— "When you reached the house, did you meet anyone?"

AG— "I talked to the girls that were in the boat."

I— "The soldiers took you to the house?"

AG— "We were all taken." (These were additional girls who were offered to the Sultan by their parents.)

I— "When you reached the house, did you meet the owner of the house?"

AG— "No, we had to be bathed and oiled and groomed."

I— "Groomed for what?"

AG— "That is what I don't understand yet."

I— "Cëta, you have been in the house for three days. I want you to go forward one month in time. You have been in the house one whole month now, tell me, what goes on in the house?"

AG— "We all have duties to perform."

I— "What is your duty?"

AG— "The marble baths."

I— "What do you do at the marble baths?"

AG— "I keep the salts."

I— "Who comes into the marble baths?"

AG— "All the women share the baths, especially the favorites."

I— "The favorites to whom?"

AG— "The master."

I— "Who is the master?"

AG— "I do not know his name. I am told to just call him master, but he is so handsome."

I— "Your duties are to take care of the salts for the baths. How many baths are there?"

AG— "There is a big marble one and the favorites are sometimes granted permission to have their own."

I— "Do you know what country you are in?"

AG— "I heard someone say Turkey. It's a strange name."

I— "What place did you come from?"

AG— "Dinea"

I— "Dinea, is it a city or a country?"

AG— "A small village."

I— "In what country is the village? Every village has a country. Do you remember that?"

AG— "No"

I— "All right, you're in Turkey, you are in the big house and you take care of the baths."

AG— "The salts have to be just right. Too much will dry the skin."

I— "This is done for the master?"

AG— "No, for the girls."

I— "Are they the master's girls?"

AG— "Yes"

I— "You are not the master's girl?"

AG— "Not yet."

I— "You want to be?"

AG— "He is nice."

I— "You are now fifteen. Go forward to the time you are eighteen years old. You are Céta at the age of eighteen. Tell me, where are you?"

AG— "I have my own wing."

I— "How did you get your own wing?"

AG— "My friend showed me some tricks."

I— "Tell me, what kind of tricks?" (At this moment Ceta became very agitated and hesitated to tell me.)

AG— "No, no, it's very private."

I— "Oh, I am sorry. I did not mean to invade your privacy, but it would be very nice to know and I am your best friend."

AG— "No" (Speaking adamantly.)

I— (Speaking reluctantly) "You can tell me."

AG— "You would turn my secret over to some of the others and then I would lose my wing."

I— "I promise you that I will not do that since I am your very close friend."

AG— "There is much intrigue here and it is not always wise to trust everyone."

I— "I understand that, but you can trust me because I am your very close friend and I promise you that I will not do this. What secrets have you learned to use for the master?"

AG— (With exultation) "The master likes young boys."

I— "And what do you do?"

AG— "I bring him young boys and the master is very kind to me."

I— "Where do you find them?"

AG— "I have a eunuch and he helps me."

I— "The eunuch helps you and so you have gotten an entire wing. Does the master like you?"

AG— "Yes, because I know what he likes."

I— "Do you go to bed with the master?"

AG— "Yes, of course." (Spoken with deep feelings of sexuality)

I— "You keep him happy?"

AG— "Yes"

I— "Do you have a maid for yourself?"

AG— "Yes, I have a whole staff."

I— "What does he call you?"

AG— "Céta"

I— "By the way, Céta, what is your last name?"

AG— "Cynea" (SYE-NEE-AH)

I— "Céta Cynea?"

AG— "It is pretty."

I— "It's a pretty name and you are beautiful to the master, aren't you?"

AG— "I have grown much."

I— "Is the master married? Does he have a wife?"

AG— "He has considered marrying me. I am the only one who has given him a son."

I— "Tell me, in what country are you?"

AG— "It is Turkey."

I— "What city in Turkey?"

AG— "This household sits by a range, a mountain range. We are cloistered here. I do not know a lot about these things. The master likes it better that way. He says, "Women do not belong involved in the daily problems." It is unfortunate.

37

I— "Do all the other women bow to you?"

AG— "They must."

I— "When you have a meal with the master, do the maids or servants serve you?"

AG— "Yes"

I— "What do you have to eat for dinner?"

AG— "I choose to eat rather lightly."

I— "You watch your figure?"

AG— "Yes"

I— "What do you eat?"

AG— "Many, many fruits and we are not allowed meats. I am told that there are some heathens who do eat meat."

I— "What is your religion?"

AG— "We are not allowed to practice any type of idol worship."

I— "And so, you take care of the master and his needs. You have your own wing and you are eighteen years old. You have a wonderful life and you have your little boy."

AG— (Speaking with admiration) "He is strong too."

I— "How old is your son?"

AG— "One year."

I— "Céta, you are going forward in time. You are twenty years old now and you can speak to me and tell me about your life. Where are you now?"

AG— "Very, very hot today."

I— "What are you doing today?"

AG— "Trying to relax."

I— "By the way Céta, what year is this?"

AG— "1519"

I— "What is the name of your master?"

AG— "Am I allowed to tell you?"

I— "Yes, I am your friend. You can tell me."

AG— "Are you sure?"

I— "I promise."

AG— "Alright, it is Chung Lee."

I— "Is this Chinese?"

AG— "One of his parents was a foreign girl in the harem and - - - ."

I— "So, Chung Lee is your master?"

AG— "This is why he does not want anyone to call him by his name."

I— "What do you call him?"

AG— "Master, I respect him."

I— "Everyone calls him master. He does not want to be called Chung Lee. I can understand that. Is his last name Lee?"

AG— "This is the only name I know."

I— "What do you call your baby?"

AG— "Shenot" (SHAY-NOT)

I— "And what is the baby's last name?"

AG— "Lee - Shenot Lee"

I— "Does the master like his little boy?"

AG— "Oh yes, he loves him very much."

I— "Does he look like the master?"

AG— "No, he is beautiful as I am."

I— "Céta, you are twenty years old. Has the master married you yet?"

AG— "No, not yet."

I— "Does he love you?"

AG— "Yes" (with feeling)

I— "And you are in charge of the entire house now?"

AG— "Yes"

I— "It's a beautiful hot day and you are relaxing. We are going forward in time. It is now five years later. What year is this?"

AG— "1524"

I— "It is 1524, how old are you now?"

AG— "25, you did not think I could count, did you?"

I— "Has the master taught you how to write?"

AG— "No"

I— "You still cannot write?"

AG— "A woman could be killed for writing."

I— "I didn't know that. Are you going to teach your child to write?"

AG— "There are scribes who will do that."

I— "That is good. Céta, you are twenty-five, tell me what are you doing this day?"

AG— "My servant has told me that she is going to have a baby."

I— "Your servant? What is her name?"

AG— (laughs)

I— "It is funny, isn't it?"

AG— "Yes, because her husband did not do this."

I— "Her husband cannot do this, but she is going to have a baby?"

AG— "Yes"

I— "Do you know who the father is going to be? Did she tell you?"

AG— "I have my suspicions, but - - - ."

I— "You're not sure. Tell me, on this day that the servant told you about the baby, what is the exact date? What month is this?"

AG— "August"

I— "August and what day is it?"

AG— "Eighteen"

I— "August 18 and it is 1525, is this correct?"

AG— "Yes"

I— "So it is August 18, 1525 and on this beautiful day you heard from the maid that she is going to have a baby. What are you going to do on this day?"

AG— "Find a way to protect her. She is a faithful servant."

I— "You mean that her husband may kill her for what she had done?"

AG— "Yes"

I— "Do you have any way to protect her? What can you do?"

AG— "I could have him killed."

I— "You have the right to have him killed?"

AG— "I could."

I— "I thought only the master could do that."

AG— "All I need to do is say one word to my master."

I— "Yes, then he would not do anything to your maid. Is that correct?"

AG— "Yes"

I— "That is good, because she should have her little baby just as you had your baby. Céta, you are twenty-five years old. Are you married?"

AG— "No"

I— "What's the matter, the master doesn't want to marry you?"

AG— "He is a stubborn man."

I— "Men are stubborn, you know that, but you will have your way. Has the master ever taken you any place to visit?"

AG— "No, my responsibilities are in the house."

I— "You never leave the house?"

AG— "No"

I— "You spend your time raising your little son?"

AG— "Yes"

I— "What else do you do to keep busy?"

AG— "I have my own stallion. It is not wise for women to ride, but I am allowed to."

I— "What do you call your stallion?"

AG— "Arabia" (phonetic sound - our-ah-bee-ah)

I— "That is a pretty name. Where do you ride?"

AG— "Around the grounds."

I— "I thought you were not allowed to leave the house?"

AG— "Not allowed to leave the grounds."

I— "Are they big grounds?"

AG— "Yes, the woods are as far as you can see."

I— "You have animals that you raise?"

AG— "You know a lot. You know too much."

I— "I am learning. Remember, you are teaching me. Céta, would you like for me to write a book about you so that everyone in the future may know how wonderful you were? Would you like that?"

AG— "Can you do this? And what would you want for this?"

I— "Nothing at all, just your friendship. If I have your friendship, I will write the book and you will live for posterity, for the future. Would you like that?"

AG— "Yes"

I— "Alright, then if you would like that, I must have information to put into the book. So, you have to answer all my questions. How many women are your maids?"

AG— "I am the ruler in the harem."

I— "How many are in the harem?"

AG— "At last count, I think there were 159."

I— "Your master takes care of all these women?"

AG— "Yes"

I— "Does he go to bed with all the women?"

AG— "No, there are many, many virgins."

I— "What are the virgins doing there? What does he need them for?"

AG— "Until they are ready, they must take care of the harem."

I— "Do they work in the harem?"

AG— "Yes, and they attend the favorites too."

I— "Besides the master?"

AG— "Yes."

I— "If the master were to tell one of the girls to go and be with a friend of his, would she go to bed?"

AG— (Speaking indignantly) "The master does not lend his women. They are all his. There are levels for women."

I— "Tell me the levels. What are they?"

AG— (With a smile on her face, she said, "I am the first favorite. All the rest who have given him a son are at the second level. And all the newly consecrated virgins are at the next or third level, and then there are the young flowers."

I— "The young flowers? What do you mean?"

AG— "They have not been deflowered yet."

I— "And then the master has his boys?"

AG— "No one knows of that but the eunuch. They are not kept here. The eunuch brings them in and takes them back."

I— "Does the eunuch take care of all the women in the harem?"

AG— "Yes, he oversees."

I— "Does the master ever kill any of his women?"

AG— "If they are unfaithful."

I— "Have you ever seen anyone killed?"

AG— "No"

I— "Do any of the women in the harem ever leave of their own free will or are they forced to stay?"

AG— "They must stay."

I— "They must stay until they die?"

AG— "It is a privilege."

I— "Is it a privilege to be with the master?"

AG— "Yes"

I— "What does the master do to make money to live?"

AG— "Tax the people."

I— "He collects from the people?"

AG— "I know this much. He goes on a campaign now and again."

I— "Does he fight?"

AG— "Such is a campaign."

I— "You mean he goes on a war campaign? Does he have many men with him?"

AG— "Yes"

I— "Is he the ruler of the country?"

AG— "He is the ruler of all Turkey."

I— "Is he called king? What do the people call him?"

AG— "The master. Some, I have heard, call him Sultan."

I— "By what name do you call him, Sultan what?"

AG— "His name is not mentioned in his presence."

I— "So they just say Sultan. Is that correct?"

AG— "Yes"

I— "So, he is either called Sultan or master?"

AG— "Yes"

I— "Does he have a throne that he sits on?"

AG— "Yes"

I— "Do you ever sit beside him?"

AG— "Not yet, but I will."

I— "If you marry the Sultan, what will they call you?"

AG— "I do not know."

I— "You do not know, but we need this for the book. In order to write the book, you will have to find the information and give it to me."

AG— "I will have to. I will ask my master."

I— "You are how old now?"

AG— "I am twenty-five."

I— "You are twenty-five and it is a beautiful day in August. You will now go forward in time and you have become thirty years old. You are still beautiful. Are you still in the Sultan's house?"

AG— "Yes"

I— "What does he call his house?"

AG— "It is called a palace."

I— "It is the masters palace and you are thirty years old. Do you still love him?"

45

AG— "Yes"

I— "Céta, how old is your little boy now, Shenot?"

AG— "He will be twelve soon."

I— "What does he do all the time? Does he go to school and learn?"

AG— "He has gone to learn to be a ruler. Young sons are generally taken from their mothers when they reach a certain age. Shenot was very, very small."

I— "You haven't seen Shenot lately?"

AG— "No, I see him at meals sometimes. He spends most of his time in study."

I— "Where does he study and who teaches him?"

AG— "In another part of the palace. He has his own wing now. There are scribes who teach him."

I— "Do you know the names of the scribes?"

AG— "No"

I— "You do not see him often, but does the master see him?"

AG— "Yes, they spend much time together."

I— "The master loves him?"

AG— "Yes, he shall be the successor."

I— "The master has not married you?"

AG— "No, but I think it will be soon."

I— "You feel it?"

AG— "Yes"

I— "He is getting up in years. How old is the master?"

AG— "Forty-five."

I— "The master is forty-five and you are thirty. Is that correct?"

AG— "Yes"

I— "The master loves you and you love him. Well, I think it is time for him to marry you, don't you?"

AG— "Yes, I have thought so for a while. I am getting old."

I— "Céta, are you happy in the palace?"

AG— "Yes"

I— "Have you ever heard from your father and mother?"

AG— "No"

I— "What is the name of your father?"

AG— "I suppose they are still calling him Cyleel."

I— "And your mother, what is her name?"

AG— "I have put my mother out of my mind. Do not ever speak of her again. I do not wish to speak of my mother again, and if you persist—."

M— "Tell me why? (I was unable to determine why she said this) I will not persist. Remember what I said. I want to write your story for the book and I said I need all information."

AG— "I will not want posterity to know about my mother." (I was never able to ascertain why Ceta despised her mother)

I— "Then, I will not write about her. Forget your mother. You are thirty years old. Céta, I want you to go forward in time. Go forward to the date of your death. Tell me how old are you when you die?"

AG— "Forty"

I— "In what year did you die? (There was silence)

AG— (Hesitantly) "1535."

I— "Do you know what day you died?"

AG— "No"

I— "Is the master still alive?"

AG— "My husband, master."(Exploding with deep satisfaction)

I— "You married him? In what year did you get married?"

AG— "Yes, moments before my death. It will insure my son the succession."

I— "So the master married you moments before your death and your son becomes the successor. Are you happy this has taken place?"

AG— "Yes"

I— "What are you dying from?"

AG— "Age"

I— "Age? At the age of forty you have gotten old. Do they have a doctor to help you? "Yes." What does the doctor say?"

AG— "It addles the brain."

I— "He doesn't know what is wrong with you?"

AG— "Poppy juice, for the pain."

I— "He gives poppy juice to take away the pain? Where is the pain? In what place?"

AG— "My heart."

I— "Your heart has pain and he gives you poppy juice to take the pain away. You are getting weaker and weaker. Céta, you are leaving this life. You are passing on and you have left Turkey and your master and son behind. But, your son will be the next ruler and you leave in peace. You have left behind the memory. Now all thoughts will leave your mind and you will forget. You will forget everything and you are at peace." (This suggestion is given to avoid any anxiety when she is conscious.) (In the entire time that I questioned A.G. all of her answers were spontaneous without any hesitation. If the answers had been fabricated I would have assumed that she needed time to think of an answer.)

I awakened AG, but she was unable to remember anything of the trance. (Very deep hypnotic subjects do not remember.) I presented her with the tape and asked her to research the story for verification. Since Céta mentioned the year 1520, Turkey, harem and eunuch, I asked her to research the time and life of Sultan Suleiman, The First, who ascended the throne in Turkey during her past lifetime. I also asked AG to investigate the home of Suleiman 1st, known as the "Seraglio." Following is a critique of the time period in which Cëta lived.

Review of the past-life regression of Cëta Cynea - circa 1499 - 1539

- Father's Name

At age 15, Cëta says her father's name is Cënal, however, minutes later the name changes to Cyleel. Cëta refers to the second name as the "one he carries now." This may mean that his name is Cënal but for some reason it was changed to Cyleel. It is possible that the father was forced to turn his daughter over to harem officials/soldiers due to a war, etc. where the most beautiful women were often gathered along with the other spoils/loot and presented to the conquering monarch. This may explain why the mother, Beenocht, "did not have time" to explain where Cëta was being taken on the boat or why, and the fact that she was loath to see her daughter go. Cënal may have changed his name as a protective alias for political reasons. Note that Cëta has no difficulty with the father's name and that the alias has remained intact.

- Harem Accommodations

New arrivals to the harem did in fact share one large room/rooms (dependent upon the number of women housed.) It remained this way until one caught the eye of the Sultan. If after she was bedded, she was not called again or did not conceive a child, it would be her fate to remain lodged in these crowded quarters. This was a miserable life for many women and quite often-lesbian acts were committed in secrecy to ease the pains of loneliness and growing old. Once the odalisques reached old age or found disgrace with the master, they were often banished to another older palace often referred to as the "Palace of Tears" until their death. It is also interesting to note that Cëta pronounces the word harem in much the same way that it would have been pronounced during the Ottoman Empire with the rem containing a long 'e' (ha reem'.)

• Harem Location

Cëta says the 'house' is "set beside the ocean" and later, with much difficulty comes up with the name "Cimönë." Cimönë does not appear as a major body of water on the maps of Turkey during this time period, however, there are some coastal cities that resemble this word in pronunciation (e.g., Sillyum.) She is either mistaken (she admits she is not sure), misinformed (which is possible because harems are cut off from the outside world totally), or such a place just does not exist.

Later she says the household sits by a mountain range. This is supposedly at the age of eighteen. However, it is difficult to believe that after three years in Turkey she still does not know the city in which she lives. Although this is hard to acknowledge, it is not totally improbable. Harem women, as stated above, had little or no contact with the outside world. She admits this, saying "We are cloistered here…" This is a totally accurate statement. The only access these women had with the real world was through eunuchs (almost always wrinkled, old and black.) Her ability to provide the master with young boys for his sexual amusement was accomplished through such a castrated male to whom she refers very often during the transcript and always in context.

Further on, Cëta, when talking about the stallion she is allowed to ride says that the grounds are large and that there are forests also. This also is not improbable. Turkey does have mountainous regions that go down close to the coastline as well as thickly wooded areas.

• Bathing

During the Ottoman Empire, bathing was all important. Hours each day was spent at great public bathing halls. The harem being a secured area had vast bathing facilities and the women were required to bathe many, many times during the day. Maintenance of these baths and the oils, scents, and spices used were included as major duties for the minor odalisques. Therefore, the mention of bathing, oiling and grooming before presentation is correct.

• Cëta's Homeland

Not knowing in what country her village of Dinea was makes it difficult to verify its existence. Since she had to get on a boat, it is probably not a province of Turkey but there is no way to be sure. Small villages in that era did not make headlines on many maps, partially because village life itself was such a transitory thing. People were constantly migrating to other regions because of recurring battles, etc. It may be interesting to pursue the organization of the Delian League (compare: Delian - Denea which was formed in 479 BC) to prevent the recurrence of Persian invasion along coastal cities such as Lycia,

Pamphylia and Cilicia. Mention of this league appears in history books as being in effect even as late as 1874. It could be that Denea was named after the revered league of protective nations; however, this is purely theory and conjecture.

• Foods

The women did indulge in favorite exotic fruits (e.g. dates, plums, prunes were imported from Egypt as delicacies for rich men's harems.) Contrary to Cëta's statement about heathens eating meat, she could well be calling her own master one. The men of the Ottoman Empire often ate beef preserved in barrels called Pastromani (forerunner of today's pastrami), which was from cows in calf. Sheep were often the main course. Unless there is some peculiarity in this master's lifestyle/religion/preference, this declaration must be discounted.

• Religion

The Moslem faith (prevalent at that time and now) did not condone idol worship or the consumption of meats. If this was Chung Lee's faith then the comments discussed above and the exclusion of meats from the diet would be quite accurate. If Chung Lee's mother was Chinese, she may well have followed a sort of Buddhist Cult, however, sons without fail followed the religion of the man who fathered them.

• Master

Name: It is not unlikely that the master would be called a foreign name because the harem women were often a collection from all parts of the world. If the mother wheeled any influence over the current ruler (Chung Lee's father) a name such as this could have slipped by. However, it is entirely possible that as the young boy reached his majority (full legal age) the name would/could be a negative influence over his future subjects and thusly hinder his ability to command the respect of his people.

Ruler: Cëta refers to the master as the ruler of all Turkey. During the period of 1520 - 1566 the Ottoman Empire began its decline with the reigns of the 10th Sultan, the Great Suleiman I (ascending in 1520) and the 11th Sultan, Selim I (Suleiman's son, ascending in 1566.) Therefore the thought that Chung Lee was "ruler of all Turkey" must have been the over zealous whim of an aspiring harem princess. There were lesser principalities along the coast however, and they are given little or no recognition. These despots were financially well off due to campaigns they lodged against small villages/towns which were plundered for capital gain and territorial rights. Suleiman owned a harem of over 300 odalisques. The size of the harem in comparison with Chung Lee's 159 girls indicates that Chung Lee did not have reign over all Turkey because the harem size was a sign of wealth, status and influence. Cëta was correct in saying that there was much intrigue in harem life. Harem influence was a major factor in the decline of the mightiest empire of that period.

- Female Education

Women were <u>not</u> formally educated and the possibility of receiving a death penalty for learning was not uncommon. Though some women picked up knowledge of numbers, etc., they rarely, if ever, displayed their talents. Therefore, Cëta's comments concerning death for writing are accurate.

- Harem Levels

The levels described were <u>totally accurate</u>! In addition the statement concerning women never leaving of their own will was correct. Only on occasion and then usually only for political reasons (marriage as a show of good faith were as good as a signature on a contract) were married to lesser leaders. Also male heirs were taken from their mothers at a very young age (sometimes as early as 4 or 5 years old) to be educated.

- Date Discrepancies

1499 - Cëta's birth

1514 - Cëta, 15 years old

1517 - Cëta, 18 years old/Shenot a year old

1519 - Cëta, 20 years old

1524 - Cëta, 25 years old

1525 - August, 18 - servant pregnant

1529 - Cëta, 30 years old/Shenot 13 years old/master 45 years old

1539 - Cëta's death (Shenot 23, master 55 years old) Cëta age 40

If the first date given is accurate, then the following are discrepancies:

• The year could not have been 1525 when the servant became pregnant because Cëta was 25 in 1524.

• If Shenot was a year old in 1517 (when Cëta was 18) then her statement that he would be twelve soon in 1529 is wrong. He would be 13. A possible explanation is that fratricide was commonplace among heirs usually instigated/initiated by the harem mother of male heirs to ensure her own son's succession to the throne. If such a plot was successful and the woman conceived and bore another child, it was not uncommon for this second son to be renamed after his dead brother. If such a thing happened to the original Shenot, it is not impossible that she could have had another child. Note that she is never asked if Shenot was her only child.

• The date of Cëta's death at age 40 would be 1539, not 1535. Poppy juice, a favorite narcotic extracted from the opium poppy native to Asia Minor (between the Black Sea and the Mediterranean), administered to her by the physician for pain could account for her inability to relate dates/facts properly.

• The Ottoman Dynasty. The tenth sultan of the Ottoman dynasty, Suleiman the magnificent.

• The Years Of Decline	Date of accession
10 Suleiman I	1520
11 Selim II	1566
12 Murad III	1574

13 Mahomet III	1595
14 Ahmed I	1603
15 Mustafa I	1617 (deposed)
16 Osman II	1618 (murdered)
Mustafa I (second accession)	1622 (strangled)
17 Murad IV	1623
18 Ibrahim	1640 (deposed)
19 Mahomet IV	1648 (deposed)
20 Suleiman II	1687
21 Ahmed II	1691
22 Mustafa II	1695 (deposed)
23 Ahmed III	1703 (deposed)
24 Mahmud I	1730
25 Osman III	1754
26 Mustafa III	1757
27 Abdul Hamid I	1773

POSSIBLE CASES FOR REINCARNATION

Through the technique of past life regression hypnosis, it seems possible for people to see themselves in scenes from their past lives, going back thousands of years, into ancient cultures, wearing the clothes of that period, speaking the ancient language of that time and even writing and translating from that era. They find these experiences stirring, gripping, puzzling, but also calming and reassuring. Some people believe that persons who are regressed always relive a life as a famous person to satisfy their ego, not so. Through the many thousands of regressions I have witnessed, most come through leading ordinary lives, similar to their present life. Very few come through as wealthy and powerful.

A story told me by a friend named A.S. (initials used to protect the person's privacy) helps to substantiate that reincarnation is possible. She said, "in the early part of 1970, I visited Czechoslovakia for the first time to visit a friend. We decided to take a walk through the small town. As we strolled along the street, I sensed a feeling as though many things looked familiar to me, though I knew that I had never been here before. As we reached the top of a hilly roadway, I exclaimed to my friend, "What happened to the church that was at the top of the hill?" He said that he had been living in this town for sixty-five years and had never seen the church, which I described to him, at this location. Since I was so insistent, the following day we checked in the local records office and there had existed a church at that spot which had been removed seventy years ago, before my friend was born.

Another story recounted to me, about two women who came to see me for a past life regression, because of an incident that happened in their lives. A year before they entered my office, they had been introduced to each other through a mutual friend and found themselves enjoying immensely each other's company. They would eat together; visit places together, and felt closer than loving sisters and yet could not understand this caring relationship for each other. I brought one of the women into my regression room, while the other remained in the waiting room. Under hypnosis, she regressed to the time of the French Revolution, where she was arrested, declared a witch at her trial, was condemned to death to be "burned at the stake." I awakened her, brought her into the waiting room and escorted her friend into the regression room. I did not permit them to speak to each other. Her friend regressed to the same period in France, was also condemned and placed in the same jail cell. Three months later they were burned at the stake, where they died together. However, they had developed such an affinity and closeness for each other during the time spent in jail, that this feeling carried over into their present lifetime and that is why they unknowingly felt so close to each other.

CHAPTER 5

INTRODUCTION TO ALVIN LEARY AND RUDOLPH VALENTINO

Knowledge is the greatest treasure of all gifts - anonymous

In the year 1970, while attending a lecture on metaphysics in the basement of a church, I was approached by a young man. He was twenty-seven years old, slightly over six feet tall, with an easygoing charismatic appearance. He introduced himself as Alvin Leary and said, "I have recently had the opportunity to hear your tape on Harry Kantroff. Since the age of three, I have had dreams and nightmares that constantly repeated themselves." Every night until I was six, they repeated and later returned off and on, spilling over into my waking adult life. When I was five years old and other children were outside playing Cowboys and Indians, which was the rage at that time, I would remain inside the house. I would drape a large bath towel over my head to resemble the crown worn by the Pharaoh Kallikrates, casting orders out to his subjects. What my parents never stopped to realize was that at that time I had never been to a theater, there was no television in the house and there were not any books in the entire house that mentioned the word 'Pharaoh' or how a pharaoh acted. When they asked me why I was not outside playing Cowboys and

Indians, I would reply in a stern voice, Royal Falcon not to be as other children. Must learn to be king. In their ignorance, my parents only laughed believing that it was my imagination. In the many dreams that I have had, I dreamt that I am in a war and I am a young boy who is killed. In another, I would be riding a white horse named Firefly, through the desert sand. In one dream, I was on a ship heading back to England. I remember this dream where I put up a terrible struggle as these men forced me to my knees. Then I saw a hooded man swing a great ax, decapitating me. I saw myself bend over in an attempt to pick up my head and place it on my shoulders, but I was unsuccessful. My most powerful dream was when I saw myself as an adult with bronze skin and light golden hair. I was dressed in a white robe while running through the field of a bloody battle. I remember reaching a large river and climbing into a boat made of reeds and the boat traveled a long distance through a wide space of water with a sandy wasteland on both shores. Then the geography changed and the land became green and verdant. It was very hot. The boat pulled ashore and my group of people was attacked by black men clad only in loincloths. I saw a man in my dreams that I felt was my brother and during the fighting this man was killed. I would wake up screaming and shout that my brother had just been killed and yet I knew that the man bore no resemblance to my present living brother. These were not dreams but self-induced trances at which time I was parentally regressing into highlighted scenes from my previous incarnations. These dreams have repeated themselves over the years. For the past four months, I had a woman hypnotist working with me who placed me in hypnosis and was able to draw forth three of my past lives. However, I feel that there are many more that I have never been able to reach. I believe that you are qualified to help me. During my incarnation as the pharaoh, I would stand up while in trance, give orders in a domineering fashion and the hypnotist became frightened that I would hurt her and therefore did not care to work with me anymore. Would you be willing to hypnotize and regress me? "Why not," I replied.

In Baltimore, Md. began fifteen years of off and on research with Alvin Leary. The researchers were Joseph M., Marilyn C., Dr. Stanley F., Nela R. and myself. (Names shortened to avoid invasion of privacy.) We were known as the Metaphysical Research Society and we arranged it so that every Friday evening we would hold a trance in the living room of Alvin's home. I would place him into hypnosis while he was stretched out on the carpet and I would regress him into several of the lives with which he was familiar. I would sit beside him with a tape recorder and hold the microphone to his mouth. Before long, people heard about our experimentation and they asked to join the trance sessions. We would have fifteen to thirty people watching the trance each Friday. As the months passed, we were receiving more and more information on his previous lives. I had been working with Alvin for two months securing information when a woman in the crowd asked, "If he can tell you about his lives, maybe he can tell you about my lives?" I answered, "We have never attempted it, but it is worth trying." This is not a new idea. Edgar Cayce, the world famous psychic had been giving past-life readings since the early 1920's until his death in 1945. I spoke to Alvin while he was in trance and said, "I would like to have a life reading on the following entity," and I fed him her name, address and date of birth. I believed that with a name, address and date of birth, it would be unlikely that he would give me the wrong information. Who on the entire earth would have the same name, address and date of birth? The odds would be against it. If

Alvin could find this one specific person we could secure a correct reading. Five seconds later he began to speak.

"This entity born in 1815, Madrid, Spain under the name ——-(name withheld to avoid invasion of privacy), dies in 1885; born prior to that period in 1620, and Alvin continued going back, speaking of each life, who she married, how many children and what transpired in each lifetime. We taped his remarks so that the woman could have a record of it. She was very happy with the tape. I did not try to verify whether it was true or not. Soon I was getting calls from other people who wanted a past life reading. Alvin began to give readings on a regular basis.

I asked him while he was in hypnosis, where he was getting his information, He said, "I have a vast book before me with all the knowledge of the universe. I can tell you anything you wish to know." Many months later I tested much of the information that came through Alvin and it proved to be correct.

After two months of personal life readings, I said to myself, "Alvin must be fantasizing all the lives that he spoke about because some of the names he gave were so peculiar. I would not be able to imagine these names." The following letter was received from Robert T. (name changed for protection of privacy), who came to my office on January 31st, 1981 for a past life regression. (See page 147, exhibit A, a copy of letter received from Robert T.)

Since Alvin was giving past life readings, I decided to check out his own previous lives to determine whether they were true or if he was creating fictional stories. The following week, unknown to Alvin, I placed him in hypnosis and fed him his own name, address and date of birth and asked for a past life reading for all of the lives of Alvin Leary. (See page

148/149, exhibit B) for a list of the sixteen lives that came through Alvin Leary while in trance.

Now that I had all the lives of Alvin Leary, I began the major job of verifying each life for accuracy and validity. I decided to begin with the top name, as it would be easier to check the lives, which were closer to our present time. Before a large crowd of curious people in Alvin's living room, I placed him in hypnosis and asked him to go back in time to 1940, which was two years before he was born. "Where are you?" I asked. He did not answer. I took him back to 1930 - No answer - 1920 - no answer. The year is 1910," I said. "Who are you? What is your name?" In Italian, he replied, "Rudolpho Gugliemi." "How old are you?" I asked. In Italian, he answered, "Fifteen." Then I said, "Speak to me in English, Rudolpho. You have the power to speak in English. What is the name of your father? In Italian-accented English, he said, "Giovanni." "The name of your mother?" He answered, "Beatricia." "Do you have any brothers or sisters?" He nodded, "one brother, Alberto, one sister, Maria." "What is your religion?" "Catholic," and he crossed himself as he spoke. "Where do you live?" "Cassalanetta, Italia."

"Rudolpho, the year is 1910, you have the power to go backwards and forwards in time. Go forward to the year 1913, and tell me where you are?" "I am on board the SS Cleveland, and I am going to America with my friend, Luigi Abruzzi." "What does Luigi do for a living?" "He is a barber."

Now, go forward to the year 1914. "Where are you?" "I am in New York City. I work on Long Island for Mrs. B., (name withheld to avoid invasion of privacy) I take care of her flowers." "Do you like her?" "She is stinky."

"Go forward to 1915. Where are you?" "I work at Maxim's and wait on tables."

"It is now 1916. What are you doing?" "I am working at Bostanobi's. I dance with women." "Do they pay you?" "They pay me five dollars and for ten dollars, I teach them the finer attributes of love."

"It is now one year later. Where are you, Rudolpho?" "I am in San Francisco with my friend, Eddie Foy. We are in a musical."

"The year is now 1919, what is happening to you?" "I am in Los Angeles and I work for Mr. Belasco. I am in pictures, and am known as Rudolph Valentino."

I was understandably stunned by this revelation, and as I brought Alvin out of his trance, I knew I couldn't rest until I proved or disproved his startling claim. Was Alvin trying to show his macho image of being a lover by fantasizing the story?

Since Alvin had mentioned sixteen previous lives while in hypnosis, I decided to research each life for verification of any facts that came from the trances. The next morning I rushed to the library to borrow every available book on Rudolph Valentino. For three weeks, I poured over the pages of eight books, to compose the most comprehensive test it was possible to devise. As soon as I read a page, I would write a question and take the answer from the book and I created a list of five hundred questions and answers.

The following week before a well-known women's organization, I explained to the audience of one hundred members, that I was going to regress Alvin Leary to his previous alleged incarnation as Rudolph Valentino. I would then ask him the five hundred questions and tape his answers. The results of our experiment were incredible. Alvin answered four hundred and ninety-eight questions correctly and on the remaining two, claimed I was incorrect. The books could have been wrong, as I had no way of checking.

I was amazed that he had answered four hundred and ninety-eight questions correctly, since I had forgotten half the answers after listing them. I ask myself, "How did he do it?" "How could he accomplish such a feat?" Unable to accept him as Rudolph Valentino, the only reasonable answer was, that he must have gone to the library before me and read the same books, and with a photographic mind, had memorized them. This is not easy to do, but it is possible.

In my library research on the silent-screen actor, I had read that Rudolph Valentino and actress, Pola Negri, had been sweethearts, and had he not died so prematurely, they would have married. She was a Polish actress and in the year 1970, she was still alive. It was quite by chance while reading a movie magazine that I came across a story about Pola and that she was living at the Chateau Hotel in San Antonio, Texas and resided in a suite on the top floor. "Alvin," I said, "get on the telephone and call Pola Negri. Maybe as you talk to her, memories of the two of you together will surface." Through the information operator, I secured the phone number of the hotel, and Alvin called and was told, "Miss Negri accepts no calls. She must call you." Alvin then left a phone number and message to be called back collect. A week passed without a call from Ms. Negri. Not discouraged, I asked Alvin to sit down, close his eyes, try to visualize any memories that he had shared with Pola Negri, and then to write to her. "Put on paper whatever pops into your mind concerning Pola and you."

Two weeks passed without receiving an answer. I said to Alvin, "It could have gotten lost in the mail. Write a second letter and I will have it registered at the Baltimore, Arlington post office with return receipt requested." Five days later the letter was returned to me. On the outside of the envelope was the stamped word "refused." Since my efforts to reach Pola Negri had come to naught, I decided to forget the entire incident.

It was to come to an understandable conclusion, however, with my receipt of a letter a month later, from a stranger in California, a Florence H. (Name withheld for privacy.) Below is a copy of the information that I received from her.

> August 15, 1970
>
> Dear Sir;
>
> You do not know me, but I am a very close friend of Pola Negri. (I found out that she was her secretary for forty years.) I was in San Antonio, Texas the day your first letter came and Pola read it and said to me, "This is my Rudolph." (Pola and Rudolph believed in reincarnation.) However, in the letter you write that you are twenty-seven years old and she is much older. Because of the difference in age (Alvin was 27 and Pola was 70) she did not care to get involved again. Therefore, she never answered your first letter. When your second letter came, she refused to accept it and it was returned to you. She asked me not to write to you, but because of the effort you put forth, I felt that I should at least answer. Make no effort to contact me.
>
> Yours truly,

PS: On September 23rd, of this year, Pola and I will be at the services for Rudolph at Hollywood Memorial Cemetery at 2 p.m. If you and Alvin Leary can be there at that time and he can show her the identification mark on the second toe of his left foot, she will accept him 100% as her Rudolph.

Sincerely,

Miss Florence H.

(Name withheld for privacy.)

Miss F H. gave no return address. All I had was the circular rubber postmark on the envelope with a Los Angeles imprint. I called Alvin to come over immediately and quickly pulled off his shoe and sock from his left foot. The only place he has any mark is on the second toe of his left foot ————- a large, dark circular mole! Regrettably, Alvin developed a bad case of pneumonia and we were unable to attend the services at Hollywood Memorial Cemetery.

Since I could not reach Pola Negri, I decided to try several more experiments with Alvin. I believe, that in order to speak and write in a language, it must be learned. The following week, while he was in trance, stretched out on the carpet as Rudolph Valentino, I said, "sit up Rudolph and cross your legs." As he followed my instructions, I placed on his lap a breadboard supporting an 8 ½ by 11-inch sheet of writing paper. Handing him a pen, I directed him," Write a letter to your brother in Italy, and I will mail it." While his eyes were closed and taped he wrote in Italian the following letter and translated it for me. (See page 150, exhibit C)

The translation was perfect, which was witnessed by a schoolteacher who taught Italian. She also spoke to him in Italian while he was in hypnosis as Rudolph. She said he spoke the language correctly with some Spanish words interspersed. Valentino's family had a Spanish background.

I wrote to the M.G.M. studio in Los Angeles and secured an autographed picture of Valentino. I cut the signature off the picture and also off the letter he wrote to his brother and mailed both signatures to a world famous handwriting expert in Philadelphia for a comparison and to verify what was already evident to my own eyes. She wrote back, "written by the same hand."

In 1970, I discovered that there was a club in Los Angeles known as the Troupers Club. The membership was composed of the old-timers, the carpenters, electricians, etc. who would get together once each month and talk over the old stories about Rudolph. I wrote to M. M. (to protect privacy) the president, to get ten of the troupers, each to write a question and answer to which only Rudolph and that person would know the answer. I believed that Alvin would not be able to get these answers from any books. I asked her to place all the answers to the questions in a separate envelope. I was not going to look at the results until Alvin had answered the ten questions, because mental telepathy does exist and I did not want people to say that he was reading my mind. The following week before a large crowd, I placed Alvin in hypnosis, regressed him to Rudolph Valentino and asked him the ten questions. He answered every one correctly. One of the questions was. "On the first day while you were driving up to Marion Davies' party at the Hearst Castle, how many people were in the car with you, who were they, and what happened to the car?" Alvin mentioned the names of three men and said," the car is going down a mountain road, and the right front wheel just came off and rolled down the road." That was the exact answer to the question.

I tried one final experiment with Alvin as Rudolph Valentino. Rudolph was known as a smooth, sexy tango dancer during his acting career. One Friday night we held the trance in a dance studio. I had invited a qualified dance teacher and I told her that I would play an old 78-tango record after Alvin was placed in a trance as Valentino. I was able to ascertain that Alvin had never taken dancing lessons so that dancing the tango would be difficult for him. I placed Alvin into hypnosis, regressed him to when Valentino was twenty years old. I then turned on the tango record and said, "Rudolph, I have a fan of yours here who would like to dance the tango with you. Please stand up" While in hypnosis, Alvin arose from his supine position on the hardwood floor and I ask the dancing teacher to stand close to him while facing him. Suddenly, he reached out, placed his right hand in the middle of her back, his left hand reaching out for her right hand and they both began to glide across the floor in perfect rhythm to the 1920 record music being played. Although Alvin's eyes remained closed at all times while in trance, he was able to lead his partner in the most intricate tango steps that I have ever seen. When the record ended, I asked Rudolph to lie down on the floor, relax and sink deeper asleep. I questioned the dance teacher as to whether she felt that Alvin was faking the tango steps. She said, "This man is a fantastic dancer. He led me so easily and we were doing dance steps that I have never seen or tried before and yet I was able to follow him without any difficulty." I awakened Alvin and questioned him, but he had no remembrance of having danced the tango or of having spoken and written in the Italian language.

In 1973 Dr. Stanley Z. Felsenberg, a Baltimore physician, decided to join our research group. Each week he would check Alvin Leary's blood pressure reading before he slipped into trance. The first time he took his pressure, the reading appeared as 120/80. Once I hypnotized him and took him between lives, the blood pressure reading dropped to 60/30. The doctor became upset as this is considered a coma state. However, as soon as he slipped into one of his previous lives, the pressure returned to 120/80. After many years of associating with our research group I asked him to give me a testimonial as to what he had witnessed. (See page 151/152, exhibit D.)

By 1974, I had regressed Alvin through all of his past lives with the different writings and with some translations for these lifetimes, all written with his eyes taped or blindfolded. The only life he did not write in was the life of Andanee, an intelligent ape-like creature. I decided that Alvin should be checked out by other researchers in the field of reincarnation. In April of 1974, Dr. Walter Panke, a psychiatrist, doing research in reincarnation at the Maryland Psychiatric Research Center in Baltimore, Md. began experimentation with Alvin as per the testimonial letter he sent to me. (See page 153/156, exhibit E)

Since I had a list of Alvin's sixteen lives, I decided to continue with my research on Alvin Leary to determine whether he was able to write and translate the languages of his other lives. To a researcher, such as the author, there comes a, *hunch* that the ability to speak and write in different languages, of which the hypnotized subject has no prior knowledge, would help to conclude that the soul continues to carry knowledge from life to life and that reincarnation does exist.

CHAPTER 6

HIGHLIGHTS OF ALVIN LEARY

Life is all memory, except for the one present moment
that goes by you so quickly you hardly catch it going. -
Tennessee Williams

As a hypnotherapist, Alvin Leary posed a very special problem to me. What were his motives? This was not going to be a superficial investigation. I had no desire to simply copy down and report what he said in trance. I wanted to know where his information came from. What secret sources were opening a flow to his brain that allowed him to change personalities, to recite almost perfectly, life in an English city as it had existed two centuries before his death? I realized as I began to practice with past-life regression in the early sixties, that people would look upon seekers of the occult as not fully oriented with the technological society in which they lived. These skeptics of society, for the most part, dictated the actions of individual human beings; that human beings do not dictate to society as a whole. To these skeptics, researchers into the occult were a strange lot. It was, as if they needed power, power over nature through the use of witchcraft; power over their own destinies through an understanding of astrology, and also the reincarnationists, who demanded proof of power over death itself. To these non-believers, they seemed to be on the fringe of sanity, to be rapidly losing their grip with the real world around them. However, my belief in reincarnation had increased after the investigation of Leo Vincey, because of the correct results that were found on his data, certainly placing into the realm of the paranormal, any explanation that could be offered. He couldn't have read it, so where did it come from? Leo Vincey and Rudolph Valentino were only a small part of the entire mystery of Alvin Leary. There were fourteen more lives to question and there was the phenomenon of health and life readings yet to be checked, and maybe even more important, there was the life of the man himself.

Alvin Leary was born in May, of 1942. He is the second son of a middle class family. His eyes are a cool green cat's eyes that has overlapping traces of joy and sadness, a sense of youth, yet a feeling of age and fatigue. Then they will change and become dark and heavy, big brown spots circling in an ocean of white that cut off the light and gave a sense of power, yet despair. As you gaze into his eyes, they will change again. This time they become large ovals of red and white, like fiery super-nova floating in an endless universe. This is a disquieting transformation, and you will quickly turn away. For you will know that you have seen a man who can look deep into your soul and dredge up your deepest secrets, your greatest fears, your most ambitious hopes. You will feel that you have looked into history itself, and turned away from the impact when it returned your glance.

Alvin seemed to be the perfect example of an American of his generation. He had moved from city to city in his youth. Cherishing dreams of fortune, he had once hoped to become an actor. But he had changed jobs many times, and after marriage, had settled into the

74

respectable mold of a middle class suburbanite. Why had Alvin consented, even asked to be the subject of a reincarnation experiment? What were his motives?

In the years that I experimented with Alvin, the life of Kallikrates would overpower other lives that he was reliving and would immediately take over. It would begin by his bottom lip quivering and vibrating very fast, an activity, which is not easy to accomplish while awake. Suddenly, Alvin would quickly arise from his supine position on the floor, gaze around the room with his eyes closed, with a domineering attitude and begin to bark orders in a strange tongue. I asked myself," why had the memory of Kallikrates continued to override his other lives?" The answer was comparatively simple. In the trances, Kallikrates, the Pharaoh, is most dominant. No matter what personality I elicited from Alvin's subconscious, we always were faced with the possibility that Kallikrates would take over. There was a reason for this; a pharaoh was treated as a God. To his people he was the living Ra-the sun God. Not just a symbol, he was the real thing. The most feared and absolute ruler in the ancient world sat on the throne of Egypt. If someone so much as brushed the garment of the Pharaoh, an instant and unpleasant death was the penalty. It is a logical explanation that such a pleasant memory of being adored and of having absolute power would linger in his subconscious through many lifetimes.

A third dream, which Alvin said he had "quite often," was not as frightening. In it he saw himself riding a white stallion. He remembers sand dunes, an oasis and a beautiful woman. He recalls embracing the woman, kissing her and attempting to seduce her. Again, this is a memory of a previous existence.

There is an explanation for its surfacing during this lifetime. Alvin in trance, as I have said earlier, has given a fair amount of evidence that his last lifetime was Rudolph Valentino. If so, it would be his most recent memory and the one most likely to come through. The scene he recalled as a child is an accurate portrait of Valentino's greatest triumph, "The Sheik." This would make it even more likely that the memory would come through.

I asked myself, "Of what importance are the dreams?" Some would ascribe them to the overactive imagination of a creative child, but they are not the normal hallucinations of a two or three year old. In all of the dreams, Alvin saw himself as a fully mature adult, although the physical characteristics changed with each life recall. Also, in all of the dreams, he knew he was watching his own actions. Not only watching, but reliving with great feeling, the pain, fear, or joy of the moment.

Few children of that tender age are capable of understanding the implications of death, much less a violent one. Most children in their formative years are limited in their sexual imagination to asking their parents, "Where do I come from?" One doubts that any are so advanced as to dream of making love to beautiful women in an oasis. Few would even know what an oasis was. How many small children would have such a great knowledge of Egyptian history as to accurately describe the dress, physical appearance, the Nile River, Temples and Pyramids. What child could give the name of a Pharaoh of whom no record exists?

Where did the name Kallikrates come from? This is before television. He could have learned it from radio, perhaps, but how could a child of this age have taken all the other parts of Egyptian history and combined them? That's an illogical conclusion.

76

Alvin's parents had reacted the way 99% of the parents of America would have, and just smiled and gone along with their child's "daydreams", in an attempt to humor him. But when I realized that the substance of these dreams compared favorably to the information we received from Alvin while in a hypnotic trance, the relationship could not be ignored. It indicated a deeper memory. Where did it come from? Were they really memories of previous lives?

A possible answer has been formulated by Dr. Ian Stevenson, the chairman of the Department of Neurology at the University of Virginia. He made an in-depth study of young children from various nations who claimed to have lived before. In his book, <u>Twenty Cases Suggestive of Reincarnation,</u> Dr. Stevenson advances the theory that the best evidence of reincarnation comes from spontaneous cases of memory, especially among young children two to five years of age. He cited two cases of pre-school age youngsters who were able to recall vividly, information about people who had lived hundreds of miles away and died many years before the child was born. Most of the data collected approaches the realm of the unbelievable when it becomes apparent that those children were giving personal detailed accounts of other lives and that there was no possible way they could have known. Dr. Stevenson then writes that most of the cases he studied came to an adult's attention when a child from two to four years of age began talking to his parents or other adults of a life he had supposedly lived in another time and another place.

Tom Shroder, the author of "The Scientific Evidence for Past Lives," asked Dr. Stevenson whether he thought his research had "proven" reincarnation. Dr. Stevenson remarked that of all the cases he knew about, that at least for some, reincarnation was the best explanation he was able to come up with. He mentioned that there is an impressive body of evidence getting stronger all the time and that a rational person can believe in reincarnation on the basis of the evidence. In the forty-three years of research at the University of Virginia, he had investigated more then twenty-five hundred cases. In his autobiographical essay, he said that his beliefs should make no difference to anyone. Everyone should examine the evidence and judge it for himself.

Alvin's waking memories of Kallikrates certainly reflects a similarity to this hypothesis, but what of the dreams? Was this something new? Dr. Stevenson mentioned nothing of dreams in his book. It seems apparent that if the memories of these boys and girls were so strong that it came through while awake, then it must have been powerful enough to filter through during their sleep.

By now, I was sure that the desire to clear up the mystery of Alvin's dreams was his motivation. I began to theorize that this compulsion to go into trance was caused by his desire to know his destiny, and that his destiny would come forth as he met and knew his past lives. So, I answered my first question, but in the process raised many more, but at least, I felt a small part of the mystery had unfolded. A few clues were available to me.

The connection between Alvin's dreams and other cases of this type was plain. As in the cases Dr. Stevenson investigated, Alvin had known at an early age information that it would have been impossible for him to obtain. The question that this raises, however, would be a little stickier. Was Alvin while in trance, simply reliving fantasies of his childhood?

I answered my own inquiry with a question: do the daydreams of children include correct historical and linguistic information? No! And if Alvin were only regressed to age three, he would only know what his mind contained as a three-year-old. The memory of his adolescent and adult years would be lost. There is a type of amnesia that goes with the phenomenon of age regression that blanks out the memories of the later life. It is best explained by an example. If I, age 22, am regressed hypnotically to age 17, I will actually be living the experiences I had at that age. I will know everything I knew at age 17, but nothing later. The five years between ages 17 and 22 will be wiped from my memory.

So, if Alvin had simply been regressed to age two or three, it is likely that the body of his dreams would come out through the trances, but almost impossible that he would be able to give correct historical and linguistical data as he already had proven he could do during the investigation of Leo Vincey.

But, if Alvin was not at age three, is it possible that when he is in trance that he is at an older age, combining the memories of the dreams with learned information?

Alvin is a tenth grade dropout. He is not stupid, but rather his failing in organized learning stemmed from a complacent attitude and the spirit of a rebel. He did poorly in his studies from the first grade on and was shifted from school to school. In the fifteen years I experimented with him, he did nothing more than scan a newspaper, and he claimed he never read a book from beginning to the end. He failed high school Latin.

When the acting bug hit him, he left school for good, and traveled to Hollywood, where he appeared in two segments of a now defunct television series. After a few years, and one bit part in a class "B" type picture, he decided that the pressures and the strains of an acting career were not for him. He returned to Philadelphia.

He then went to hairdressing school, where he met his wife Nancy. There was an instant attraction between the two and after a short courtship, they were married. Later, when the trances began, the attraction for Alvin and his wife that resulted in love at first sight was explained: from information received. We learned that his wife, Nancy had been Alvin's wife in another lifetime. She had been Amenartis, Kallikrates' Queen and half-sister. This gave the researchers another fact to ponder: what were the effects of group karma, as they related to Alvin? But the first question to be answered was whether or not he could have learned the information he gave us.

With his marriage impending, Alvin decided that he needed a regular job, so he went to work as a pet salesman. He did well and was promoted to Store Manager, and finally, District Manager. His company then sent him to Baltimore, Md. to handle its chain of stores. He did so well that he decided to set out on his own. Unfortunately, he bought a pet store that was almost bankrupt. The business collapsed under him. He then went to work selling first, used and then new automobiles. Later, he made the switch to the home improvement business

As can be seen, there is little in his background to suggest a diligent scholar with a photographic memory and a sponge like retention of linguistics and history, which is what he would have to be able to know, based on his answers in trance. Because of his dreams, Alvin had developed an interest in mysticism and psychic phenomena. He began to seek out acknowledged psychics and hypnotherapists. He walked the streets of Baltimore and attended lectures and demonstrations. Most of the people he saw gave him the feeling that they were downright frauds. Anxious to obtain answers to his dreams, he experimented with self-hypnosis, which he had used in his adolescent years. With almost fanatical concentration, he was able to achieve a state of light somnambulism. But this was not enough. He found that he needed to be controlled by someone who could direct his actions and question him extensively. His curiosity about his past lives and the purpose of the present life overwhelmed him. He began to attend as many public demonstrations of psychism and hypnotism that he could find. Many of them disappointed him. He felt that the field was over-run with frauds and fakes. He began to wonder if he would ever find someone capable of making a serious inquiry into his background and bring forth from his subconscious, the memories he was certain that lurked there. It was at this period of time that Alvin heard the tape on Harry Kantroff and sought me out and we began the research off and on for the next fifteen years.

CHAPTER 7

THE CHILDHOOD YEARS OF PHARAOH KALLIKRATES

There is nothing more frightening than ignorance in action. - Goethe

By the middle of the Third Century before the birth of Christ, the land of the Pharaohs had fallen in political and military stature to that of a fifth rate power. Since 700 BC, a series of invasions from both Asia and Africa had bled to exhaustion the fierce pride and courage of the warrior kings. For 125 years, the mighty Son of the Sun had been little more than a vassal to the Persian Empire.

But, shortly after the close of the Fourth Century BC, a Royal House arose in the Egyptian Delta. It made, over a period of approximately 50 years, a vain attempt to regain some of its fallen glory. For a brief period, the Pharaonic Falcon flew again. With the aid of Greek mercenaries, Egypt was able to stave off the Asian hordes. This was the Thirtieth Dynasty. It was a time of turbulence and bloodshed.

It was during this period that Alvin/Kallikrates claimed to have ruled. He claimed to have been pharaoh for only two years. Was it possible that relics of his reign had been lost? In checking Budge's book on Pharaohs, between 343-341 BC, there is a two year gap where someone ruled, but it is not known who ruled. The records show that Nectanabo II died and Artaxerxes from Persia took over the Dynasty. Alvin/Kallikrates claims that he ruled these two years and was chased out of Egypt by Artaxerxes also known as Ochus.

There is much archeological evidence to suggest the answer is <u>yes</u>. In a similar case, the records of the boy-pharaoh Tutankhamen, who also had ruled for less than two years, had been lost. In an unnoticed corner of the Valley of the Kings on the West Bank of the Nile, a mighty pharaoh had lain unknown to the world. It was only by accident that in 1922 Howard Carter, an archeologist, stumbled upon the grave of "King Tut." In another incident, Egyptologists discovered the mummies of nineteen pharaohs in a mountain cave. Apparently their bodies had been carted away by grave robbers who were not content with just rifling the tombs.

The incidents mentioned above occurred in times of peace. But, when Kallikrates is supposed to have lived all was fluid. Ochus of Persia invaded Egypt and put it to the sword. He killed the sacred bull Apis, and destroyed temples and defaced monuments. Memphis and Sebennytos in Lower Egypt were sacked. No excess was too much for this sadistic madman. So, there is a strong possibility that Ochus would want to wipe from history the name of the Pharaoh that he routed from Egypt. To preserve his own triumph, he would almost have to do something like this, as it was a common practice in the ancient world. But how, short of taking pick and spade and hitchhiking across the Atlantic, were we to get at the truth of Alvin/Kallikrates.

The problem was solved in research. One of the major complaints against the "<u>Search for Bridey Murphy</u>" was that the hypnotist had led the subject on. Prominent psychologists, along with some irrational outbursts, did find, admittedly, that Morey Bernstein had not re-tested his subject at that period of time on specific points of information. To the contrary, Bernstein, himself in some cases, kept referring to "facts" that had previously come out in trance in order to jar the subject's memory. It was decided to do the opposite with Alvin/Kallikrates. We built a life history of this missing Pharaoh to the most remote detail. Then, over a period of months, without prompting by myself as the hypnotist, we re-checked those details. If Alvin/Kallikrates had been fabricating this great mass of information, it would be almost impossible for him to regurgitate the fabrications months after he had, on the spur of the moment, invented them. On the other hand, if Kallikrates was not fantasy, he would give the same answers that he had before. Then we could place this evidence to the theory that it fit.

The last pharaoh that history mentions is Kheper Ka Rekh Nekhtnebf, also known as Nectanabo I. Historians say this last native ruler fled before the onrushing tides of Ochus. It was he who made the last stand to keep together the crumbling 4,000-year-old empire. It was he who collapsed before his soldiers. It was he, they claim, who fled to Ethiopia, while his land and people were put to the sword and the torch. History mentions that it was Nekhtanabo I, known as Nekhtnebf, to whom this inglorious defeat is credited, or was it?

In the second year of the reign of His Majesty, Nekhtnebf I, Se Rekh Kallikrates Meri Amen was born. Alvin/Kallikrates began relating his story.

As is the case with most people, Alvin/Kallikrates' memory was faulty when it tried to conjure up scenes of his very early life as a prince. He remembered sitting on the garden wall watching the other children playing. From what he was able to recollect, the games were mostly violent simulations of warfare. He saw himself confined to a garden throughout his young life. In the garden, he remembered, there was a pool covered with flowers that he believes were lotus leaves and chrysanthemums. As he had done in the first trance that Alvin/Kallikrates appeared, he mentioned a woman named Hoshekh, who was his guardian. This is the point where the question and answer period began in earnest.

On the floor before us lay a full-grown man who claimed to be a Prince of Egypt. Alvin/Kallikrates' tanned body was unmoving.

Having finished regressing Alvin Leary to five rises of the Nile (the age of five), I began to have a conversation with a boy who had been dead for 2,300 years. "Why do you not play with the other children, Kallikrates?" "Pharaoh has said I not to be among others. I will be Pharaoh after Pharaoh. They must respect me as young falcon." I had to facilitate that fact-finding mission and told Alvin/Kallikrates to speak only in English, unless otherwise told not to. "Do you ever get a chance to play with the other children?" "At times Falta will bring with her Rahotep and Neri to my chambers. We see to the others, and they bring offerings fine." "Who are Falta, Rahotep and Neri?" "Falta, sister of Nekhtnebf, Rahotep, son of Falta and Rashahotep and Neri, sisters of Rahotep."

This is the first type of factful information we wanted. Weeks from now we would go back over the tapes, and test the subject on these names and the information that was brought forth from the regression. Again, we acted on the belief that the subject could not correctly remember all these names, places and ages if they were invented when the question was asked.

"Who is older, Rahotep or Neri?' "Rahotep is first born. Nile rises two times before Neri came into being. (The Egyptians counted the years by the rising of the Nile, once each year.) Neri came into being after Rekh (the sun) had rested in the western horizon of heaven ten times after Rashahotep was killed in battle North." "Who is older, Falta or Nekhtnebf?" "Falta first born. Nile rises three times before Nekhtnebf came into being."

This was enough of Kallikrate's early life. From trances held before, in which the personality of Kallikrates had manifested itself, we knew that some traumatic event occurred when Alvin/Kallikrates was about six years old. What had happened to the young prince at that time we did not know, but it was an eerie feeling to be a witness to a drama that had played upon this earth long before we were thought of, and long after the principal characters had become dust. It was this next scene, with its raging passions that made believers out of many of those involved in the investigation.

"Clear your mind Kallikrates. I want you to clear your mind. You are now moving forward in time, I want you to see yourself at six rises of the Nile." The figure of Alvin/Kallikrates had shifted. Although still lying on his back, the young Prince had drawn his knees up and his head was lifted. "Tell me, Kallikrates, what is happening? What are you doing?" "I am hiding behind throne of Nekhtnebf in Great Hall. Sappho (the queen) asks of Nekhtnebf to journey to Macedon to visit her cousin Feeleepakh, and Nekhtnebf orders, "no". Sappho asks of Pharaoh if she is prisoner in his land. He strikes Sappho and Sappho tears like Auset and falls to floor crying. Sappho is running away. Nekhtnebf shouts after her, "How dare you question the decision of Pharaoh." No! Oh, no! A look of horror and fear scrunches up on the young prince's face, "Nekhtnebf has seen me."

It was interesting to note that, unlike the Bridey Murphy case, Alvin/Kallikrates did not have to be reminded of his mother's name nor his father's. Also, in the legend of Isis, who Alvin/Kallikrates called correctly, "Auset," she cries over the loss of her beloved husband Osiris, thus the expression "She tears like Auset" was a poetical Egyptian expression for someone who was crying.

"Please continue, Kallikrates. What does Pharaoh say to you? What does he say to you?" I asked.

"Nekhtnebf puts me on knee and speaks the words: "Little prince, my little Heru, you are very young, but try to understand that her life would be in danger if she left these lands of Rekh. Her place is here to protect the throne for you, should harm befall me. Your reign here will be most important of all kings, for under your majesty, Tamerech (Egypt) will rise up or fall to ashes. Tarisush (Ochus) is making strong his army again to come to our two lands. We must be friends to those of Macedon and Laconia and to be ready for Tarisush. Your mother, Queen Sappho and I, your father, agree that your spiritual body was given to your spiritual father Rekh, and your spiritual mother, Auset, for you are to be the next living Heru (Horus), Pharaoh of upper and lower Tamerech, (Egypt). There is much wisdom that you must learn and much of this wisdom was entrusted to the Prophets of Auset by the Lords of Atlan (Atlantis) in the days of old. It is my wish that you go together with Prophet Chief Karis to dwell within the Temple of Auset (Isis) in Menefer (Memphis) to be educated as a prophet of Auset. Just go now Kallikrates, beloved of Amen." Then the figure on the floor shifts. A lone tear dribbles down his left cheek. His words are slurred. He cannot be understood. "What are you saying? What are you saying? I questioned. "Please, Kallikrates, speak so we might understand."

"Samentep, Prophet Chief of Amen, when Rekh was at rest put thoughts into my head of the tomorrow. I had seen a man of black come for me to take me away to a far place. What is this meaning for me? What does Samentep, Prophet Chief of Amen say? Samentep has said," great tomorrow's are there for me. These thoughts are good things." The tear has dried up. The Prophet Chief evidently had allayed the boy's fears. Kallikrates lay back as if sleeping. Peace and innocence spread across his face.

The jump in time had confused us. Most likely the two scenes were related —- the dream and the encounter with Nekhtnebf, but how? So far, there had been no real traumatic experience, at least not of the type we had expected.

"Go forth to the next day, Kallikrates. I want you to see yourself as you rise. What is happening now?" "Day come for me to take to Pharaoh. I stand before Nekhtnebf and he speaks words to me."

The prone body suddenly stiffened all of its muscles, as if standing at attention. The breathing was quicker, as if Alvin/Kallikrates was nervous and excited. He wrinkled his forehead with the sheepish look of a little boy caught in some act of mischief.

"Go on Kallikrates, what does Pharaoh say?' He speaks: "Karis, Prophet Chief of Auset, take my son, Se Rekh Kallikrates Meri Amen, into your hands. Allow him to dwell within the Temple of Auset at Menefer. Educate him and teach him the ways of the Gods, until the day he returns to Uisa as the new Pharaoh. Protect him with your own life, for if any harm should come to him, I shall have your life, and I shall crush your temples and your Gods along with them. Journey to Menefer under the protection of Haypee."

"Now Kallikrates, I want you to move forward in time one day, I asked. Ra has gone and appeared again. It is morning and Ra has just risen. What is happening?" "Samentep, please help me!" Alvin's voice is the shrill and high-pitched tone of a frightened child. Tears stream down Alvin-Kallikrates' face. The arms flail wildly. "This is the far away place of my thoughts. I not to go. Karis is evil. Go to Pharaoh, and tell him you have spoken with the great Amen, King of Gods, and it is the wish of Amen I to stay here in Uisa. He will listen to you. Nekhtnebf is one with Amen."

"What is Samentep's answer? Please give us Samentep's answer," I quickly requested. The figure shook with sobs. Only his low moans were heard. It was obvious that this was not acting, that he was actually living this scene that had happened 2,300 years before. It was like stepping through a window into the past.

Samentep say, "As much as I would like to do this my prince, I can not be false with Pharaoh. Suten Net Kheper Ka Rekh Se Rekh Nekhtnebf is a wise man, and he will know if I speak false words to his ears. Go with Karis, and one day you will return home to become Pharaoh."

"You have now gone forward in time again. It is later in the morning. What is happening, Kallikrates?"

Two priests of Auset come to me in my chambers. They wash my body and dress me in a white robe. They do not allow me to take my belongings. No need of these any longer. I run to Sappho. I say to Sappho, "I do not wish to go with Karis, he who is evil." Sappho says to me, "My child, my little Heru, you must go and do as your father has ordered. This too is a part of your tomorrows. There will be a young priest in the Temple, called Bako. Make of him your friend, and when you return to Uisa as the new Pharaoh, bring him with you. Become wise and strong, for you will one day be called the King, greater than all kings. The day will come when all kings will bow before your feet as the True Living God. Your destiny is many, many years and more than years. In the days to come you will be angered with Nekhtnebf, but remember that he does that which he must do, and even he does not know the reason for that which he hast done. Trust the Gods my little one. Go!"

During the parting from his mother, Alvin Kallikrates' hands had outstretched as if to encircle someone. He had spoken like a frightened little boy, not like a husky twenty-nine year old man. The tears had been real. The minute information he had given was just what we were hunting for. So we ended the trance at this point. We wanted to wait a week to see if his memory could pick up where it had left off. When the trances resumed there was to be no suggestion on my part of what had taken place. Alvin/Kallikrates would just be taken to that exact spot in his sixth year. We wanted to see if his memories would produce statements that conflicted with his earlier testimony. So far his information that could be validated proved to be correct. Uisa was a name for Thebes. Menefer, which means the Beautiful City, is now known as Memphis. Hapi was the God of the Nile, and Auset was the Egyptian name for Isis, according to Budge's book "The Mummy." Speaking of the death of Rashahotep, Alvin/Kallikrates had mentioned a great battle in the North. He was correct. According to the book "Ancient Egypt under the Pharaohs" by John Kenrick (Vol. 1, 1883, John Alden Publisher) Nekhtnebf had fought a battle with a large force of Persians under Artaxerxes Mnemmon in the Egyptian Delta in the early years of his reign. The forces involved included thousands of Greek mercenaries on both sides and over 100 ships at sea. It was a decisive victory for Egypt, allowing the Pharaoh to rule autonomously for the first time in more than 100 years. It must be noted that the source books I used were sequestered in a University library that Alvin had no access to. The public libraries in Baltimore and surrounding counties were notable for their lack of books on Ancient Egypt. There was no explanation for his correct answers.

So far, in this early stage of the Alvin/Kallikrates investigation, the depth of emotion shown in the scenes with his father and mother, pointed to either reincarnation or possession. For a genetic memory to be that strong is doubtful. Equally doubtful is that proposition that Alvin/Kallikrates could become so emotionally disturbed if he was only tapping into this scene via a vast psychic consciousness. But, it was not proof enough. The next week the trance was again held in his private home. More members and guests were present than at any previous trance. Alvin, his summer tan beginning to change under the autumn skies, was again placed in the center of the gathering. I moved his slim frame closer to the chair I was in. Once more I placed him into a profound hypnotic trance. Alvin's eyes rolled toward the top of his head. "You are now going back hundreds and hundreds of years, and you will be able to answer my questions. You are going back, way back. You will go back in time to the life of Kallikrates, in the land of Egypt at five rises of the Nile." Alvin's stomach muscles jerked with each word. It was apparent that another personality had entered. "What is your name?" "Se Rekh Kallikrates Meri Amen." We all nodded. Now to test whether his story could be continued, or if it was a dream that had abruptly ended the week before. "You are going forward to the age of six. You are halfway through your sixth year. What is happening?" I inquired. Alvin repeated the words of Sappho. Then he was moved forward. "I want you to move forward. You see yourself. It is the next day, speak in English. How many boats are going on the journey?" "Twenty boats in all." "How many men are in each boat? Who are these men? You will speak in English unless I direct you to do otherwise." "Nineteen boats have twenty Royal Immortals, twelve rowers and one rudder man. Our boat has ten Royal Immortals, ten priests of Auset, twelve rowers, and one rudder man, Prophet Chief of Auset, Karis and me, Se Rekh Kallikrates Meri Amen." "Describe the journey in full detail," I requested. "Uisa grows smaller and smaller until Uisa is no more. I say to Karis, when do we arrive at Menefer-Ikuptah?" Karis answers me, "Menefer, Beautiful City, is name. Ptah will soon be in second seat in city. Auset will rule!" He smiles wickedly, and says, "Many days we must journey forth. Fear not little prince, for now you are in hands mine." Not much time, we passed the cities of Nebi on the left side of the river, and Gesau on the right side of the river. Then we come to city Gebtiu on the right side of the river. We rest there for a short while, and to eat of food and drink the blood of the vine. Once again on the river, we pass by city Hut, on the left side of the river, and city Nushenuset, on the right side of the river. I now see very beautiful city. Yes, this must be Menefer at last. I run forth to Karis and he smiles wickedly to say this will be city of Abtu. We arrive at riverbank, on left side is Abtu, and we rest the night within the Temple Satet. Priests of Satet good to me." The childish voice that emanated from so large a man faltered. He seemed to stumble as if tired. The inclusion of the names of so many cities was an unexpected

92

surprise. I knew I would have much more research work to do when this trance was finally finished. One could actually, with a little imagination, see the strain of the journey on the young prince. Alvin/Kallikrates was sweating. Every once in a while, he began to scratch his arms and neck. He would flick his wrist out around his ear. His voice began to get weaker.

"Yes, Kallikrates, we understand. Please, go on," I requested. "When Rekh risen in horizon, eastern of heaven, we continue journey to Menefer. Day all we journey, and soon, before Rekh rested in horizon western of heaven, I see city of Menefer. I run to Karis, and he smile to say Menefer not, for this city of Khmun." A flood of tears and a child's wail stunned the onlookers. Fighting back his sobs, Kallikrates continued.

"Tears roll down face mine, for to me seemed journey without end. We rest night within Temple Tehuti. Again, priests good to me. Next day we pass by city Stetoui, and city Dashur. After Rekh had begun his journey toward the horizon, we see beautify city. Me not think Menefer for to give up hope this time." Karis come forth to me and say, "We now here, city Menefer. Soon you will be no Prince of the Two Lands, but will belong to Auset. You have life new ahead of you." Alvin/Kallikrates' face began to smile, but again his hands kept smacking and flicking at his face, arms and neck. He looked happy, but irritated. "Why do you keep hitting your face?" I asked. "River gnats are many this time of year." "What time of the year is this?" "Auset is mourning for Ausir, and her tears are making to rise the River Nile."

"You will move forward a few minutes. You are now arriving on the banks of Menefer. What is happening?"

"People of Menefer are chanting. Priests of Ptah offer tributes for me. Menefer is beautiful city of the Gods. We now go forth to Temple

Auset. All maidens cast down lotus flowers before me to pass on forth. We now arrive at the Temple Auset to enter."

"Describe the Temple of Auset to me. What does it look like? What is it made of?"

"Wall large around Temple Auset. Steps many to large doors. Temple of granite, Priests of Auset chanting hymns to Auset and Ausir. Karis says to me to come forth to sleeping quarters all together with Karis. Door opening to Temple gardens. Young priest beautiful in garden. Karis says called of him, Bako Neysu Auset. Go forth to he in garden."

"Yes, go forth, what is happening now?" I asked.

"Young priest beautiful, he says to me," name mine is Bako Neysu Auset. You must be Kallikrates Neysu Auset. Eokh! Nuk pa ba en ta khat hate, Se Rekh Kallikrates Meri Amen, suten se en neb en tuai, Suten Net Kheper Ka Rekh, Ankh, Tchetta...."

A terrible change has come over the young prince. Alvin/Kallikrates' long face had screwed up with anger, and he had shouted the words with added emphasis on his name.

"What have you said? Speak to me in English." Still shaking from anger, he spits forth: "Bako called me Kallikrates belonging to Auset. I shout, No! I am the soul of the body great, son of the Sun, strong and beautiful beloved of Amen, royal son of the Lord of Two Lands, King of North and South, Soul of the Sun comes into being, Son of the Sun, Mighty lord, living forever." "Does not this Bako know your name?" I asked.

"Prophet Chief of Auset, Karis, is to take away name mine to give name of Temple to me. I will send words to ears of Pharaoh not to please him."

"What do you do next? Continue, please."

"Bako takes me to share sleeping quarters together with him. Bako says to me, I will not be at peace here for many days, but I must learn to be like others all, for it is the wishes of the Pharaoh and the Gods. Bako asks of me to be his friend always. Bako has promised to protect me from evil all."

"How many rises of the Nile is Bako?"

"Sixteen rises of the Nile of God Hapi in age."

"Do you like Bako?"

"Sappho has told ears mine that Bako is good. Sappho has said for Bako together with me return to Uisa in many tomorrows, not yet to come."

It was interesting that Alvin/Kallikrates had remembered this detail from among the hundreds of pieces of information he had given the week before. How much better than the "Search for Bridey Murphy" this investigation had become! More and more, Alvin/Kallikrates was dispelling our feelings that he had fabricated this story of the last Egyptian Pharaoh.

"What are you doing now?"

"Priests all go to eat of food. I tell to Karis is not enough? I want food plenty. Karis says to me, I am Kallikrates Neysu Auset. I am to be like others all. I am no prince in Temple of Auset. I will go to Bako to run from this place, when Rekh rests in Horizon Western of Heaven."

"I want you to travel forward a few hours. It is now night and Ra has rested. What do you do?" I asked.

"Bako tells me to go forth not from this place. Karis is wise. Karis will make unhappy things to me. Karis is within Temple Auset, like

Pharaoh is within Royal Residence of Uisa. Bako says to me to trust him always."

Where do you sleep?" I inquire.

"I sleep together with Bako. He is to teach me the ways of the Temple of Auset."

"It is now late in the next day. What have you learned?"

"Auset, mother of all, thou art all good things. Protect the Pharaoh from our enemies. Protect our wisdom given to us by the Gods of far away houses. Let the Nile flow freely, and let the Two Lands be fruitful that all should prosper. Grant us long life, strength and health for eternity, Auset, mother of all, hear our words to you now and forever and eternity all."

The second hypnotic trance relating to Kallikrates came to an end at this point. We were satisfied that Alvin was not inventing his stories on the spur of the moment as a reaction to hypnotic suggestion, as many psychologists had suggested when they called the phenomenon, "fantasy." He had successfully fulfilled his story, given names and places. He had not forgotten his mother's last request to him. He knew the Osirus myth well enough to describe the time of the year with it. But, still there were his factual dates that now had to be checked.

During the story of Alvin/Kallikrates' journey up the Nile to Menefer, the subject had named several cities. In a list of places of Upper Egypt, I was able to verify most of his statements. Kallikrates mentions passing Abtu. There was a city Abtu. Its chief God was Anher. Our phonetic spelling had come up with the city of Gebtiv. Closest to this pronunciation was the city of Qebt-herui. He mentions that Ptah was the chief deity of Memphis. (Menefer) He was correct. Ikuptah, or City of Ptah, was another name of Memphis. The cities of Nebi, Gesau, Dashur and Khmun were also mentioned. This list, admittedly incomplete, did not have records of Nushenuset or Hut. However, there was a city of Het in the "Nom of Sechem". Again, Alvin had come through with amazing information. He was again correct as best we knew. But, still one question remained: What is the basis or the cause for the inexplicable behavior of Alvin Leary in a trance state? That we still did not know. However, by this time, we had crossed off genetic memories in the belief that no memory could last so long and be so clear to cause violent emotional changes in the subject. Reincarnation and possession were the two propositions being forwarded by the Research Society's members, but we still had a long way to go.

CHAPTER 8

ADOLESCENT PERIOD OF PHARAOH KALLIKRATES

Where thou art, that is home. - Emily Dickinson

We moved on to the middle period, the adolescent years of Kallikrates. For the next trance, we brought prepared questions for points of fact, rather than allowing the subject free reign to build a story. By moving back and forth between these two techniques, we began to zero in on our proposed theories. As more information was accumulated, these ideas were discarded one by one. By process of elimination the one true theory would be revealed.

The excitement among the researchers had been growing week after week. Now when Alvin was in trance, we were able to see him not as a full-grown man, but as a child, dressed in his robes, frightened yet defiant. Imagination played a great part in our excitement. For we felt we had overcome man's limitations. That now, we could break the time barrier, so to speak, and travel through space/time at will, talking to characters that heretofore had only inhabited history books.

For centuries, man had been challenging his limitations and slowly pushing back the barriers. Man dreamed of soaring through the clouds for centuries, now he flies. Man dreamed of walking on the moon, and now man has conquered this too. And man's other limitations are slowly falling. This experiment, we hoped would push back yet another frontier. No longer would history have to be a dull collection of dates and events. It could become a living science, as men who lived in other time periods were brought back to life within the limits of the trance state. We had expanded man beyond his physical and temporal limitations. Our excitement knew no boundaries. We knew there would be many scoffers, yet, we felt it would be impossible for someone to deny what the eyes had seen, to turn their back on what the ears had heard.

We had to check our confidence, for we were not yet finished. We still had more of Kallikrates to research. There was other phenomenon within the investigation that had not yet been touched.

The subject lay prone on the rug. I, again, induced a hypnotic trance. "You are now sinking into a deep state of sleep."

Alvin/Kallikrates was regressed to his years as a priest of Isis. Then the questions began again.

"What do you eat and drink for your morning meal?"

"Meat and blood of the Nile."

"What is that?"

"Nani."

"What is Nani in English?"

"Water."

"What prayers do you say in the morning?"

"Homage to Rekh who rises in Horizon Eastern of Heavens."

You will now travel forward to the twilight hours. It is evening. What are you wearing?"

"A white robe, ankh made of gold, waist down around."

"Is your head shaven and do you wear anything on it?"

"No."

"Are you barefooted?"

"Yes."

"You are going to your mid-day meal. What do you eat for your mid-day meal?"

"Rekh…Horizon Western of heaven."

It sounded like gibberish. The names, everything, but here they made no sense. In reality, as the next question shows, he was trying to correct me.

"Do you eat a mid-day meal?"

"After Rekh has set in the Western horizon."

"Thank you, Kallikrates. I want you to move forward in time. Rekh has set in the Western horizon. You are going into the dining hall. You see yourself in the dining hall. What are you eating and drinking?"

"Meat, herb from the land, and blood of the vine."

"Kallikrates, what do you say at the evening prayer? What happens after the dinner?"

"Karis speaks to ears prophets all, priests all be. Karis tells Kallikrates belonging to Auset will be priest, day for to prepare."

"What is the exact day of today?"

"Year eight, month two, day one, under Majesty of Heru Life of Births, Two Ladies of Births, Heru of Gold Life of Births, King North and South, Soul of Rekh comes into being, Son of Sun, Mighty Lord, living forever."

"I want you now to go back in age to seven rises of the Nile. You are seven years old. What is the first thing that you do in the morning? Speak in English."

"Welcome Rekh for day new."

"How do you do this? What do you say?"

"Homage to thee O Rekh, who riseth in the horizon eastern of the heaven. Shine forth your rays over the two lands and cause all to become awake and alive. Make the beasts of every kind and the fish of the waters green, and the fowl of the air to move about. We wash our bodies of the day past and begin a day new. Homage to thee O' Rekh, that you might cast your beams over the Two Lands, causing life, strength, health and prosperity for all. Protect our mighty Pharaoh, grant favor of Prophet Chief of Auset, Karis, in the eyes of the Pharaoh, and shine forth upon the Temples of Auset. Homage to thee O' Rekh, that your journey to the horizon western of heaven be glorious."

"What do you do next?"

"We wash our bodies and put on our garments."

"What type of garments?"

"Robe white, band of gold around waist, band of gold hanging from waist, with Ankh of gold."

"Is your head shaven?"

"No, that is of past days."

Here we repeated several questions in an effort to test the subject's earlier information. He did not, as is shown, contradict himself.

"Is there anything on your feet?"

"No, for we are within the walls of Temple on sacred ground."

"What do you do after you wash your body and don your garments?"

"We eat of the food of the Temple."

"What do you eat?"

"Meat of the Nile waters."

"Do you drink anything?"

"Blood of the Nile."

His answers jelled with the earlier information he had given. But, we seemed to be getting no closer to our solution. A vast psychic consciousness theory had fallen to our solution. Alvin/Kallikrates had used the third person when referring to the statements by Karis at the evening meal. Instead of saying Karis tells me, he says "Karis tells Kallikrates Belonging to Auset." It is almost as if he was watching that scene rather than living it. We were more confused than ever. However, one thing was certain, unless Alvin/Kallikrates had a photographic memory, his information was not subconscious fantasy.

"What do you do next?"

"Learn of the wisdom of the Gods."

"What wisdom do you learn today?"

"During the days of Shekkemyeb Peren Matchre, the gods came forth to Tamera in their fiery chariots from their faraway houses. They bring with them good things many; the power of mighty Rekh comes forth, from their hands to build up or tear down. Their knowledge is great of things all. Their magic is great to take away their bodies, and make again to appear. With stick of silver that glows on end, they can heal wounds instantly, and can cure things more." (I believe that UFO's appeared at that time and were treated as Gods.)

"When did Shekkemyeb Peren Matchre rule in Tamera?"

"Before the days of Peribshen."

We now switched our questioning to again re-test information given in earlier trances. Alvin/Kallikrates had not yet contradicted himself, but proof positive was needed. As I stated earlier, we believed we had broken the fantasy theory, but in cases of this type, one is never totally certain. Alvin/Kallikrates looked tired, so I brought him up to the present and aroused him. The following week I placed Alvin again in hypnosis and regressed him to Kallikrates to the moment we had stopped the previous week, and began once more to question him.

"What do you eat for your noon or mid-day meal?" I asked, trying to trick the subject. In the trance a week earlier, Alvin/Kallikrates had said there was no noon or mid-day meal. Would he fall for my suggestion that there was, or would he stick with his answer?

"After Rekh has nested in the horizons western of heaven, we chant songs to Auset, sit in silent meditation and then eat the meat of cattle or fowl of the Temple. We also eat herbs of the land," came the answer, exactly as it had been given earlier.

"After you have finished eating, what do you do?"

"I go forth together with Bako belonging to Auset to a place in the gardens. Bako belonging to Auset speaks to me of beautiful things many."

We broke the hypnosis off at this point. Alvin had come through this part of the testing with flying colors. Now we needed more information that could be historically verified. Throughout all these questions Alvin had not contradicted himself. Yet, in future trances, we would still double back, and ask questions that he had answered earlier. We also moved Alvin forward in time in an effort to get more writings.

These hieroglyphics were, of course, our basic proof. No other subject, not even Bridey Murphy, had written in the languages of the times they claimed to have lived. (See page 157, Exhibit F)

Another interesting phenomena occurred after this study of Alvin/Kallikrates' adolescent years. The subject, after the trance, claimed to recognize one of the researchers as the reincarnation of Bako. This researcher, a young man in his 20's was willing to be hypnotized in an effort to check the subject's information, but he froze and we were unable to induce hypnosis. However, later information led us to believe that Alvin's waking memory of the trance state was correct.

The next tape started with Alvin/Kallikrates' youth and moved up to the time just preceding his coronation as Pharaoh. Again, the same words and general system was used to induce the subject's deep hypnotic state.

"You are now ten rises of the Nile. You have just finished your evening meal."

"I go forth with Bako belonging to Auset to a secret place in the gardens. We make to exist love between our bodies."

"Who taught you to do this?"

"Bako belonging to Auset is kind and gentle, and he has taught me to love better than hate. He has told to me that making to exist love between our bodies is good, and he to me to he is only." At this point I had realized that Kallikrates had developed a homosexual relationship with Bako.

"You are now fifteen rises of the Nile in age. You can see yourself at fifteen rises of the Nile. What are you doing? Speak to me in English. In English."

"Make welcome them who visit from the land of the mother mine."

"Where is this land located?"

"Land North across great, great waters."

"What is the name of this land? How do you call it?"

"Thau Nebunet."

"What does this name mean in English? Can you translate into English for me?"

"Distant land of North."

"What names do you call these visitors by?"

"Plato and Euripides."

"Why have these men come to Tamera?"

"Learn of hidden wisdom in Temple. Learn of wisdom brought forth by Gods of faraway lands. They come forth also to speak with my mother Sappho, who sits in Uisa together with Nekhtnebf. They say Sappho not well, and to bring to her the words of her cousin, King Philip."

Alvin/Kallikrates had sat up. He kept rubbing his hands as if washing them. Then he reached over and moved as if to pick something out of the air. He began to rub the air just above his fingers, as if washing something that he was holding.

"What are you doing with your hands?"

"I am to helping Prophet Chief of Auset, Karis, and Prophet of Auset, Setrekh, take out evil demons from head of Plato."

We were really excited now. It was a known fact that the ancient Egyptians had practiced brain surgery. Although it appeared Alvin/Kallikrates was only a scrubber, we hoped he could give us enough facts to tell us just how advanced in brain surgery the Egyptians had been.

Also, it is known that Plato traveled among the Egyptians to gain knowledge, but historically there is no record of the Greek philosopher ever undergoing surgery. Had we beaten the historians to an interesting historical discovery?

"How does Karis take them out?"

"Plato drinks much blood of the vine. Karis makes Plato to breath the green smoke of sleep. Setrekh open head of Plato, and makes to chase evil demons away. I make to keep clean from blood."

Most books on Egyptology mention the proficiency of the ancient doctors in dealing with head wounds. We know stories of men wounded in battle whose lives were saved by brain operations. And, to our great amazement, we had just had one of these described to us. Unfortunately, beyond the fact that Sekrekh opened the skull of Plato, we were unable to get more information from Alvin/Kallikrates. He was not surgery trained, and thus could only report what he saw.

We moved on, keeping to our schedule. But the emotional thrill running through our bodies refused to leave. Over and over, we whispered among ourselves that we had actually talked to a man who took part in an Egyptian brain operation. Were we proving the existence of more than one life, of man's ability to defeat the finality of death? Yet, there was more to come.

We turned back to the subject, who was again lying flat on his back.

"You are now twenty rises of the Nile. Where are you? What are you doing? Please, speak to me in English."

"I am together with Prophet of Auset Bako. We will go forth from the Temple gardens to walk among the people in the city, Menefer."

"How will you leave from the Temple?"

"Hidden opening in wall gardens known to Prophet of Auset Bako and Prophet of Auset Kallikrates only."

"What will you do in the city?"

"Prophet of Auset Bako wishes to visit together with woman Keeshta, who waits for him near the city end."

"Who is the woman Keeshta?"

"Woman Keeshta, one who raised boy child Bako."

"How many years did she care for Bako?"

"Thirty years past, during days of Nektharheb, soldier of high rank to Keeshta brings boy child, Bako, new born."

"But how long did she care for him?"

"Ten rises of the Nile had passed, and it was the first year of the reign of Nekhtnebf when the soldier of high rank and same woman, then heavy with child, came forth to the house of the woman Keeshta, and did take Bako to give to him of the Temple of Auset in Menefer."

"While Bako is visiting the woman Keeshta, what will you do?"

"I will visit together with friends in city."

"I want you to move forward in time. You will go into the city. What are you doing?"

"Armies of Pharaoh camped outside city end. I will go forth to speak to Nekhtnebf."(His father)

"Go on, you have arrived at his camp. What do you say to Nekhtnebf?"

"Royal Immortals stop me to say, "Not you go forth to Pharaoh. I say, stand aside as Son of the Royal Falcon is in your eyes." They believed me to speak words false, but one soldier recognizes me and tells to others:

"This priest is the hair golden son of Pharaoh." Let him pass to go forth to see his father."

"You have now reached your father Nekhtnebf. What do you say to him?"

"Father mine," Alvin/Kallikrates' face had adopted a wide smile and he reached out his arms as if to grasp someone, "rises many of Hapi has passed since eyes mine have been cast upon face yours. I am longer not a priest of Auset, for I have passed over to become a Prophet of Auset. Is father mine pleased with me?"

He stopped, arms still outstretched, face glowing with the pride of a young man.

"Go on, I said."

Nekhtnebf says to ears mine, "Royal son of mine has pleased me. You will make a good Pharaoh of the Two Lands."

"Why has Nekhtnebf come to Menefer with his armies?" Kallikrates questioned.

"Battle against people from the eastern horizons, who have come forth into Delta land of Lower Egypt," answered his father. I ask of the Pharaoh, for me to go forth together with he into battle, and Pharaoh tells me I an to remain here at Menefer, for day when I become the Pharaoh new of Tamera all."

"Where will the battle take place?"

"Near the city of Teb-neter."

"What news has the Pharaoh brought you from Thebes?"

"Royal Princess Amenartis is a beautiful woman who waits for the return of Kallikrates."

Now we decided to re-test that piece of knowledge about Amenartis that had been learned from the first trance in the investigation. It was almost three months later now. Would Alvin still remember?

"What does the name Amenartis mean in English?" I asked.

"Praised of Amen," he answered correctly, and exactly as he had months before.

"What else has the Pharaoh told you of Thebes?"

"All well and good in Uisa. Rahotep and Neri well. Rahotep image of Kallikrates, having hair black. Surtan and Raoul well."

Again we went back to earlier trances. Without my suggestion to jar his memory, we wanted to see if Alvin/Kallikrates could again pass the fantasy test.

"Who are Rahotep and Neri?"

"Rahotep, son of Princess Falta and husband Rashahotep. Neri, sister of Rahotep." Again he did not change his earlier answer. Still, we had never really tried to overly trick him. Now we did.

"Falta, sister elder to Nekhtnebf, and daughter to Nektharheb and Nitkoteb-Iribent."

"If Falta is daughter of Nektharheb, and sister of Nekhtnebf, how did your father Nekhtnebf become Pharaoh without marrying Falta, since the throne and succession passed through the Royal Princess?"

"Princess Falta, not daughter only of Nektharheb. Nekhtnebf had taken Royal Princess Bashptah for a wife, but took Sappho as his Royal wife and queen."

Those two answers were sufficient to relieve the most nagging doubts. Many people have claimed that prenatal regression was simply the subject's desire to please the hypnotist; and that he was, through his own words, leading the subject on. They felt that by asking a direct question, the hypnotist was suggesting an answer. But here, Alvin had taken the direct questions with implied answers and given a different response. He had not contradicted himself. He gave no information that conflicted with data received in earlier trances. We had tried to trick him with the question of the Royal Princess Falta, and Nekhtnebf's succession to the throne, but it did not work.

The investigation had proved that the genetic and fantasy theories could be jettisoned. Remaining theories remained intertwined. Alvin was now definitely in the realm of the transcendental. More, even than during the Leo Vincey investigation, he had built an entire early life of this Ancient Egyptian, Kallikrates. We were being treated to an intimate view of the life and languages of people who had walked the earth three centuries before Christ was born. To many, this transcending time and space was the most exciting personal experience. But, we hoped to reach the final answer.

Now moving into the final stage of the Alvin/Kallikrates' investigation, and his life as Pharaoh, we found that what had come before, was only an indication of the depths of Alvin's memories. We were about to learn of the violence of the times, and become eyewitness to the death of the Egyptian Empire.

The story we heard from Alvin is a strange one. It is the tale of a homosexual Egyptian Pharaoh, beset with intrigues, spies and traitors within his Royal Palace. It is a dramatic story of the collapse of an empire. We now turned to Suten-Net Rekh Ankh Tchetta Meri Amen Serekh, Kallikrates Meri Amen, and the last native Pharaoh of Egypt.

CHAPTER 9

ADULT PERIOD OF PHARAOH KALLIKRATES

No man has a good enough memory to be a successful liar - Abraham Lincoln

We started this final hypnotic trance at 20 rises of the Nile and moved swiftly through the last questions of the years preceding the Alvin/Kallikrates inheritance of the throne.

"You are now 20 rises of the Nile in age. Tell me, what will you do for your people when you become Pharaoh?"

Taking his fist and swinging it toward the researchers, the future pharaoh answers; "None will stand up against me or they will stand no more. I will chase out of Tamera, Persians all. The two lands will be fruitful and prosperous. No more will be famine or bloodshed in these lands mine. I will make this place for the Gods to dwell forever and eternity all."

"You have just left your father's armies at the cities end. You are back in the Temple of Auset. What is happening?"

"I am in garden alone. I look at water in pool. It is at peace. Second Prophet of Auset, Hashashun, comes forth to me. He places arms of his upon body of mine to make to exist love between our bodies. I shout out for Bako. Bako runs to pick him up and to cast him into pool."

Earlier, we had told of the first indications that Alvin/Kallikrates was a homosexual when he talked of his relationship with Bako.

"You are now 24 rises of the Nile in age. What is happening?"

"I travel by the horse; I do not use chariots because only royal Immortals use chariots and I prefer to sit upon the mighty horse Nekht in Rekh who is as white as the rays of Rekl."

"Who is with you on the journey?"

"Prophet Chief of Auset, Karis, has taken me below to the flames of Auset. He says to me, when I go forth to pass through the cold blue flames of Auset, I will be sworn to keep her secrets within these walls and within mind mine. I pass through flames. Prophet Chief of Auset, Karis asks of me to decree him 'Rank of Lord High Priest' of Tamera all."

"What is your answer to Karis?"

"I will keep my sacred vows to Auset, but I will decide Royal appointments when I become Pharaoh."

"You are now 25 rises of the Nile in age. What is happening?"

"Three thousand Royal immortals have come forth from Uisa to Menefer to carry out orders of Pharaoh to return Son of Rekh, the strong and beautiful beloved of Amen to the Royal residence in Uisa."

"I want you to move forward now. You see yourself on the journey. How do you travel?"

"Prophet of Auset Bako rides a chariot to my right. Prophet Chief of Auset, Karis rides a chariot together with Prophet of Auset Setrekh to my left."

"Why is Bako returning with you?"

"My mother Sappho has asked me this to do. Only to do as mine, I have promised Bako that day when Pharaoh dies, I am Pharaoh and he will be pharaoh with Pharaoh."

"You now can see yourself entering Thebes. What is happening?"

"People are falling to their faces as I passed them by. Priests are many along way to Royal Residence, and they chant sacred prayers. As I reach Royal Residence, trumpets sound 'The return of the Pharaoh,' but I do not see Pharaoh. I turn to Karis and say, "What is happening?" He tells answer to me to say Pharaoh is dead. 'Thou are now Pharaoh of Tamera all." I get down off Nekht en Rekh and walk up steps of Royal Residence with Bako at my right, and Karis at my left. I reach top of steps, and turn to people mine to speak.

Alvin/Kallikrates had suddenly stood up while in trance state. The crowd in the room backs up; some look frightened and pale. He raises his left hand as if holding something and begins to shout in Egyptian. He spoke loudly, as if addressing a throng. His body quivered with nervousness. He looked neither left nor right, but up in the air, as if addressing the Gods. His face shone with splendor. In our imaginations we could see him clad in the golden robe, his tan body reflecting the golden Royal Residence, as he reached for his imaginary crown.

"What do you say to your people? Speak in English I asked quietly."

"People of Uisa and Tamera all, hear my words. The Royal Falcon has flown unto his nest. I claim for me the name, Heru Life of Births, two Ladies Life of Births, Heru of Gold Life of Births, Prince of the Royal House of Haskor, Prophet of Auset, Prince of Uisa, Lord of the Two Lands, Living God, King of North and South, Rekh living forever beloved of Amen, Son of Sun, Kallikrates Beloved of Amen. May I be granted life, strength, and health for eternity." His voice rose in a crescendo that peaked, and then got stronger as he finished his chosen Royal name.

Still shouting, as if trying to be heard over the chatter of a large crowd, he continued: "Bako will be Pharaoh with Pharaoh. Words of Bako will be words of Kallikrates. I decree Bako will be Lord of the Two Lands, Ptah-Kheper-Rekh, son of Rekh, Bako, the ever living."

Exhausted, Alvin/Kallikrates turned and began to stalk from the living room. Six men tried to catch him. His demeanor became one of anger. No one was allowed to touch the Pharaoh, a living God. He shouted and pushed. The six men, each of whom weighed 200 pounds, fell aside like paper mache figures. Alvin/Kallikrates would not listen to me. He kept moving. Suddenly he drew back, and pointed to the floor. He spit and signaled. Taking an imaginary dagger from his belt, he slit it across the air and continued on.

"What has happened?" I asked.

There is no answer. (Later, under conscious recall, Alvin claimed he was touched on the foot by a slave girl, and had paused to kill her for being so bold.) The researchers encircled Alvin/Kallikrates. His arrogance knew no end. I yelled, "Someone get a mirror." (We knew from previous trances that when Alvin saw himself in a mirror he instantly collapsed.)

"Thais, Nagado" Kallikrates raged. (This means shut up. Nagado was my name as his vizier, when he was Pharaoh of Egypt and he always recognized me as Nagado when I regressed him to the time of the Pharaoh.)

Alvin/Kallikrates kicked out at me, striking me on the shinbone.

"Get the mirror, someone shouted."

We began an effort to draw Kallikrates back to reality. The personality of the Pharaoh was overwhelming the individuality of Alan Leary. Finally, the researcher who had been recognized as the reincarnation of Bako shouted: "Kallikrates, come here and sit beside me. We must talk."

An unbelievable change came over Alvin/Kallikrates. He calmed down, and extended his hand to the modern form of Bako. Speaking in a fast, slurred Egyptian, he made motions of pointing at the researchers, as if to say they didn't understand him. Finally, now that he had calmed down, I was able to regain control.

"You will move forward in time. You are now twenty-five rises of the Nile and have been Pharaoh for one day. What happens to you?"

He stood up, began clapping his hands and shouting. His demeanor became, black and ugly again. It was our imagination, of course, but many of us claimed we saw Alvin/Kallikrates as though wearing his robes and double-tiered crown. It was eerie to watch the Pharaoh give orders. It was like being present at a historic drama that was not fiction. He was real!

"What are you saying Kallikrates? In English, what are you saying?"

"Why Sappho not comes forth to me? Karis tells me Sappho put to death by orders of father mine, Nekhtnebf. He says Sappho did adultery and treason. I tell Karis why he tells me not this in Menefer. He say I not have understand when child."

He turned and began to whirl about, stalking back and forth across the carpeted, living room floor.

"Bring forth Samentep to me," he clapped his hands, and shouted at the top of his voice. "Samentep will tell ears mine of Sappho." (Samentep was the Prophet Chief and Lord High Chief of Amen, and a close friend of Alvin/Kallikrates while he was growing up in the Temple of Isis.)

"Samentep is here. He is speaking to you. What doe he say," I suggested.

"He says, during day of Nektharheb, after Nekhtnebf had taken Sappho for his wife, Sappho and captain of Royal immortals, Surtani, secretly made to exist love between their bodies. Not long after that time, Sappho journey to live in Gebtiu. When heavy with child, Sappho sends for Surtani, and boy child came into being.

"Surtani and Sappho did take the boy child to a woman's house for her to raise up. At the end of the first year of Nekhtnebf, Sappho did journey, together with Surtani to house of woman, and did take the boy to the Temple of Auset in Menefer. After blessing given by Auset for birth of child, Sappho and Surtani did return to Uisa, and Son of Rekh, the Strong and Beautiful Beloved of Amen came into being."

A lone tear dribbled down Alvin's/Kallikrates' cheek. He looked pale and shaken. He groped for a chair, finally settling in a sitting position on the floor.

"Go on!" I urged.

"This brought to ears of Nekhtnebf by Falta in year seven of Nekhtnebf. Nekhtnebf send away the Son of Rekh, Strong and Beautiful Beloved of Amen together with Karis. Royal Son not to be made known of these things. Pharaoh orders Queen Sappho be put to death for eternity and eternity."

"Continue Kallikrates."

"I say to Samentep, 'What name of this boy?' He has no knowledge name." Alvin/Kallikrates' voice was shaking. He looked like he was about to fall. But then he rose quickly and reaching back for inner strength, he shouted. "Bring Karis to me."

"Karis has arrived. What do you say to him? Please continue to speak in English."

Shouting loudly, and angrily, Alvin/Kallikrates began: "Tell me name of boy child of Sappho and Surtani." Then Alvin/Kallikrates answered his own question: "Bako," then lower and lower in the form of a question, "Bako?" Alvin/Kallikrates walked across to where the modern reincarnation of Bako was sitting, and embraced him, tears streaming down his face. "This is so, for Sappho did tell me to bring forth Bako to Uisa." Alvin/Kallikrates wrinkled his forehead as if remembering the story he had related in trance months earlier about his mother's last request.

To the researchers, it was like watching a Greek tragedy, except it was real. No one could have so great an imagination as to dream up this tale, but the most tragic part was yet to come.

"What do you do now Kallikrates?"

Alvin/Kallikrates began to pace about the room. His movements were quick, and made in anger. His jaw jutted out over his chest. With a sneer, he commanded: "Bring me Surtani."

The researchers looked back and forth at each other. This was the most impressive demonstration of Alvin Leary's past lives that we had yet seen.

"We have brought Surtani, your majesty. He is here. What do you say to him?" I asked.

"Surtani, you have brought shame to house mine, and shame to name of mine fathers all. You have made black your rank of high favor. You have caused a queen in high place to commit acts of treason and adultery for pleasure your own. You did place yourself before the well being of your king and his house, which of your rank you swore in names of Gods all to protect. I decree Surtani to be stripped of his rank, titles, property and claims. You will be made to face death without organ part that took this pleasure. Come forth to feet mine!! (His voice rose, crescendo like to a high point) His anger seemed to know only hate. There was no mercy in his demeanor. With a flourish, he reached to where he kept those imaginary daggers on his hip and grasping something at his ankles, made a crescent in the air, as if performing an act of castration. Then with disdain, he rolled over something, probably Surtani, with his foot. Placing one foot in the air, where the body would have been, he slit across what would have been the nape of the neck.

We sat back, stunned, astounded and quaking with fright. The violence of the ancient world had caught us unprepared. Again, we felt positive it could not be that Alvin/Kallikrates was just tapping a vast past-lifetime consciousness. The depth of emotion displayed during the loss of his mother, the finding of his half brother and the castration and death of Surtani, Captain of his Royal bodyguard, could not have just been seen. It had to be felt. If Alvin/Kallikrates was an actor, he deserved an academy award for this performance. The tears, the movements, the hatred were real. We were now convinced that for months we had actually been watching the movements of a modern pharaoh from Philadelphia. All the information in the world meant nothing when compared to this outpouring of emotion, in the tragedy we had just witnessed. We now moved on. We were getting closer to the end of the Egyptian Empire. It was like being present at one of the great turning points of history.

"You are now twenty-six rises of the Nile. What monuments or buildings have you or your father built?"

"Temple of Auset at Pa-Alek."

"What is the modern or Greek name of Pa-Alek?"

"At rivers end in Pa-Alek. Rocks sent to Temple of Auset at Pa-Alek up the Nile to South."

"Yes, but what is its modern name?"

"Philae-Pa-Alek, "Alvin/Kallikrates answered after a short pause.

"Thank you, your majesty. What other monuments were built by you or your father?"

"Nekhtnebf began to add more to great Temple of Amen at Uisa. I have built more to Temple. I have dedicated it to Amen, King of Gods, together with Montu, God of War, that we will put end to Persians all."

"I understand Kallikrates. What else have you or your father built to last for eternity?"

"Temple of Khmun at Iabu, Temple of Anur-Shu at Teb-Neter, Temple of Bastet at Basta, Temple of Net at Sau, Temple at Djedi, Temple of Net at Bzu-Bzu-Per-Meri, Temple of Auset and Temple of Heru at Hebenu-Bed-Het."

"What is modern name for Iabu?"

119

"Iabu-Elephanteen."

"What is the modern name for Teb-Neter?"

"Teb-Neter, Sebennytos Teb-Neter."

"What is the modern name for Basta?"

"Bubastis Basta."

"What is the modern name for Sau?"

"Sais."

"What is the modern name for Bzu-Bzu-Per-Meri?"

"Naucratis—old name."

"Tell me, who is the man entrusted to build your tomb?"

"Chuma is master builder of Tamera all. Shakhta is helper to Chuma."

"Tell me your majesty, where is your tomb located?"

"No!" giving a loud shout like I have never heard before. "Chuma has knowledge." (He was the builder of Kallikrates' tomb. At the hypnosis sessions, Alvin Leary always recognized Leonard G. as Chuma from his lifetime as Pharaoh.) (Alvin Leary once mentioned that he was instructed to go to Baltimore, through an unknown voice in his head, to bring together those people who had been with him when he was Pharaoh of Egypt.)

"I wish to know so that I can see that all is protected, your majesty. Please tell me where your tomb is located."

"From Valley of Kings is in direction of horizon western of heaven at the first Oasis, outside Valley of Kings so to not be found by people robbers of the Gods. Divine House mine not to be violated. Protected by Anpu for eternity and eternity all."

"Where is the tomb of your father Nekhtnebf located?"

"Nekhtnebf rests in North. Funeral procession taken him down Nile."

We now entered the final stage of Alvin/Kallikrates. We had taken him from the cradle, through his early life, now we were to take him to the grave. The last trance of this part of the investigation was a study in fear. Egypt was about to lose the autonomous rule it had held for 4,000 years. This was a turning point in the history of mankind. We were eyewitnesses to it.

After the trance was induced, it became apparent that something important was happening. Alvin/Kallikrates had stood up and began stalking the room, his condition appeared on the verge of collapse. Rage filled his face. "Your majesty, you have just said your land is being invaded. What king or leader is behind this attack?"

"Ochus, King of Persia."

"Where are the armies of Ochus, right now?"

"Ochus did first take city Sinu in north. News brought to ears mine. Ochus now take city of Djedi, then city Zedu, not city Basta. Armies to Onu and Khemo. Words tell Ochus will take city Menefer Iku-Ptah. After my beautiful city of the Gods, Ochus' armies will move through Gebtiu, Nebi and enter Uisa No-Amen."

He moves like a wounded dog, baying at the moon. His shouts and manner had lost their arrogance. His shoulders drooped, his body movements exhibited his state of terror.

"Surtan!", he shouted, clapping his hands. "Surround the Royal Residence with Royal immortals all, in our protection."(Surtan was son of Surtani who was killed by Pharaoh Kallikrates.)

"Raoul, call out my armies all to block North and Western sides of Uisa. Balto, take word to Lord High Priest Samentep of Tamera all to protect all knowledge of the temples, to put within divine house mine."

"Yes, go on," I urged. "What is happening?"

"Amenartis and Bako join together with me in bull rushes of the Nile to leave these lands.

"Surtan, take these things mine under protection yours. Take seal mine for day when I return to Uisa to rule again and I sit upon the throne of the two lands. I will return to take my place among the Kings."

Alvin/Kallikrates appeared to be on the verge of bolting through the front door and heading toward the street

In a state of heightened anxiety and fear, Kallikrates spoke and mentioned that Artaxerxes, King of Prussia had invaded the palace and he was forced to flee from Egypt with Bako, Amenartis and his entourage. They sailed down the Nile on two barges toward the land of Libya, which is now Africa. They traveled down the coast to the mouth of the Zambezi River. They found a cove, but were overtaken by black natives and in the struggle Bako, Kallikrates' lover was killed. He and Amenartis were taken to the native's white queen, Ayesha (pronounced Asha) who was known as "She who must be obeyed." Amenartis was set free and Kallikrates lived in the village of Kor with Ayesha for two years.

In 340 BC, at the age of 30 years, Ayesha killed Kallikrates with a dagger to prevent him from leaving her, as he wanted to return to Egypt and reclaim his throne. Just before he died, Ayesha placed his body on a stone slab and said, "Forgive me Kallikrates for what I have done, but you belong to me and now you will never leave. Perhaps some day you will return to me in another life. I shall be waiting for you."

All of this information I gathered through the research, regressing Alvin Leary to his lifetime as Kallikrates..

CHAPTER 10

LIFETIME OF NORAN FROM OUTER SPACE

Do not be too timid and squeamish about your actions.
All life is an experience - Ralph Waldo Emerson

Two year had now passed and I had created a composite picture of the life of Rudolph Valentino, Leo Vincey and Pharaoh Kallikrates through the past life regressions of Alvin Leary. I decided that I would make an attempt to regress him to his first life as Noran based on the list of names he had mentioned in the first month of the trances.

While Alvin was lying comfortably relaxed on the carpet, I placed him in hypnosis and asked him to sit up. The tape recorder was running as I held the microphone to his mouth. "I want you to go way back in time to your first life on earth. Dwell upon any scene during this lifetime and tell me, what is your name?"

Suddenly, from his sitting position, his hands and fingers began to move as though he was speaking to me. It looked like sign language. I thought he was faking so I repeated, "What is your name?" Again, he made exactly the same movements with his hands. I then asked, "Where did you come from?" His right hand, with the fingers pointing to the ceiling, began to make small circles and his hand extended completely overhead as though pointing toward the stars. He made no further effort to answer my questions and after two minutes of interrogation I asked him to clear his mind and I then regressed him into one of his other lives.

The following Friday, I invited a sign language teacher to our trance meeting with Alvin and I explained to her that I would regress him to his first life as Noran and question him and she was to tell me what his answers were to my questions. (I secured the name Noran from the list of his sixteen previous lives he gave me in the beginning of the trances.)

With Alvin Leary in hypnosis as Noran, before an audience of twenty people, I asked him to sit up and I began:

"What is your name?"

Once more he repeated the same finger movement with his right hand as he did in the previous week.

"Where did you come from?"

Again, he repeated himself. I then asked the sign teacher, "What is he saying?" She replied, "He is not speaking my language." I realized that he was signing in his own language. At this moment, one of the viewers in the audience said, "Ask him how to say "yes" and "no" and we will be able to get answers."

"How do you say "yes" in your language?" I asked Alvin.

His right hand extended straight out before him with the fingers pointing to the wall and his thumb pointing to the ceiling. His hand rose and fell one time to signify yes.

"How do you say "no" in your language?"

His right hand once more extended straight out from his right side with the palm of his hand facing the floor. He made one quick movement of his hand across his chest from his right side to his left to signify "no." I now had a means of questioning him.

"Did you come to earth from Mars?"

He made the sign for "no."

"From Venus?"

Again the same sign.

"From Uranus?"

Suddenly, he made the up and down sign for "yes."

"Did you come to earth on a flying machine?"

He answered "yes," making the up and down sign once again with his right hand.

"Is your ship powered by atomic energy?"

His answer was "no," with his hand moving once from side to side.

"Rocket fuel?"

The sign is "no."

"Magnetism?"

He makes the "yes" sign. I was getting "yes" and "no" answers, but I wanted to converse with him in more detail and so I said, "I wish to learn your language. Will you teach me? He answered with the "yes" sign.

I asked, "How do you say in your language, "I am your friend."

He made a sign by moving his fingers.

I inquired, "How do you say, "You are my friend."

Again he signed with his hands. I could not see any difference and I realized that his language was too difficult to learn. "Your language is too difficult to learn. Will you learn my language?," I asked.

He signed "yes."

In his sitting position on the rug, with his legs crossed, I placed a large Webster's Dictionary on his lap, opened to the inside of the front cover of the book, where the alphabet was printed in large letters and said, "These are the letters of my language, pointing to the inside cover. Flipping the pages of the book I remarked; "These are the words and meaning of my language. If you know all that is in this book, you can write in my language."

Leary grabbed approximately fifty pages of the book between his fingers, and as he stared at the book, with his eyes closed, I noticed that the skin on his forehead was moving apart and coming together like a shutter on a camera. He then held another fifty to one hundred pages in his hand and once more his forehead moved. After a minute, he closed the cover of the dictionary.

"You know all that is in this book?" I asked.

He made the sign for "yes." I couldn't believe this. I took a standard sized clip-board, placed an eight and one-half by eleven sheet of white paper on the board, took the book off his lap and wrote ten words on the paper from the dictionary, words that I had never seen before. I placed the clipboard on his lap and handed him a pen.

"These are ten words in my language. Can you give me the meaning?"

He began to print. When he was finished I took the clipboard and checked the words in the dictionary. Every word was defined correctly. In one word, the publisher mistakenly reversed the letter "e". His letter "e" was also reversed for the same word. Since he claimed that he was able to write in my language, I asked him the question.

"Where did you come from?" (See page 158, exhibit G)

Through the many trances with Noran, I had learned that Shan was the name of our earth, Uria was Uranus and Araton was the name of his rocket ship.

"What type of energy do you use in your Araton as you travel through space?"

I was able to determine through his answer that the dynarator would cut the magnetic field of the universe, thus giving them the thrust to move forward through space. (See page 159, Exhibit H) What a way to travel? We carry oxygen and hydrogen to the moon and dump excess material. They carry no fuel but use the existing energy around them.

"How does your Dynarator operate?" (See page 160, exhibit I)

Printing in English he wrote, "Our rate of speed has not yet been attained by your people." "How fast do you travel through the universe?" (See page 161, exhibit J)

"Do you travel faster than the speed of light?"

"We travel at unlimited speeds," he inscribed.

"Are they're many of your flying ships in the universe?"

He mentioned one Araton, and many selatons and meratons.

"Please write some simple words in your language and there meaning."

Alvin also completed drawings of three types of flying machines. He claimed he had come from Uranus as pure energy and took on physical form on earth. "Can you translate your entire language into my language?" His answer was, "You do not have enough forms in your language." (See page 162-165, exhibit K-N)

In the years of regressing Alvin Leary I had drawn a composite picture of his life as Noran. He claimed that he and fifty highly evolved human-like beings in energy form left Uranus a million years ago and traveled through the solar system to earth. Their mission was to protect the sun from being moved out of our galaxy by people in another galaxy who had lost their sun through an explosion. They took on physical form on earth. The day came when nuclear war broke out with people from another galaxy. All life on the planet was destroyed except for the few that were able to seek refuge inside the earth. They remained there for hundreds of years and became a mutated race. Noran had died, but remained on earth. Hundreds of years later he reincarnated into another physical body known as Andanee.

CHAPTER 11

LIFE OF GUILLAUME, DUKE OF NORMANDY AND ALSO ADONNA FROM ATLANTIS

Listen or thy tongue will keep thee deaf. - American Judian proverb

One Friday evening during a trance session, Alvin Leary suddenly slipped into one of his sixteen lives without my asking him to do so. He began to speak in a language that sounded to me like French since I had taken one semester of French in high school. Although he was answering my questions in French, I was unable to understand him. I asked him to sit up, placed a kitchen cutting board with a letter size sheet of paper tacked on and asked him to write a letter to whomever he wished. He wrote the following letter in French signing it Guillaume, Duke of Normandy. I then asked him to translate it into English. (See page 166/168, exhibit P, P.1, P.2)

For the rest of that week I researched the life of Guillaume, Duke of Normandy and discovered that on October 15th, 1066, William of Normandy crossed the English Channel with a large army and defeated Harold of Hastings and was crowned the next day in Westminster Abbey as King William the First. He had written the letter from England to his wife Mathilde in France. I also contacted a teacher who spoke and read fluently in French and asked her to attend the next Friday's session. I wished to determine whether or not Alvin's spoken words in French were correct.

The following Friday evening, while Alvin was in a deep state of hypnosis, I regressed him to the life of Guillaume, Duke de Normandy. I asked the French language teacher to question him in that language and determine whether or not the answers were correct. She spoke to Alvin in French and they began to converse as though they were old buddies. I asked the teacher, "Is he speaking correct French?" She answered, "Not only is he answering correctly, but he is speaking with high-class words, some that I have never heard before." Since Alvin had written a letter from England to his wife Mathilde prior to defeating Harold of Hasting on October 15, 1066, (See page 166/168, exhibit P, P.1, P.2) I decided to take him forward passed the date when he was crowned King of England. The letter he wrote is dated April 15th, 1068 and is signed William First, King. As the years passed, whenever I was able to regress Alvin to the life of Guillaume, Duc de Normandie, if I took him to anytime before the crowning in West Minister Abbey, he signed his letters Guillaume Duc de Normandie. If I took him forward to his crowning as king or later, he signed his letters William I. I was never able to catch him making a mistake. Many times when Alvin was in hypnosis and I asked to speak to Guillaume, another life would appear instead of William of Normandy. My research of Guillaume was very limited. The sixteen lives of Alvin did not appear at one time, but showed up over a period of many years. However, whenever a life appeared that I had never worked with I would have Alvin sit up and write in the language of the life he was projecting since I believe a language has to be learned through practice.

In all of Alvin's previous lives except for one, he appeared as a man. In the life of Adonna in Atlantis, he came through as a woman. In the few sessions in which Alvin appeared as Adonna, I was able to get a composite picture of "her" life and also have "her" write in the Atlantean Language. One Friday night while Alvin was in trance, I regressed him to his life as the woman, Adonna.

"Go back to the life of Adonna in the city of Tashone in Atlan during the days of Helioca and tell me of your life in that time." (I had this information from the list of lives that Alvin had presented to me when we first began the trances)

Adonna began to speak in a soft female voice and said, "There once thrived in our civilization a country called Atlan situated in the midst of the great green waters, consisting of two classes of people. One was a mixture of several races that were called "Laborers" and the other was the elite class called the "Masters" who were descendants from Uria (Uranus.) They were an advanced civilization. Into this life, I, Adonna, was born in the city of Tashone. Atlan was partially ruled by a Board of Governors, but they were only advisors to the Chief who was known as Helioca. I had an older brother named Mernatus. He was a new member on the Board of Governors and also one of the Masters of the Sciences and from the Master class of people who were also scientists. My brother was in charge of operating the giant Sub-tetran, deep in the earth, which produced the energy For Atlan.

One day, my brother put the giant Sub-Tetron to its greatest test. He knew that by utilizing all of its power, there was no limit to what could be accomplished and achieved. It caused a great explosion and more than half of Atlan was totally destroyed and slowly began to sink into the great, green waters. Volcanic eruptions were taking place over the entire Atlan. The highest mountaintop was where the city of Aseers was located and most of the people who had not been killed tried to make their way to Aseers. I was one of the people who headed for this place. While I was running through a nearby village, the ground opened up shooting flames into the air. I fell into the open crevice and died."

I asked Adonna/Alvin to sit up and placed a breadboard with an attached sheet of paper upon Alvin's lap and I handed him a pen. I said. "Adonna, write a message to your people." (Through questioning I had learned that Adonna was an educated woman and knew how to write, both in the pictorial or hieroglyphic writing and also in the higher form of script, which was reserved for the people of the scientific and political level) When she was finished writing I said, "What have you written?" She answered, "My brother has deceived people of Atlan." I placed another sheet of paper on the breadboard and asked her, "Where did your people of Atlan come from?" She wrote, "People of Atlan have come from land beyond the sun." (See page 169, exhibit O)

This ended the trance session with Alvin/Adonna as Alvin suddenly had slipped into the life of Kallikrates and so I brought him forward to the present and awakened him.

CHAPTER 12

THE LIFE OF JOSEPHUS AND HIS CONNECTION WITH JESUS

Advice is seldom welcome; and those who want it the most always like it the least. - Lord Chesterfield

In examining the list of Alvin's sixteen lives, I decided I would try to regress him to the life of Josephus, a Hebrew slave. The following week while he was in hypnosis, I spoke to him and said, "I want you to go back in time, to the time of the Nazarene, when you were known as Josephus, the Hebrew slave and describe to me your entire life." (I took this information from the list of his lives.)

"I was born during the times of Herod the Great in the hills of Judea. My father's name was Avrum, my mother's Ruchal, and I was named Josephon. We were of the Hebrew faith. As I grew older my father showed me how to tend the flock and read and write because my father was an educated man. I did not want to stay in the hills of Judea and so one-day at the age of eight I went down into the city of Jerusalem. When I returned home that evening, I found my parents murdered, the sheep stolen and the house completely burned and destroyed. I therefore returned to the city. Because I was hungry, I stole a piece of fruit and I was caught. I was taken before the Council of Elders and since I was a child and an orphan, I was sold into slavery and was purchased to serve in the house of Marcus Drusus, a wealthy Roman Tribune. I was taken to the wealthy home of Marcus who lived in Judea. It was there that I grew up learning to become a charioteer and by the time I was sixteen, I was one of the best charioteers in the land.

One day, I was brought before my master, Marcus Drusus, and he said, "Josephon, from now on your name will be Yosephus as it sounds more Roman and you will do nothing but drive my chariots in the races. In the near future, you will even race in the Great Circus of Rome. Even though you serve this house, you may come and go as you please, just as if you were a free man and you will move from the servants quarters into the main house." I was treated like the adopted son of Marcus Drusus. I wore the finest clothing and had everything I wanted.

The day finally came when my master asked me to gather my things together as we were leaving for Rome because he had been called to appear before the Emperor Augustus. Since we would be in Rome, I was to race in the Great Circus. We traveled by caravan with an escort to the seacoast and then we boarded a Roman vessel for Rome. After a long and tiring voyage we arrived in Rome. I was astounded by the vastness, beauty and grandeur of this great city.

Early the next morning, I drove Marcus Drusus to the Palace in my chariot, waited outside and after a long while Marcus came outside with the Emperor Augustus. The Emperor said, "Well, who have we here?" My master answered, "This is Yosephus, my finest charioteer and after the races tomorrow in the Great Circus, I expect him to become the finest charioteer in the entire Roman Empire." Augustus replied, Well, Counsel, you do think highly of the young man, don't you?" I wish you both good fortunes tomorrow and I hope that the Gods will be with you both."

The Following morning, I was in the stable area at the Great Circus making the final preparations for the race. Marcus Drusus said to me, "remember, there are those who would stop at nothing to see you killed in the race today. You are more important to me than a million races. Take good care of yourself and keep clear of all trouble. May the Gods be with you."

I was dressed in black and gold, offset by a red cape and red plumes, as I paraded before the cheering crowd, my chariot drawn by four white horses. Finally, the race began. In a few moments there were several fatal accidents. I kept clear of the others, but I was only in sixth place. I finally moved up to fourth place, then third and then I was challenging for the lead. I could feel the uncontrolled frenzy of the cheering crowd. The one in the lead was Caligula, the grandnephew of the Emperor's stepson. I was running neck and neck with him and finally with a last sudden burst of energy I pulled out in the lead and won the race. The crowd was cheering wildly as I brought my chariot in front of the Emperor's box to receive my winner's crown of laurel. As the Emperor Augustus placed the crown upon my head, he said, "To the victor of not only these races today, but the victor of all the Roman Empire. A job well done Yosephus of the House of Drusus."

After the races, I returned to Judea with Marcus Drusus and learned that a new governor of the district had been appointed, by the name of Pontius Pilatus. Marcus invited Pilatus to his house for supper and I was present. I heard Pilatus ask, "And what of this Hebrew Prophet called Jesu." (Jesus) Is it true that he preaches treason and calls himself the

Son of God?" Drusus answered, "I have never head him speak treason. Just because the man is a religious fanatic, is certainly no reason for Rome to become alarmed." Pilatus replied, "Let me inform you, my dear Consul, and say to you that the Empire has been threatened by these fanatics in the past. Just recently there was a fanatic called Spartacus, who was only a mere slave, and I don't have to tell you what problems he caused. After killing every army sent against him, it finally took several of our best legions to eventually and completely crush him. We cannot afford a second occurrence like that, can we."

I answered Pilatus by remarking, "I too have heard Jesu speak, and he speaks only of love and peace. He speaks nothing of treason. Pilatus said, "Well, you may be right, and what of Herod Antipas, how is he taking to this Jesu who calls himself the King of the Jews?" I said, "He does not call himself a king. It is the people of Judea that call him a King." Marcus spoke and replied, "Herod Antipas has become a man with a twisted mind. He is so greatly obsessed with partaking in incest, that he has no time for anything else." Several weeks later I asked Marcus Drusus if he would allow me to follow the Nazarene for a while and Marcus replied, "There are those masters who would flog a slave for even thinking such a thought, but I have never felt that you were a slave to me, but more like a son, the son that I never had since I have never taken a wife. You are my best charioteer and one of the best in all the Roman Empire, but if this is what you must do, I won't try to stop you."

"I traveled into the hills of Judea and became one of the many followers of Jesu; the Nazarene. I watched him do many miracles, such as pointing a small instrument towards the eye of a blind person and after a bright light struck the man's eyes, his eyesight returned. I watched him take the same small instrument and place it upon the leg of a lame man and again there was a light that appeared around the instrument. The man seemed to tremble and suddenly he began to walk without any lameness.

One day I saw Jesu walk into a small village of one hundred people that were starving and only had two or three loaves of bread between them. Jesu placed a tablet below each person's tongue and told them to drink plenty of water. Their stomachs were then filled and they were no longer hungry. Not knowing what Jesu had actually done, they passed the word that he fed the entire village with three loaves of bread, meaning that the village had three loaves of bread and not that he used the bread to feed them. One must understand that most of the people of these towns and villages were poor, uneducated peasants and they did not know how to express themselves grammatically correct.

Jesu was also able to bring back to life several people who had suffered from catalepsy and appeared to have been dead, but in fact still lived. This was also done with a small instrument held in his hand. The instrument probably attacked the central nervous system, stimulating the body to come out of the cataleptic state. As far as the peasants were concerned, Jesu had brought the dead back to life. These very advanced accomplishments were considered, at that time, to be the acts and deeds of only a God or Son of God.

Many days passed and news was heard in the streets that King Herod was angered at the popularity of Jesu, and that Herod had ordered his guards to arrest the prophet. To escape being arrested, Jesu and his followers went to the outskirts of Galilee and camped out in the hillside. I followed Jesu to the hillside. People from all over gathered by the hundreds to hear what the Prophet Jesu had to say. Jesu then spoke and said: "THOSE OF YOU WITH GOOD THOUGHTS ARE LOVED BY US IN THE KINGDOM IN THE HEAVENS. THOSE OF YOU WHO MOURN WILL BE COMFORTED WHEN YOU ARE REUNITED WITH YOUR LOVED ONES. THOSE OF YOU WHO ARE AGAINST VIOLENCE WILL INHERIT THIS PLANET. NONE OF YOU WILL EVER HUNGER OR THIRST AFTER RIGHTEOUSNESS HAS BEEN MADE UPON THIS PLACE. THOSE WHO BELIEVE IN MERCY WILL BE GIVEN MERCY UPON THAT DAY TO COME. THOSE OF YOU WITH PURE HEARTS WILL LIVE TO SEE MY FATHER. THOSE OF YOU WHO LIVE IN PEACE WILL BE AS THOUGH YOU WERE MY FATHER'S OWN CHILDREN. THOSE WHO HAVE BEEN TREATED WITH CRUELTY, BECAUSE YOU HAVE LIVED WITH RIGHTEOUSNESS, WILL BE LOVED BY US IN OUR KINGDOM IN THE HEAVENS. THOSE OF YOU WHO STAND BY ME WILL BE BLESSED BY ALL IN MY KINGDOM. REJOICE, FOR YOU WILL BE REWARDED BY OUR KINGDOM IN THE HEAVENS. THE GOOD PEOPLE HERE WILL BE LIKE A SEED UPON THIS PLACE, AND YOUR GOODNESS WILL SHINE FORTH LIKE A LIGHT TO BE SEEN BY MY FATHER IN OUR KINGDOM, WHICH IS IN THE HEAVENS. FROM THIS TIME FORTH, YOU WILL REPEAT THESE WORDS, UNTIL ANOTHER SON OF MY FATHER COMES TO YOU, FOR YOU ARE NOT YET AT THIS TIME READY FOR US. MY FATHER WHO LIVES IN THE HEAVENS, HAS ESTABLISHED HIS NAME HERE UPON THIS PLACE AS HE HAS DONE IN THE HEAVENS. PEACE WILL PREVAIL HERE AS IT DOES IN THE HEAVENS. WE SHALL HAVE FOOD AND BE LOVED BY OUR FATHER, ONLY IF WE LOVE ALL OTHERS. LET

US NOT BE TEMPTED TO DO EVILNESS, FOR OUR KINGDOM OF PEACE IS ALL POWERFUL AND GLORIOUS, FOREVER AND ETERNITY."

I continued to follow Jesu after he left the hillside of Galilee and traveled to the town of Dekapolisham, also called the "Land of Ten Cities" and then he returned to Galilee. Soon thereafter when Jesu decided to enter the city of Jerusalem, I did not follow him, as I sensed trouble was coming since many of the people referred to him as a "God" and others called him the "Savior," all of which made him an enemy of Rome. That was a serious charge since Rome was cruel to those that stood in her way. The day after I decided not to follow Jesu, while walking through the streets of Jerusalem I noticed Marcus Drusus in the market place and he invited me to stay with him.

That afternoon Jesu was apprehended by the guards of the Council of Elders and cast into prison. I spoke to Marcus and told him that Jesu was not an enemy of Rome and that he only spoke to the people of peace and love, telling the people to love their enemies, which in this case was Rome. It was then that Pontius Pilatus sent his soldiers to bring Jesu before him.

The soldiers of Pontius Pilatus, who was Governor of Judea and the entire district, broke into the prison and took Jesu to the Palace, where he stood before Pontius Pilatus. (Marcus Drusus, a close friend of Pontius Pilate, was invited to the trial and took Josephus with him)

The Governor said, "So you are the prophet known as Jesu?" Jesu answered, "Yes, I am Jesu of Nazareth." Pilatus continued, "I have brought you here to answer for the charges of treason against Rome. I was content to allow the People's Council of Elders to deal with you.

However, Yosephus here has spoken to me on your behalf and he tells me that you have been working for Rome and not against her, as you tell the people to love Rome. Tell me exactly what you have been saying to the people."

Jesu spoke, "It is true that I have told the people to love their enemies and if Rome be their enemies, then I have told them to love Rome." Pilatus asked, "Have you ever told the people that you are a King or a God?" Jesu answered, "I have never told them that I am either a King or God. I have told them that I am the son of my father who is King of the Heavens." Pilatus asked, "And what is the name of your father?" Jesu replied, "He is known by many names in many different places." Pilatus remarked, "Oh, then you are referring to Jupiter?" Jesu said, "If that is what you call him." Pilatus answered, "I find this man not guilty of treason or any of the other charges brought against him and I therefore release him."

Jesu was then set free by Pontius Pilatus; however, he was warned against stirring up any further trouble in the district. Pilatus told him not to hold any gatherings of people and not to cause any disturbance for he could not be responsible for the actions taken by the Council of Elders. His responsibility in the district was to maintain order.

Jesu then left the Palace. As he was walking through the city streets on his way back to the hillside of Galilee, just as he reached the city outskirts, he was overtaken by guards, sent after him by the Council of Elders and taken back to their prison. During this time, Manrishi, who had been head of the Council of Elders, went to the Palace to protest to Herod and Pilatus. Yosephus was there with Marcus Drusus.

Manrishi said, "We of the Council were willing to accept the decision of Pilatus, but the prophet was no sooner turned loose, than he began to gather the people together again to cause another disturbance. There had been fighting and stealing in the streets and I then ordered our guards to arrest the prophet Jesu and cast him into prison again, to await further trial by you."

Yosephus replied, "Your Excellency, surely you do not believe his lies, do you?" "Marcus Drusus added, anyone can see that they were just waiting for an opportunity to apprehend the poor man again, and for no reason!"

Herod Antipas said, "I say to do away with the man, just as we did with the last prophet that called himself, John The Baptist. My father had his head served on a silver platter and I say that we do the same to this one."

"Very well, bring the prophet Jesu before me the first thing in the morning, and I shall pass judgment upon him," answered Pilatus.

"The next morning Jesu was brought into the Palace. Hundreds of people lined the streets and stood outside the Palace gates, awaiting news of what would happen to the prophet. I sat in the courtroom as Jesu was brought in."

Manrishi said, "Pontius Pilatus, we bring before you the man called the Prophet Jesu, King of the Jews, Prince of Peace, Son of God, King of Kings and the man who will save the Jews from Rome. This man preaches to the multitude of people, holds secret meetings with his followers, causes riots and disturbances, and defies you and the Roman law. He also places himself above King Herod, yourself, and the Mighty

Tiberius Claudius Nero Caesar. We insist that you find him guilty of treason and heresy, and we further insist that you sentence him to death."

"So long as I am at the head of this district, no man insists upon anything," Pontius exclaimed. "I am, as Caesar in his absence, and let us not forget this —-and, now, lets once again hear from the accused. What answers do you have for these charges?"

Jesu replied, "I answer to no man but my father."

"Do you mean to tell me that you set yourself above me and above even Caesar?"

"I am the son of my father, who is King of all Kings in the Universe. I shall answer to him alone."

"Then you leave me no choice."

As I sat so near to Jesu, I felt that I had to speak. "Sire, I said, you do not understand what he is saying. He has told me that he comes from a far away place, a star in the heavens."

Pilatus interrupted.

"Precisely! I shall hear no more from anyone! By your own words, you have admitted to the charges and crimes brought against you. By the power vested upon me by the glorious Tiberius Claudius Nero Caesar, Emperor of the Roman Empire, I, Pontius Pilatus, Governor of this District, do hereby sentence you to death. Whatever means of death, that I leave to the decision of King Herod Antipas, King of this Province."

The people present then began shouting, "Crucify him!, Crucify him!"

Herod then spoke and said, "You, Jesu will be crucified, by the will of the people."

So, along with dozens of condemned criminals, not just two, they marched Jesu to a hill called Golgotha. I followed the crowd. They first crucified the dozens of others and then they placed a crown of thorns upon the head of Jesu, stripped him naked, nailed him to the cross and also bound his body to the cross with pieces of wet rawhide, not only for additional support, but also, as the wet rawhide dried, it became tighter, cutting into Jesu's wrists and stopping circulation.

Two days passed, and many people and I remained gathered upon the hillside. There were also Roman guards that remained there at the front of the cross, gambling with one another. Finally, Jesu dropped his head, appearing to have died. His family was then permitted to take him down from the cross and his body was taken away.

Marcus Drusus and Pontius were returning to Rome and I accompanied them. Then I traveled to Antiochia where I lived a quiet existence for many years. During this time Rome had three more Emperors. After Tiberius died, Caligula became the Emperor and when he was assassinated, Claudius became the Emperor. After Claudius died of poisoning, Nero became the leader of Rome.

These were bad times all over again, for Nero was even a worse tyrant than Tiberius had been. He hated Christians with a mad passion. He would cast hundreds of Christians to the lions for only his pleasure and amusement. I had returned to Rome at this time and upon my arrival I met Paulo, who had been one of my closest friends and a follower of Jesu. One day later I was walking with Paulo and saw him struck down by a Roman soldier. "I began to run and hide in a narrow alley and was overtaken and killed."

I saw that Alvin Leary looked very tired as he had been in a hypnotic state for two hours and so I brought him back to the present and awakened him. As I gazed at the crowd in the room I could see the awe and amazement in their faces as to what they had witnessed.

Alvin asked for a glass of water and after he had finished, I said, "Alvin, what do you remember?"

He answered, "Nothing, I have just been sleeping." I now realized that I had been sitting in on history as though I was there.

CHAPTER 13

WRITINGS OF ALVIN LEARY

EXHIBITS OF ALVIN LEARY'S WRITINGS FROM HIS PREVIOUS LIVES AND VERIFICATION OF HIS READINGS

The following copies of the writings of Alvin Leary and those persons connected to him were obtained over a period of fifteen years. While in a hypnotic trance, I would ask Alvin (who was lying flat on his back on the wall-to-wall carpeting) to sit up. He would cross his legs in the yoga position and I would place a breadboard on his lap with an eight and one-half by eleven sheet of white paper attached. I would then tape his eyes so that he could not see, hand him a pen, and ask him to write in the language that he was living at that time. All of Alvin's writings were completed while in a very deep hypnotic state. When he awakened from each trance, he had no knowledge as to what had taken place.

To we ght Central   feb 5, 1981
Institute Inc:
    on Jan 31st, 1981 I come home to recieve a
life Reading. the first "Life" was that of Mario
Antonio who was born in Napoli Italy in 1890.
Mario relocated to New York city in 1915 and worked
for Bernies Custom made clothing, on 42nd st.
he relocated to philadelphia in 1935 where
he owned his own shop at 4th and Spruce streets
on July 1, 1938 he and his wife went on a
vacation to Atlantic city he stayed at the
Chelsea hotel   on July 2, 1938 he and his
wife went to the Beach to swim. Mario was
caught in an undertow and drowned

    I returned home to york and on the following
monday, I contacted the Atlantic County
New Jersey Coroner who verified that
Mario Antonio did in fact drown in
the surf at Alantic city N.J on July 2, 1938.
The document listed his wife's name
his address and his hotel (the chelsea)
documentation of the Above facts is
being sent from Atlantic County in the
near future.
    The Above statement is factual
and accurate to the best of my knowledge

ROBERT T.

(Last name removed for protection of privacy)

Exhibit A

THE MANY LIVES OF ALVIN LEARY

<u>Rudolpho Gugliemi (Rudolph Valentino)</u>

Born in Castellaneta, Italy on May 6th, 1895. Died in New York City on August 23, 1926.

Jamie Brewster

Born in Atlanta, Georgia on May 7th, 1847. Father - George, mother – Katie, sister – Margaret, brothers – Billy Jo, Eddie and Johnny. Jamie owned a horse named Dinomite. He died in the Civil War on July 4th, 1863 at the Battle of Gettysburg.

Sequoya

Born April 22nd, 1788. Died April 30th, 1847. He was a member of the American Indian Tchalagi Tribe. The tribal name of Tchalagi meant "People of a different speech."

Leo Vincey

Born in Southampton, England on May 10th, 1761. Died in Southampton, England on April 21st, 1788. Was buried at Holy Rood Church.

<u>Guillaume (Duc de Normandie)</u>

Born in Falaise in 1027. Became King of England (William The Conqueror). Died in 1087.

Valentinianus

Born in 321. Became Emperor of Rome with his brother Valens. Died 375.

Apollodorus Delphus Vindictus

A Greek General beheaded for treason. Dates of birth and death, unknown.

Yosephus

A Hebrew slave, living during the time of the Nazareen. He was present at the trial of Jesu.

Kallikrates

Complete name: SUTEN NET REKHANKH TCHETTA MERI AMEN SE REKH KALLIKRATES MERI AMEN. Born in Uisa (Thebes) in 369 B.C. as the son of SUTEN NET KHEPER KA REKH SE REKH NECHTNEPF and his queen Sappho. Kallikrates became the last native Pharoah of Tamarekh (Egypt) in 344 B.C. He ruled for two years, at which time he fled from Egypt due to the land being

Exhibit B

invaded by Ochus (Artaxerxes and the Persians). Kallikrates died in Africa, which was then part of Libya in 339 B.C.

Senewe

Born in 1391 B.C. The son of Pentu who was the former physician to the Pharoah. In 1366 he became physician to the Pharoah Amenhotep IV, who became Ankhenaten. Died in 1331 B.C.

Adonna (a woman)

Born in the city of Tashone in Atlan (Atlantis) during the days of Helioca. Her brother Mernatus was "Master of the Science" and was responsible for putting the Giant Subtetron (giant energy crystal) to its full test, which exploded and caused the destruction of Atlan. She tried to make her way to the mountaintops, but was overtaken by volcanic fumes, fire, water and lava.

Manameter

Born in the city of Meliat-Aseers in Atlan. Not much known.

Agonorus

Born in the village of Adeve in Mu (Lemuria). He was the son of Agonor. Agonorus became the leader of his village and then became the first head (king) of all Mu. He ruled Mu from the City of Manakai. He died when the gods became angry and took back the lands into the great waters.

Agon

Born in the city of Adeve in Mu. He was a leader in the village. He proclaimed to his tribe that the son of his son Agonor would be born to rule all of the Mu Empire and unite all of Mu. He died before his grandson was born.

Andanee

Lived in Godah. He was an intelligent, ape-like cyclop that was a mutant of a prior civilization. (Possibly the missing link.)

Noran

Portated from Uria (Uranus) to the second house of Solara and took on physical form. Helped to build the Araton and came to Shan (earth). Died in a nuclear war.

28 Dicembre 1920

Fratello mio Alberto,

Io sperarò tu avere
Natale allegro. Io ho incontraro
donna nome di Natacha Rambova
e io amaro molto la donna
Noi avevamo ballaro lo Tango
in lo Albergo Ambasciatore tutto
notte. Natacha essa pittora buona
molta e io avevo dico la donna
mosto essa stata Italiano in
vita pasato. Io sarò scrivero
presto molto.

Amore sempre,

Rudolph Valentino

Exhibit C

STANLEY Z. FELSENBERG, M.D.

11 E. Chase St.

Suite 5 A

Baltimore, Maryland 21202

TELEPHONE 537-4324

July 30, 1984

To Whom It May Concern:

I have been requested to write this testimonial concerning my professional observations and opinions regarding Alvin Leary.

I first became acquainted with Alvin Leary in 1972, when I had attended an open demonstration of Alvin being placed into a hypnotic trance state by Irvin Mordes, a well-known hypnotist in the Baltimore area.

While in this state, Mr. Mordes prenatally regressed Alvin back into several of his past lives. I saw him act out his life as the Pharaoh Kallikrates, along with several other lives, and although the entire episode was very interesting and convincing, being a doctor of medicine with a scientific mind, I required more concrete proof of this incredible phenomenon.

The next session proved even more interesting, as I was permitted to actually take part in what was happening.

Prior to Alvin being placed into the hypnotic trance state, I took his pulse, which registered 72 beats per minute, and his blood pressure, which registered 120 over 80. While he was between the incarnations, I again took his vital signs. His blood pressure had dropped to 80 over 40, and his pulse now registered 40 beats per minute. Such a sudden and drastic

Exhibit D

drop had me extremely worried, as anyone else would have gone
into shock. His signs returned to a normal reading as soon
as he was back into one of his lives. The readings of his
vital signs, although normal while in the several lives, did
vary slightly from one to another. Each time he was taken
back to the same life, the readings were exactly the same
as the previous time in the same period. Although it is
possible for some people to raise and/or lower their
pressure at will, it is not possible for them to control
exactly what it will read.

When I discovered that Alvin Leary was capable of doing
health readings, such as the famed Edgar Cayce, I arranged
to pull three cases from my patient files. While in trance,
and only being given the name, address, and date of birth,
he was able to give an exact diagnosis and prognosis on each
case, as a matter of fact, more complete than even I could
have given. I know he was not reading my mind, because he
came through with a few things that even I did not know, and
by a more extensive examination on my patients, I found that
his information was correct.

I have also witnessed other phenomenon concerning Alvin
Leary, such as precognitions that all happened when he said
they would, Etc.

In my professional opinion, Alvin Leary, is one of the most
extra-ordinary and incredible people I have ever known. I
believe him to be an extremely gifted individual and to be
one hundred percent valid in all of his metaphysical areas.

Very truly yours,

Stanley Z. Felsenberg, M.D.

Walter Pahnke, M.D.

April 8, 1974

S U M M A R Y

(EXPERIMENTAL CASE OF ALVIN LEARY)

Our subject is Alvin Leary, a Caucasian male born May 4, 1942, entered the Maryland Psychiatric Research Center on Monday, April 1, 1974 and remained until Friday, April 5, 1974 in order to be tested under the most clinically controlled conditions in certain metaphysical areas.

AREAS EXAMINED:

REINCARNATION - (Prenatal Regression)

ESP - (Extrasensory Perception)

ASTRAL PROJECTION - (Separation of Non-Physical and Physical)

HEALING- (Laying of Hands)

MEDICAL DIAGNOSIS AND PROGNOSIS - (Possession by Physician)

PRECOGNITION- (By Extrasensory Means)

3RD PARTY REGRESSION - (Other Person's Previous Lives)

APPORT - (Astral Projection of Physical Objects)

It is, in my opinion, that Alvin Leary, is the most convincing case of reincarnation ever studied and documented.

While the subject was in a hypnotic trance state, he was prenatally regressed into sixteen previous lives. While between lives his blood pressure registered at 60 over 30, a sudden drop from his normal 120 over 80, and his pulse decreased to 20 beats per minute. This should normally result in a state of shock, but it did not. When we registered the subject's vital signs during his death as Rodolpho Guglielmi (Rudolph Valentino) and compared them with

Exhibit E

those appearing in the Medical Records at the New York Polyclinic Hospital, they were precisely the same.

The subject was capable of writing in the correct languages of whatever period he was experiencing at the time, and he was able to speak in the languages of those same periods. One other interesting finding was that while the subject was in a certain period, not only could he speak in the language of that period, but was also able to speak in the present day English. This tends to prove that all audio was coming from the same mind or being. If this were a case of possession, the entity would not have been knowledgeable of our present day language.

While in this state, the subject has been found to speak and write fluently in American English, Italian, English with Southern accent, Cherokee Indian (Tciloki), King's English, Norman French, Idiomatic Latin, Classical Greek, Hebrew, Egyptian Hieroglyphic, Egyptian Demotic, Egyptian Hierasic, Atlantean, Lamurean, Godean, and Urian. With only having completed the 10th grade in school and never learning any other languages, this too tends to further add to the validity of this case, especially since half of the languages he speaks and writes are languages that are not and have not been taught for centuries.

We have researched dates, people, places, etc., that the subject has mentioned during this state, and everything consistently checks out to the letter.

I have no doubt that this most extraordinary case of reincarnation is absolutely valid.

In the area of ESP, while the subject was in a sealed booth, we conducted a flash card test. In the conscious state his score was ten below chance. Through our audio system, I mentioned a post-hypnotic word that I had suggested one hour prior to the test. This word would place the subject into a semi-trance state that would raise his conscious level. Upon mentioning the post-hypnotic word, the subject began to press the flash card buttons with a rapid rate of speed, raising his score to 98 above chance, almost a perfect score. My colleagues and I looked at one another in amazement.

In the combined areas of Astral Projection and Apports, I must admit that these are areas I have not experienced testing, however, the results were astonishing. While the subject was in a hypnotic trance state, I prenatally regressed him back to this Egyptian incarnation, when he lived as the Pharaoh Kallikrates. I then asked him to leave his physical body and travel to his tomb in order to return with an object of his choice. We then noticed his body twisting and vibrating. We all noticed a mist rising from the subject's body. In exactly 34 seconds the subject's body began to vibrate again, and in his open palm of his right hand appeared the top half of a small statue of a female Egyptian mummy.

Prior to this experiment the subject was examined, including all openings such as the nose, ears, mouth, rectal cavity, etc., and he was given a pair of white shorts while in our sight at all times. This experiment of an Apport is when the non-physical body leaves the physical body and astrally projects itself to another location. It then disassembles the molecular structure of the object, causing the object to become non-physical, and then returns to the physical body. Upon entering the physical body, the molecular structure of the object is reassembled and the object once again becomes physical.

This object has been authenticated by the Smithsonian Institute, as approximately 2400 years old.

Healing by the laying on of hands is an area that we spent very little time in experimenting. However, I personally have had a trick knee that has been giving me trouble recently. In the privacy of my office, I asked the subject to place his hand upon my knee. I felt a slight vibration from his hand and heat as he concentrated on my knee. It could have been the power of suggestion, but my knee has been fine thus far.

In the area of Precognition, the subject has given information of a plane crash: however, at this time I am not able to comment on the results or his validity in this area.

In the areas of Medical Diagnosis and Prognosis, the subject was placed into a hypnotic trance-state. I asked for a medical doctor to possess the subject's physical body and examine the physical body of a person in my family. All I gave the entity was this person's name, address, and date of birth. I personally did not know the diagnosis nor prognosis at that time. When I compared the information received with the results of the findings of the patient's physician, they were identical.

In the area of 3rd Party Regression, I placed the subject into a hypnotic state, and I gave him the name, address, and date of birth of my cousin. I asked the subject to regress back into her previous lives.

In her most recent past life he mentioned her name, the date she was born, her place of birth, whom she married and the date, when she died, and that she died in a fire.

In checking out this information, we found that all the facts were precisely as the subject stated. I might also make mention, that my cousin has always been deathly afraid of fire, and will not enter a house that contains a fireplace.

In closing, I can only say that last week has been a great experience for us all here at the Center. We look forward to future experimental work with this subject and others like him.

Walter Pahnke, M.D.

Walter Pahnke, M.D.
Maryland Psychiatric Research Center
April 8, 1974

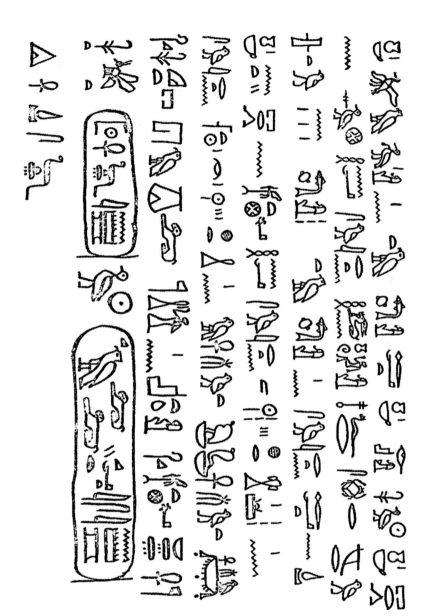

Exhibit F

157

Irvin Mordes

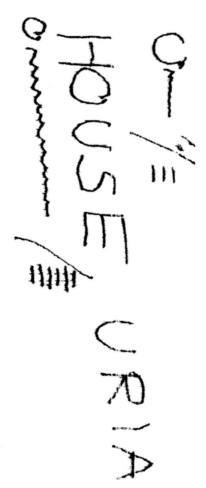

Where did you come from?

Exhibit G

What type of energy do you use as you travel through space?

SINCE YOU ASK FOR PROOF OF MY KNOWLEDGE, YOU SHALL HAVE IT.

MAGNETIC ENERGY IS ATTRACTED BY OUR POSITIVE MAGNETIC DYNARATOR. BY INCREASING THE FREQUENCY TO A DEGREE TEN TIMES GREATER THAN NORMAL, A REVERSAL FROM MAGNETIC POSITIVE TO MAGNETIC NEGATIVE TAKES PLACE, THEREFORE CREATING THRUST POWER. YOUR SIMPLE GENERATOR AND DYNAMO CONSISTS OF A SIMILAR PRINCIPLE. THE ELEMENT ARU, WHICH ATOMICALLY APPEARS AS ⚛, WHICH YOU REFER TO AS YOUR THIRD ELEMENT LITHIUM, IS USED TO A

(energy dissipated at this point)

Exhibit H

159

How does your dynarator operate?

Exhibit I

How fast do you travel through the universe?

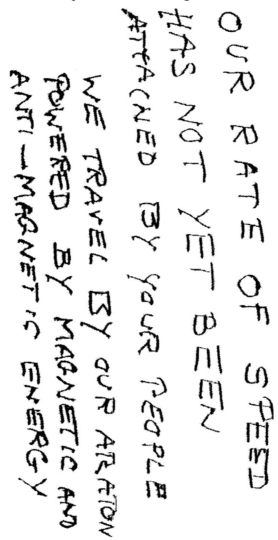

OUR RATE OF SPEED HAS NOT YET BEEN ATTACHED BY YOUR PEOPLE WE TRAVEL BY OUR ARATION POWERED BY MAGNETIC AND ANTI—MAGNETIC ENERGY

The writings of Noran after having learned the English language

Exhibit J

Can you translate your entire language into my language?

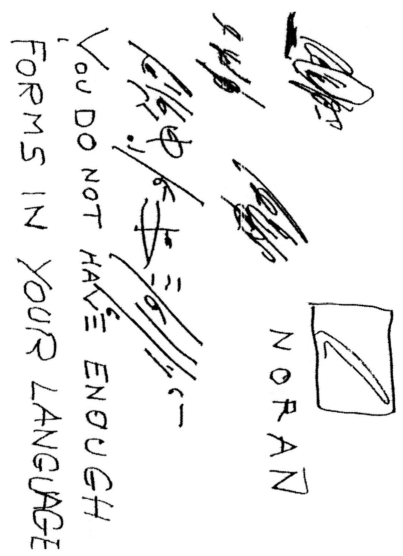

FORMS IN YOUR LANGUAGE

YOU DO NOT HAVE ENOUGH

NORAN

Exhibit K

Some word translations by Noran and his drawings of UFOs.

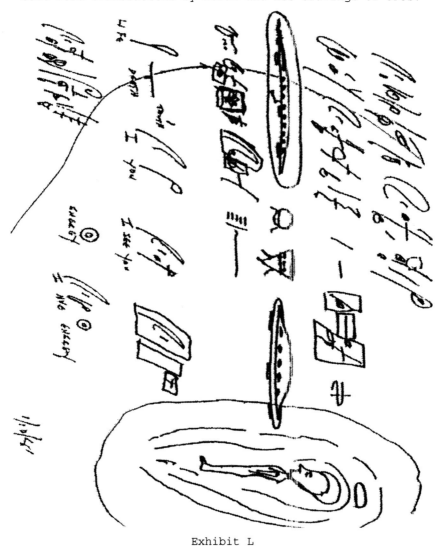

Exhibit L

163

Are there any flying ships in the universe?

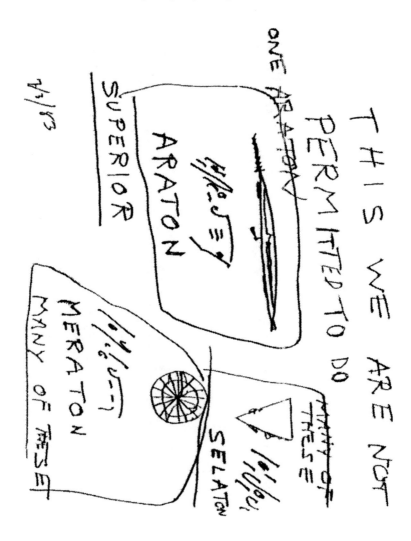

Exhibit M

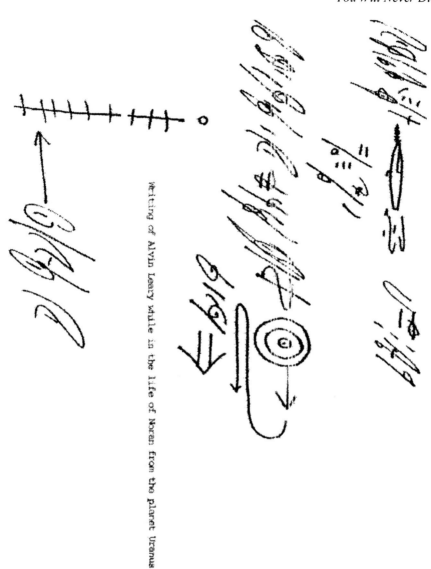

writing of Alvin Leary while in the life of Noran from the planet Uranus

Exhibit N

Translation on next page

Exhibit P

ALVIN LEARY'S ENGLISH TRANSLATION WHILE IN THE LIFE OF GUILLAUME, DUKE OF NORMANDY (SEE PRECEDING PAGE)

SUNDAY AT HASTINGS, 15 OCTOBER, 1066. MY FAIR MATILDA, I WAS VICTORIOUS AGAINST THE ENGLISH AT HASTINGS, KING HAROLD WAS CUT DOWN BY FOUR OF MY KNIGHTS. HENRI, SON OF ROGER OF BEAUMONT, FOUGHT BRAVELY AND IS MY MOST LOYAL AND TRUSTED OF SUBJECTS. I SHALL NOW MOVE ON TO THE ABBEY OF WESTMINSTER, OUTSIDE THE WESTERN WALLS OF LONDON TO BE CROWNED AS KING OF ENGLAND ON CHRISTMAS DAY. I SHALL TAKE RESIDENCE AT THE CASTLE OF BARKING. AFFECTION MY BEAUTIFUL DUCHESS AND FUTURE QUEEN OF ENGLAND.

WILLIAM, DUKE OF NORMANDY

Exhibit P.1

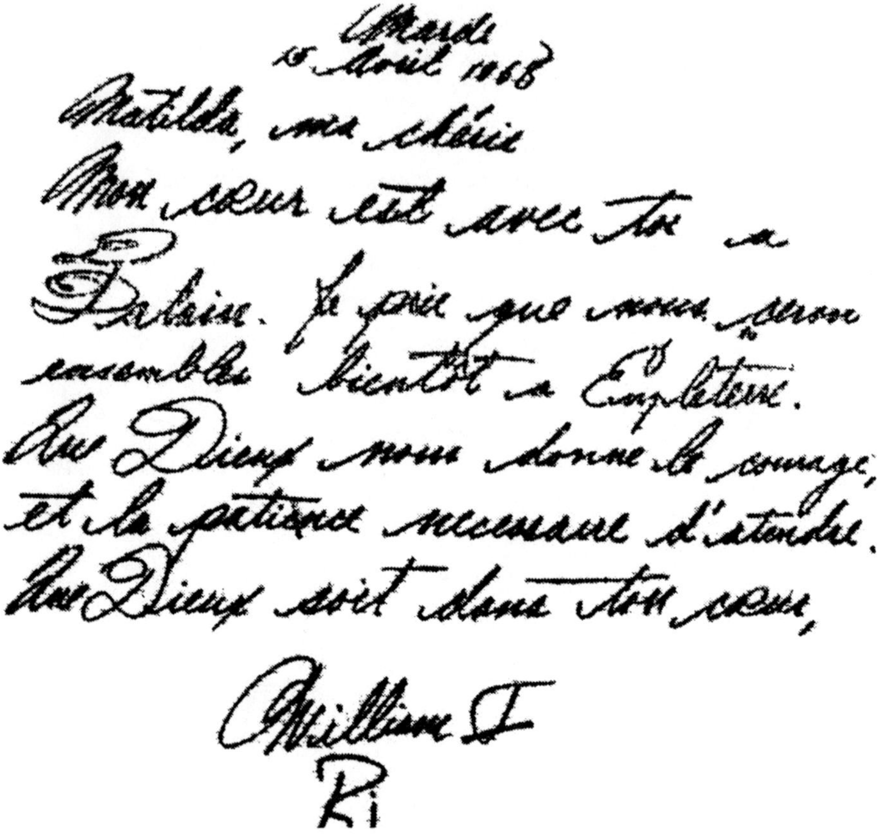

Mardi
15 Avril 1066

Matilda, ma chérie

Mon cœur est avec toi a
Falaise. Je prie que nous serons
ensemble bientôt a Engleterre.
Que Dieu nous donne le courage,
et la patience necessaire d'attendre.
Que Dieu soit dans ton cœur,

William I
Ri

Exhibit P.2

Where did your people of Atlan come from?

PEOPLE OF ATLAN
HAVE COME FROM HOUSE BEYOND
THE SUN.

ADONNA

Exhibit O

169

Irvin Mordes

PART II

TRANCES

ABBREVIATIONS OF THE PEOPLE WHO SPOKE TO EILEEN GARRETT AND JAMES AT THE MONTHLY RESEARCH SESSIONS

WHICH WERE HELD FROM 1995 - 1999

I— Irv Mordes (Researcher)

M— Marlene Stewart (Psychic Medium)

S— Spenser Gardiner (Researcher)

R— Ruth Barr (Researcher)

V— Visitors

ABBREVIATIONS FOR SPIRITS SPEAKING THROUGH MARLENE,

THE PSYCHIC CHANNELER

E— Eileen Garrett

J— James (Brother of Jesus)

VO— Voice of unknown spirits

The word "home", "here" or "over" with quotes refers to the "other side."

The word home or here without quotes refers to the real world.

5/95

INTRODUCTION TO EILEEN, JAMES, AND MARLENE

Through the past one hundred years in the testing of psychics and mediums, scientists have been unable to find a single test or theory to totally explain how psychics are able to give evidence about those people who have died. To this date, we have only stenographic writings, tape and disc recordings as a record of the rate of accuracy of these readings.

After years of research with past life regression, I became fascinated with the idea that someone could communicate with the dead. In all my years of experimentation, my general attitude towards reincarnation was on of open-minded skepticism, although I conceded that there were things for which we have no true explanation. After reading George Anderson's book, "We Don't Die", in which he, as a psychic, was able to converse with the dead in the spirit world, I decided that I would look for a psychic medium with the ability to channel spirits from the "other side". If a spirit, speaking through a psychic channeler could reveal information that was unknown to the psychic, about a person who had died, then the premise could be that there is a constant awareness from one stage of life to the next.

In "Life After Life" by Dr. Raymond Moody, in which he interviewed patients who had "died" for a short while but were resuscitated, writes that the patient sees himself outside his physical being, but in a spiritual body. This spirit cannot be seen or heard by those who are watching the patient lying on the operating table. Since the spirit has no physical body he can easily move through any solid object and cannot hold on to any person he attempts to touch. Dr. Moody was able to secure this information from hundreds of interviews. His assumption was that the spirits were weightless since they were able to float right up to the ceiling of the room, as described by the patients who were interviewed.

In my many years of experimentation with spirits, I was able to concur with Dr. Moody that a spirit can move from one place to another instantaneously, has a form and shape like a misty cloud and similar to the physical body that departed. When the spirit enters the body of the psychic, he or she can pick up the feeling of warmth and the sensation of touch, taste and odors.

In late 1995, I was invited to appear on a talk show in Miami. I was to be interviewed on the subject of reincarnation by Alan Burke, on station WIOD. He was a well-known radio announcer from New York City. During the interview the public was permitted to call in with their questions on the subject of reincarnation. After four hours of being interviewed, Mr. Burke gave out the name of my business and the phone number. The following day I received a call from a gentleman named Spenser Gardner. He mentioned that he had been researching the field of reincarnation since his early years with the Long John Neville psychic show out of New York City. He was presently working with a psychic channeler by the name of Marlene Stewart who wished to be researched to discover why she saw spirits and ghosts and was able to write and speak in strange languages. I was invited to speak with him and we found that we both had a fascination for the subject.

In February 1995, I attended my first session held in the living room of Spenser's home. A committee of three people was selected to research Marlene, comprised of Spenser, Ruth Barr and myself. There were also ten visitors who had been invited. After Marlene seated herself in a comfortable chair, Spenser then asked her, "Can you reiterate some of the things we talked about the last time we were together (Prior to my first visit) with regard to when you first saw a trance medium? What your impression was and how you felt about it at the time?"

M "I will give you a brief run down on my life and involvement. I kept pretty much to myself. And everything I ever learned came from the James and Eileen combination. (These two spirits spoke though Marlene.) My first encounter with somebody who claimed to be a medium was in my late thirties. There was this man who worked in a shop in the village in New York. I went to see him and was impressed with his methods. But, it wasn't the type of work I was familiar with. However, I was able to respect what he was doing. I called societies like the Theosophical Society, Rosicrucian, and the Madam Blavatsky Society, as I did not know who to contact or where to turn. After writing to these people, saying and describing what I do, they would send back brochures inviting me to take a course for "X" number of dollars. I would then re-write these people explaining to them that I was not interested in taking a course, but, desired to find out what I am about, what is going on with me and could they introduce me to people with my common interests. I have been teaching in this field for a long time and have years behind me teaching psychic development courses, meditation and yoga. The intent and purpose of the experiments that we are doing and the reason for being here is to probe mediumistic ability, not past life, not reincarnation and not future existence. If that happens, great. If it does happen, I would like to know about it because I am curious. I probably am one of the biggest skeptics in the room. I do buy into it with my heart and soul, but I cannot prove anything on a scientific level. Therefore, I am called a major skeptic. I do this work with an open mind and heart in the belief that one day I will make a dent in the already wonderful "survival theory" that life continues. As Marlene, I can tell you of thousands of things that have taken place. Many of you have experienced it too and just are not aware. I am also a teacher in the field of all phenomenons under the umbrella of paranormal studies. That means all. That includes healing, telepathy, psychokinetic energy, telekinetic energy, altered states of consciousness and various degrees of how deep you go into a trance state. Two spirits speak through me, Eileen and James. I refer to them as my angelic forces. Are they angels to me? They are angelic. No angels with flapping wings. The first spirit is James, who claims to be the brother to one called Yeshua, who is Jesus. I have been tested and re-tested by psychiatrists, psychologists and therapists who make sure I don't have a split personality, multiple personality or any other matter that might be residual on my conscious or supposed unconscious, that I might not be aware of. I tell you now, I came from a mixed family with no religion and it was not practiced in my home. I have respected all religions. Roman Catholicism and Roman Catholic relatives are in my family tree. All religions to me truly are clubs and a way to get to your own spirituality, but that is your own personal belief system. It has zero to do with my belief system. I am super partial to Roman Catholicism. I don't know why. The first point is that James, a spirit, sometimes will stick to one subject when he comes through. Many of the words he speaks are in tonal sounds. He will speak by using tonal words from the Kaballah of his time. You have to know, it's not like you are hearing words as it comes out in ancient Aramaic. It is tonal and has a different meaning for each sound in the Kaballah. I know nothing about the Kaballah. I have never had a human teacher in my entire life. My existence has been totally with spirit. I have also another, wonderful lady who claims to be Eileen Jeanette Garrett, a spirit, founder of the Parapsychology Foundation of Manhattan, and she claims to be an entity that is speaking through me. Again, I don't know who she is. If she wants to be Eileen, then I am going to be respectful and say,"howdy." The purpose of mediumship, in my opinion, is to bring together the so called bridge, make it less of a bridge, a gap, so to speak, so that communication can take place from the dearly departed or undearly departed to us here in mortal life. Has this occurred in your life? I think there is at least one or two of you in the room who would say, "Yes, it has." I do séances too. Yesterday I did a lovely haunting in a place called the Hills in Coral Springs and this particular home has four ghosts! Concerning the research on me, once a month the research team of Spenser, Ruth, now Irvin, and myself meet at Spenser's house. I have no control when I "go under" and relinquish my consciousness. What you are going to see here is not the typical channeling like what you see with James Von Pragh on TV. That is the kind of work I do when I do my international readings and I am connecting to people because I have to be in full consciousness. The second point I am going to make is that I am going into a deep trance. My temperature and blood pressure will change. At one time it was 148 over 138 and the doctor who was checking it was afraid that I would flat line. As soon as Eileen barrels through, it goes all the way down to normal. Be aware that my physical body goes through changes and I may wake up soaking wet from perspiration. When Eileen and James come through they do not claim to be speaking in their own voices. My voice box is different from theirs when they were alive."

S. What was the first experience that you can remember that you had which could be labeled veridical in nature, namely, that it tied in with some external event, whether from the present, past or future, something you did not know but was on a psychic level?

M. It happens every day in my life. It happened when I was five years old.

S. At five years, did you know how to interpret it at that time?

M. Of course. My grandfather said good-bye. I said "Good bye Grandpa." And a day later he was called "dead." I thought at that age everybody did this.

S. Didn't you tell your parents about this at the age of five?

M. I spoke to my mother and told her about my dream of grandfather saying good-bye. When he passed on, she would encourage me to go to sleep for a little while. Then she would tell me a little more of what was occurring and I did not understand it because I did not have any concept of death.

I. You never saw actual visions?

M. Yes, I did.

I. Did you see a spirit too?

M. Yes, I was always going to funerals. You knew that the family would always be invited to funerals and I would actually see, but could not comprehend why the casket was there, as they were putting the casket into the earth while the spirit, the entity, the essence of what was going into the ground, would be sitting on top of it. It reminded me of a humorous ghost story but I did not know how to interpret that.

S. There are many movies showing the spirit standing beside the physical body, is this a true picture?

M. I would concur with that. I have seen that myself. I have other friends who have that kind of sight. We have seen it together. We have witnessed it and can describe the same body shape, wave-light or what have you.

S. Were you influenced by what you saw in the movies?

M. No, no, no. I recently met a woman who was in many of my dreams in my youth and that was a friend of Ruth (Marlene's girlfriend) and who now channels Feda, spirit from the other side. This woman is B.H., (to protect her privacy). She used to come to me in my dreams when I was that little five year old girl and I saw myself running through catacombs and I would see this mother superior ahead of me and she turned around and I knew I had to catch up with her. When I met her five years ago here in Florida. I said," It is like meeting somebody who was part of my life." It was incredible, how in my five year old state I remembered her face in detail. We were able to elaborate on similarities and stories of her being a mother superior somewhere in Germany wearing a brown habit, and here I was this little waif running after her. It was beautiful. I was in some kind of crypt where they buried the dead.

S. This was something that happened in a past life?

M. I have no idea. All I know is that I related to it in this life and also in as far as the other experiences happening. I have a whole list of events that are verifiable that I told to people including the crash of Pan Am flight 103 where a woman was saved. Also the attempted assassination on President Reagan, the fall of the stock market a year and a half before it happened, the Yankees regaining their fame and winning the series many years back, Michael Jackson's hair catching on fire, and while sitting in a restaurant with my girlfriend and just having a chat, the glasses of water on the table began to shake. I told my friend I was not doing this and I did not know why it was happening at our table. These were some of the things that I was able to hone into. Recently I re-read my diary for the summer and I was unaware that I was told that a Tsunami was supposed to occur in Japan and apparently it did and wiped out thousands of people. But it was not Japan. It was an island close by. So these things come to me and I can't say how, where, when or why.

I. Do you personally accept that spirits exist on the "other side?"

M. Yes. I also wish to say that Sheldon did meet and speak to Jeanette Garrett when she was alive. She passed over in 1970 at the age of seventy-seven.

S- Let me explain how that happened. I was a good friend of the author of "The Search for Bridey Murphy", the book that became a best seller in the year 1958. The author, Morey Bernstein, was temporarily staying in Manhattan on West 16th Street near 74th Avenue. One day after "The Search for Bridey Murphy" was published, Eileen Garrett expressed an interest in meeting with him and invited Morey, some of my friends, and me to come to her office and we had the chance to meet her and ask questions. She was nice to all of us. The people who came with me were very impressed because they had heard so much about her. We were talking basically about the Bridey Murphy story and the publicity and flack that were associated with it. That was my introduction to Eileen Garrett.

M. For those who have never visited these trances, I am totally unconscious and remember nothing when I awake. I must listen to the tapes in order to understand what has been said. Please begin to sing, "When Irish Eyes Are Smiling," which is necessary for me to relax deeply enough to permit the spirits to come through, take over my vocal chords and verbally speak to you.

After a half a minute had passed, I noticed that Marlene's eyes were closed. Her breathing had slowed down as though she was asleep. Her body remained perfectly still with no movement in her arms or legs. Suddenly, her mouth began to move, but the voice spoke with an Irish lilting brogue and said," Hello everyone." I was totally taken by surprise. "Who are you?" "What is your name?" I asked. Marlene's mouth began to move, her eyes remained closed, and her facial expression was blank.

"My name is Eileen Jeanette Garret."

"Where were you born?" I questioned.

"In Mead, Ireland." (This is why she spoke with an Irish accent.)

"What did you do for a living?"

"I was a writer of seven books and a few articles. I started the Parapsychology Foundation in New York City and I was a publisher of forty books. I also published a newspaper called, "The New Age Press.""

"When did you die?"

"I died in the winter of 1970."

"Eileen," I said, "I would like to write the story of what takes place on the "other side," where you are. Once I cross over, I will not be able to write the book."

"I will permit you to write the book if you do not change the meaning of my words." she answered. I promised to abide by her wish.

The next day I stopped by the library and discovered that Eileen Jeanette Garrett had written seven books. I reserved three and read them. Eileen Garrett had been a fabulous writer. The following week, I called the Parapsychology Foundation in New York. It was still operating. Her publishing business had closed. I was able to verify as true many of the answers that she had given me concerning my questions.

Thus began five years of questions pertaining to life on the "other side" and receiving answers from the spirits. W would meet once each month inviting people who were interested in our research. Marlene would slip into a trance, Eileen would come through and we would record the question and answers on my tape recorder. The sessions would last approximately two hours. A month after the first session with Marlene, I was surprised suddenly while questioning Eileen. The voice changed and a man with a deep guttural, gravely voice as though he was forcing the words out, began to speak.

"Who are you?" I asked.

My name is James and I am the brother of Yeshua (Jesus).

I will only answer questions relating to my brother Yeshua, my family and the Bible.

V- Hello James.

I- James, did you ever sing in your time?

J- I regarded my voice as too important to share, but you might ask me about my Yeshua. (Jesus)

V. What do you want to tell us about Yeshua?

My name is Yakov Ben Joseph that translates to son of Joseph. And my mother's name is Miriam. My number one brother is Yeshua, my third brother is Daniel, and then David, then Ruth, then like your word for Elizabeth and like your word for my Mom's name Mary/Miriam. When my brother Daniel died, it broke my father's heart. My life was a carpenter's life. We were not poor. I lived with my wife and five children in Qumran. We did hard and toiling work, always busy. You understand that Yeshua was Hebrew. He had nothing to do with your Christian religion. That is Paul's work, not Yeshua's. I like the good Yiddish word, meshuganah (means crazy). We didn't know this word then. Mostly, people are coo-coo. You don't know my father's father and you don't know about Sofia, the momma of my father's father. You don't know my father's family. In mom's family, she had a beautiful sister named Ehrfria. Oh! She was a beautiful girl. People would fall in the streets when she walked by. My God, she was gorgeous.

S- What kind of clothes did she wear?

I. Sack cloth. Not fine merchant cloth.

S- What made her so special?

I. She had blue green eyes with nice skin. Please understand that we are also Jews. You are being fed a book wrapper story about Jesus and the cross. That never happened. It certainly never happened. Paul invented that lie and made Yeshua "God-like." My brother was a fine teacher and was ordained by God himself to be his "bris." (Circumcision at the beginning of a male life.) He was so good among men. My brother would never put his face on what you wear, for that is not good. My brother had dark hair and dark skin. He was not as handsome as you make him out, nor was I.

V. Did he have a beard?

I. Of course, we all had beards. We were pious.

I. James, where is Yeshua buried?

J- I will not tell you because we know that my work is going to be uncovered very shortly when the Israelites will piece it together correctly.

11/95

CROSSING TO THE "OTHER SIDE" AND QUESTIONS ON REINCARNATION

(While Marlene is in trance Eileen comes through, using Marlene's vocal cords to speak)

I— When a spirit decides to reincarnate into the physical, how does a spirit know if a woman is pregnant, to be reborn in her body?

E— The best way to answer this question is very simply to picture an entity. Call it a ghost, soul, energy or a collective consciousness. Call it a spirit or whatever you want. But, the factual statement is that it is the continuation of energy. The energy has intelligence and has emotion. It has already been pre-ordained so to speak, pre-destined. It has a pull to the female pregnant lady who will become its mother. The baby that is being nurtured in the embryonic state has no mind other than the development of itself, but it has not been encased with our "breath of living." So, what we are going to do is simply say, "I know this woman here has to be my mother." Therefore, it is not a big deal for me to just feel it and be drawn to it, thus creating what you call a "living life" with a soul and intelligence.

I— For how long does the embryo have to grow for the spirit to enter?

E— There are many levels "here." It depends mainly on the learning process of what the entity feels. For some it might be to have what is called an abortion or a "spontaneous" abortion. For others, it might be an entry from the fifth month and yet still for others it may be just before the woman gives birth. I would say that the general feeling is between two and five weeks before the birth is actually happening and those spirits who do not have to feel the birth itself may go into the "sentence of living" when it is just about ready to come out.

I— Is there someone on the "other side" that decides when this spirit shall enter?

E— Nay. It is an entity decision. It encompensates for the first of your collective consciousness. Keep in mind that "here" there is no past, present and future so the word time is not a normal feeling for us. While we are entering the baby, we can simultaneously experience a life into the future. You think in terms of division. In fact, it has more to do with the thirst for experiencing the lives that you must have.

I— Then you are telling me that there is no one, such as masters?

E— Of course not. You are thinking in terms of ascended masters and such gobbledygook. That is a silly notion. There are people making a lot of money from this idea. I tell you and caution you that if you limit yourself and believe that you are not as high as a so-called master, then you will never get there.

I— If I am going to enter and begin life anew, why shouldn't I pick some woman who is wealthy? Why should I pick one who has no money?

E— Because the wealthy woman has already offered you, perhaps, a living. The woman in poverty is one, which you have to exemplify because you have never chosen that ever before. The experience of what you would gain from this life preordains doing what is mapped into that life which is something you had to do. You do have free will in a very odd way.

I— You have free will all the time?

E— You think you do, but it is in a very strange way. I have to answer it this way, that if I told you one has free will, but you are also talking about destiny, it almost sounds like a contradiction. I am understanding of that. But, keep in mind, again, that to the intellectual, free will means that you are never under the domination of destiny. But, I can tell you that it is destiny?

I— In other words, if I am born, and lets say I am fifteen years old, and I walk along a street, and a brick comes down from the top of the building and kills me, who created this destiny?

E— You did. You had to be there at the exact time, and if the brick did not smash into your head, but hit you in the toe, then you wanted an easy way of learning that you are a fool, because you never checked the building that you walked past. That is like telling me that walking under a silly ladder with a black cat is superstitious nonsense.

I— Yet, my mother loved me and she would suffer if I am killed with the brick.

E— That is correct. That would have meant that you had to be the foolish child to have that accident. You brought it upon yourself. You were ignorant. You had to experience stupidity, and thus, your mother had to pay for the suffering of your stupidity.

I— Am I stupid to walk on the street and a brick falls down.

E— You did because it was mapped in, you chose a very silly thing to have an accident with. It was your choice right down to the color of the brick.

I— You are saying that all accidents that happen - - - -

E— There is no such thing as an accident.

I— You create this?

E— Of course. You bring it to your life, to the experience and to the pleasure of growth.

I— You say we have to grow. Are we growing all the time?

E— Correct.

I— At what time do we grow to the point where we don't have to grow any more?

E— This involves the theory of limits. Again, you are trying to talk about the infinite and finite. Keep in mind; everything is not as it appears. Therefore, it involves other conceptions "here." The question was based upon the man made conception of limits. I cannot imagine having limits. There are no limits.

I— Is there a God?

E— If you believe when you come "home" that you have created the essence for the God vision, then you will meet a God vision. If you do not believe that, then there will not be one "here" for you.

I— Can you answer how the world was created?

E— I can tell you that your scientists are one hundred percent correct. They are not always correct, but with the creation of your planet, they are.

I— We are talking about the big bang theory.

E— Yes, and it is true.

I— So, there is not such a thing as a God who created the "Big Bang."

E— I will tell you that I don't wait at this moment to examine what you said to me. Examine that thinking. What are you trying to do, create chaos?

I— I am trying to see if there is a God.

E— Why don't you say, Eileen, did you see a God?

I— Eileen, did you see a God?

E— No, I am still looking.

I— Eileen, I'll call you Jenny. (Eileen enjoyed being called Jenny based on her middle name) How do you, coming from the spirit world, interpret reincarnation?

E— I do change it, a bit. I no longer feel that you necessarily have to collect or fulfill the commandment because you have left. It has more to do with gathering debts in life. You live from day-to-day and you are either what you call good or bad, guilty or guiltless, loving or loveless. It is a way of seeing that you collect the debts, that you have to pay back that debt. But, as you live your daily life you rise to the occasion of feeling the power of love. When you feel the power of love you are dealing in an essence that is fulfilling, so that the karmic debt has more to do with a philosophical term applied to the correct way of living a decent, healthy life, almost like the ancient Hebrews had prescribed, a manner of how to live with healthiness and cleanliness.

I— So, actually love is the strongest of all emotions.

E— There is only one emotion and it all comes from love.

I— So, you should love your fellow man and everyone.

E— No, you should be discriminate whom you love. But, the essence of love should be within you.

I— Is it better to give than to receive?

E— It depends on what you are getting. If you are getting an elephant, you don't want it. But, to answer that, you are speaking in an unhumorous way, relating it of course to the gesture and kindness of man. Once you release the giving aspect of what nurtures your life, you then bring back to you a feeling of empowerment.

I— I ask you that because I thought we could have discussions with them.

E— I would love nothing more, but I am busy involved with this lady's life (Marlene), and talking to you. Do you know I spend between two and fifteen hours a day talking with her? That means while we are driving, I am driving her car. That is fun for me.

S— When you passed over to the "other side", did you meet with people you used to know when you were living in this world? Did you meet any of your relatives or friends?

E— Yes, of course I have. Better than that, I brought with me my "yew" tree. (Eileen at age five in Ireland used to play with her unseen friends near a yew tree) I could not leave it behind. I wanted so to see my children, and I had that with me. I knew that it was only by just thinking of them that I was amazed to learn how easy it was for me "here" to see and feel the emotions of everyone I ever knew. Even though people learned about my work and they never knew me when I was very young, it made me feel so good that I expressed it with lots of gifts. By allowing this lady (Marlene) to speak, one-day she will have to take my whole connection focus.

I— Jennie, what made you pick Marlene Stewart?

E— We did not choose her. She did not choose us. We came from the same nucleus. It can only have happened this way.

I— What do you mean by the nucleus?

E— One day I will grant you the knowledge of knowing that the creation of man came from ten single nuclei. Think of that! We call them the ten ancients and from those ten ancients a geometric progression occurred and people began to be born. Through trial and error you have the first human race, which will once again change.

V— Are there males and females on "your" side?

E— We deal in ying and yang philosophy, which is female and masculine, ying being female and yang being masculine. Understand that we can project our thoughts and create whatever we want. So that if there are men and women "here", of course their essences are remaining with their consciousness as they present it. But, there is a very neutralizing feeling. So it is mostly just an energy that can think.

I— Is there such a thing as sex over "there?"

E— You have heard fantastic stories about spirits having sex, but it cannot take place without bodies. But, you can have mental sex if you take it to that extreme. But, truly it is boring. Why would you want to? (Laughter from the group) From this last measure, we can feel that with your laughter.

I— Does anybody on the other side hate each other?

E— Not even Hitler is hated.

I— If you have hate for someone on this side, and you both cross over and you meet, what happens then?

E— Then you have agreed to settle it when you reincarnate, and then what occurs is disaster. But, that too is an act that must be played out because those lives needed that in order to go on.

I— Are there spirits known as "walk-ins" who take over the physical body and remain until the physical body dies?

E— Yes indeed. Oftentimes when people have their psychic experiences, they have agreed that there is no such thing as a stranger walking in. Everyone "here" must be invited by you. This cannot happen unless there was a deal made regardless of the time of life it occurs. So, most people call it a walk-in near the death time of the other human, but in fact, it is a deal. The term "walk-in" is a very sweet way of saying, "We have arrived. Keep in mind we come with our consciousness. Our consciousness will develop out of the present time that we are taking in your world."

I— Eileen, on the physical side, are there such things as aliens?

E— I can tell you one hundred percent it is a truth. The woman here known as Marlene does not believe it, but I can tell you, "yes, aliens do exist."

I— Also, can you tell me whether or not the United States government has captured any aliens or bodies of aliens?

E— I can tell you that there is a lot of quietness in your government, but not so in other governments, especially south of the border, I will tell you that the governments of many nations have not captured any, but have been friendly and communicating with certain of these aliens from other worlds.

I— Do you feel that these other worlds are trying to take over this earth?

E— No

I— Are they much more intelligent than we are?

E— No. They just have a less complicated manner of living, so it frees up their thinking and they seem more intelligent, but they are not. They are not as cumbersome as humans. They can plan. They only have to worry about themselves for survival.

V— Are these so called aliens, the same entities as people on the earth?

E— Do you mean, "did the people come from aliens? I will tell you this that this is true.

I— Are there many aliens in human form?

E— I did not say that. When you asked about creation, you remember I spoke of the nucleus and the original ten. It did not start by itself.

S— Do you have any ideas as to why aliens have come to visit us in this time in our history?

E— It has not been this particular time. They have always come. What occurs is that the machines you now have track them easier. It is no more greater now than it was a thousand years ago.

V— What is their main purpose in coming here?

E— One of their purposes is to assist the human race and make them understand that all humans came from them and therefore are theirs, that we are their offspring. That is a concept that will gather momentum as mankind develops and loosens the shackles of the silly notion of what an alien is. You are as much alien to them as they are to you.

I— Do they look like us?

E— No, they are testing to see why you all turned out to be so ugly.

V— Do the aliens wish to do us any harm?

E— Never, you are their children.

V— Did the alien's put, what we call mankind, on this earth?

E— Yes, they are your seeds.

S— Explain the significance of the fact that many people who dream of departed ones often see them as they were when they were very young rather than as they were when they passed on. They seem to see themselves sometimes as young girls or boys rather than as mothers and fathers. Is there any explanation for that?

E— It is the psychology of the human mind and the nature of man to find that we want to have people in their beauty and wholeness, in their healthiest state. Then what happens is that when we vision them that way, then we are according ourselves that same loveliness.

I— Jenny, does the "other side" give you any clue as to what the future will be like, as to whether people will be more understanding, tolerant and open?

E— "This side," which I really feel is your side too, you understand, but for demarcation purposes————.

I— Yes, but we have physical bodies and you do not.

E— Oh, but I am sitting in your brain; so now I do. Understand this. I just want to tell you that the day of the proof that I am trying to conjecture up will come and it will come through this lady (Marlene), and it is not going to be with her last breath either. There are many good mediums out there to help us. So we are going to do it. Isn't it wonderful! Life does continue!

I— Does the "other side" say anything about what is going to happen regarding dangers such as nuclear war?

E— Indeed. There are many "here" who feel very free to talk about it and I too have been telling this lady (Marlene) about certain events that are going to cause greater hardship than the natural events. They will come in the manner of illnesses and disease that you will eventually overcome.

I— Dr. Jones Salk died recently. He was working on Aids.

E— He did develop a vaccine. It has not yet been refined. He will get credit for it.

I— Does he work on this on the "other side?"

E— He is finding out that he can now do it. There will be somebody who will accommodate him, a thickheaded woman who doesn't know that it isn't her own. (Eileen laughing) We do not dare. It will still be done.

I— How soon?

E— It has already been done. It must go through refinement. In the year 2003 there will be a vaccination.

I— It was all due to Jonas Salk?

E— He was the primary man. He already created it.

I— Why is it that people die at different ages on the physical side?

E— That has been answered with regard to children. Think, if you will, that all you had to exemplify was the kind of living you had up to that point. A better question is, "Why is it that people can be so friendly and then have the most horrible relationship, be it in marriage or among friends?" Then you have the other case. "Why is it that enemies will become friends?" The answer to that too has to do with exemplifying those needs that you require during the time that you had the likeness, passion and pull to each other.

I— Have the spirits ever told you why you were chosen with psychic abilities and if you have a purpose as a spiritual medium, what is it?

To talk, to annoy, to let you know that life of light continues, to make sure that those of you who are open-minded will teach others, to allow this to convey to many lives out there. You don't have to take certain things because it was given to you that way. You had to understand that you had to accept certain "ouches." You did not have to stay in them. We are trying to teach you over and over again that you can exemplify good health and you will become healthy. Exemplify the lessons that you must learn and you will go to perfection. Our purpose is simply to communicate and to convey the easiest journey for your living. If it has to do with winning things, then we would convey that feed. We would love to convey love and a brighter day. It sounds very super, but you don't do it. The purpose is to communicate love, because through love, as often used as it is, we are going to grow.

I— If you can alter something that is going to happen by seeing ahead and doing something to prevent it, is it not predestined?

E— I can tell you now that is the same point that is mentioned when you talk to me about quanta and space time continuum. If you have dynamics in a space-time continuum, then you would understand that your question is an entrapment to a human life. If something is predestined and you have to fulfill it because it is predestined, keep in mind the concept of what we said, that you might have a dynamics going on. Only when the issue comes about as to whether or not you have fulfilled your destiny, do you exemplify your freedom. But before that, you are not even aware that you are doing it. You are not conscious of the fact that you are destined to do it, though it is non-existing, which is giving you that impetus. It means it is all destined anyway.

I— Are you saying that when a spirit is reborn and twenty years later commits suicide that is predestined?

E— Indeed, the sacrificial act just simply means that the human no longer had to be with the body. Either the emotional, mental or physical status was beyond repair and it knew it was going to deem itself out of this life. Why would it want to stay with it? It is not a matter of hopelessness, but indeed more like, let's get on with growing. Do not sit in judgment of all those suicides.

S— How do the senses on the "other side" compare to our senses here in the physical body, based on hearing, vision, touch, taste and smell? Do you see colors?

E— What I do is that I simply feel. I say to my thinking, "I would like to feel what is that I am talking about or touching." It is like my senses gather to my thoughts, visualizing scenes. The difference is that I do not have the five senses as a concrete thing, but I have it as a thought. I cannot say it is anything other than knowing that energy is an intellectual thinking machine.

V— The answer you just gave, "Could that be equated with imagination on this side?"

E— I can tell you that there is imagination on both sides. That is not a seeing thing. I do not think of it in the sense of being a sick mind that can hallucinate or fabricate. I am simply thinking of it in the creative sense. Yes, imagination plays a role.

V— Is what we call imagination here a reality on your side?

E— Depending upon the imagination, the inventiveness of man is so wonderful for us to watch. In a way, what you have created and we take "here", is a passion for that creating. We know where it is going, so understand; we prepare first and then live the life.

S— Eileen, can you see colors and hear sounds that we cannot hear normally in our physical world?

E— I would say that the heightened sensitive can hear what you describe and I am going to say, yes, we can do that. We can also choose to feel your life or anyone else's life without having to touch you. If I saw yellow I would feel the liver and kidney areas, which of course, does not always follow what the average person might find. Color radiates in different places for me and of course they can disappear. Sometimes colors can show where a sickness is.

I— Jennie, do you believe in free will?

E— Indeed, and I practice it.

I— Have we predestined ourselves to our own free will?

E— I would say from a man's conception, definitely.

I— If you are going to come back, do you have a choice to come back as a female or male?

E— Of course. I can choose to elect to be a female again.

I— Are there any animals on the other side?

E— If you create the thirst for an animal it will come. It is your perception. If you had no humanness near you and all you knew was a chimpanzee, then you will find your chimpanzee.

I— If the chimpanzee dies on the physical side is there no soul to transfer over?

E— That is a wrong assumption. That is the wrong theory that has been given to man.

I— Are you saying that the animals have souls?

E— I am telling you down to the blade of grass you are all from the universal law and I can tell you not to be so arrogant that the chimpanzee has no soul.

V— Are you saying that we can come back as a chimpanzee?

E— I am not saying that. The specie evolves on its own level. Man chooses to only be man. The animal kingdom only chooses their way. But, it is not a consciousness like what humans are engulfed with.

S— Can the souls of the lower forms of life eventually evolve to that of human beings?

E— The animal world does evolve on its own through natural evolution, but no, they cannot do it via soul. They can never do that even though that is what you read.

S— Do animals have self-consciousness such as man? Do they have the awareness that we have of what the physical world is like? They seem to show intelligence at times that parallels that of man. There are chimpanzee's that can understand sign language. They show emotions similar to man. Can we truly say that we are that unique?

E— The attitude there is also arrogance, Spenser. It is an assumption that we are unique and that animals are not, where in fact it might even be reversed.

I— Jennie, what about different religions? Does it matter whether you have been a Jew, Christian, Moslem, Hindu or Buddhist on the "other side?"

E— Oh, no, it does not matter. We all want to learn different philosophies, whether or not it sounds negative to you, it is something you must experience and enjoy.

I— On the "other side", you don't have synagogues or churches?

E— Of course not.

S— How do entities communicate with one another on the other side?

E— By thought.

I— You can move by thought?

E— We can.

V— Are there places to go?

E— Everything that has ever been created by man, what was, is, and will be we go to.

V— Mentally?

E— Yes, we are energy with intellect.

V— Is the vision of heaven, self-created? Once you don't need to cross over to this side, is that what we consider heaven?

E— The word heaven is a notion, man made, if that is what you feel, indeed. But, I cannot answer it based upon the way the question was put.

V— Perfection?

E— I knew that that was what you were aiming for. Perfection occurs only when you don't have to exemplify anything in a life.

V— Does it follow then that the perfection you are made of, and where you are presently, you can create and enjoy by thought?

E— Yes, in a manner of speaking that is a neat way of saying things. It doesn't work out that way because the obstacles that we also create come with the vision. We don't like to be bored. So that is why people leave to be reborn. It is exciting.

V— I guess there will come a time when I find out for myself.

E— Oh yes, you had a very nice one.

I— Jenny, if people are fearful of death, say they are afraid to leave children and loved ones behind, does that affect them when they cross over?

E— In the amount of time that you think of time, that they must spend thinking of that, it effects them so much that they still don't understand where they are. However, that would change once they allow their minds to expand, and they do. Everyone does. Therefore it negates those feelings.

I— But, it takes time?

E— According to you it can be from one week to ten years. We have people who are still hovering near their families and they don't even realize that they are, what you call, "dead."

V— Is there such a thing as an infinite number of entities on your side?

E— No, they come "here" because they are involved in what we call the fusion of many minds. I will tell you for instance, ten human beings can be fused and merged into one consciousness. That one consciousness can have ten different lives at the same time in ten different places plus the past, present and future of all of them going on simultaneously. So the fusion of the thinking of all that is amazing, isn't it? It even goes beyond that.

V— I would like to find out more about it.

E— It is wonderful. Because you don't simply say or talk about a parallel world, but what you really have to conceptualize is the amazing drive that humans do have in their conscious, thirst for life. So finite is the answer that I cannot offer it to you because it is too limiting. Again, we do not limit, but that was an excellent question.

I— What do the spirits on the other side say, if anything about our funeral practices, death rituals and rites in the physical world?

E— That depends on the religious club you belong to, and I say this most respectfully. But, what I do feel is that those that observe the funeral rituals do understand why it is done and why you feel you have to pay people, and to spend a lot of money on our used up bodies. That is one lesson, we feel, you all should learn. You are not paying homage to the deceased. You are paying respect in filling the pocketbook of the funeral parlor owner. I will also tell you that we look upon it as a necessary expenditure strictly from your purse.

I— Would we be better off giving our body to science?

E— Of course, you know I feel that way. Anyone who does that, I feel, is really allowing themselves a beautiful growth.

I— Jenny, how can we be better prepared in our physical life for the inevitability of our physical death?

E— This is a question I often asked myself. Is there any preparation that one goes through? Each one of you has to do it in your own unique way. I would say, simply know and just live your life to the fullest and don't allow anyone to upset you so that you are really getting sick from the upset. Rise above every thought. Understand it and rise above it and you will have won all that you had to be prepared for to come "here." Otherwise, it can be a bit upsetting and you might be one of those that needs ten years to grow.

(Eileen says goodbye to the group and Marlene returns)

2/96

THE PURPOSE OF LIFE

(Marlene slips into a hypnotic trance and Eileen steps in)

V— I wonder if there is someone in charge in the spirit world and does the leader have a name?

E— Yes, I call "it" the boss.

V— Does he have a title?

E— (Speaks with emphasis) It is not a he, sir. It is quite female.

V— There is some doubt in my mind that it would be a female.

E— I know. That is because you are thinking and conceptualizing a male God.

V— That is correct.

E— We do not.

V— Why don't you?

E— (After a pause) Because I have yet to feed it to my thoughts. And I have not yet witnessed a God. God is a conception made by human beings. You should say to me if this is a female boss, does she go by a name?

V— Yes.

E— My answer is, "I am that boss. I have to answer to another fragment of my soul. That fragment of the entire soul is already at perfection."

V— To whom do you report?

E— I report to me. Each intellectual thought that is connected to your life, you have when you come "here." Don't ask me what "here" is because that is yet a word I have to find meaning for. When you come "here" with the capacity to create a thought and to use it, you then create the vision that you need, but you sir, are already examining your previous existences, and your future existences while you are "here." We are not talking within the space-time continuum. We are transferring the thought processes to connect to your connective, collective consciousness. (It is very quiet for a moment as everyone tried to comprehend the meaning of Eileen's statement)

V— Do you really know that there is a future?

E— Yes, in terms of what you perceive, a future technically for human beings. I once wrote something on the topic of fear, and it was just before World War II ended, and I recall implying or stating, and I can't remember my exact words, but it was about all tomorrows are immortal.

V— You said you are a female boss. Are there any male bosses?

E— When you come "here" and you are a man, you answer to your man boss. That is you.

S— When people pass over to the other "side of life," do they change dramatically in certain ways and if so, how or do they stay pretty much the same as they were when living in their physical body?

E— I will use the concept "when one passes over". All that is "passing over" is an intelligent energy form to create the thinking of whom you were. You then create the vision of that one. Oftentimes, people say when they see a ghost manifested, "Why is the ghost also young or beautiful when dressed? Why isn't it old and sickly?" That is because

205

the vision that we want to project is one of love and beauty. Thus, that is the same for us. We want to create a loving, beautiful vision. We don't want to create what the lessons were during the living. So, when I came "here" I simply became my thoughts of me. I projected that first, and saw myself as me. I did not see angels. I did not see God. I did not see St. Peter. There were no pearly gates. There was no white light. There was energy. Unlimited energy. Each one a majestic quiet love.

S— We had talked about the possibility of seeing into the future and I know that you have told us that the future is pretty well fixed, that if I had the perception, I could see into the future, see what was going to happen. There was a recent case of someone who had a near death experience, and he did see certain events that were going to occur in the future, where a couple of events that he foresaw never came to pass at the time that it was alleged that it was going to happen. Yet he was convinced that they were all going to turn out to be true, but they didn't. How do you explain the fact that all these prophecies did not happen?

E— They are not prophecies. It is that the margin of error is not very often large, but it is there. And often times when we are not communicating like this, then the medium that we are using to work through, is only partially getting the information out. If there is interference, then I cannot speak freely, but if there is no interference I have no conception of time and often I have to stimulate Marlene's thoughts to show me the four seasons.

S— What would cause the interference?

E— The mind of the human being has fear that if it relinquishes itself completely it won't be able to come back to its full consciousness. Thus, even though Marlene has us using her voice there have been occasions that she has interfered with her thought and has not even considered that her thought may be my thought but I would not have worded it as she has. Oftentimes, just the reversal of two words changes the whole reading. I will say this, when I think of the occasion of the earthquake to occur in San Diego soon, I have to say to myself, what season am I examining. Then I have to think about the climate, and visualize this fault line and then I have to say, I see the town. Where is this town? Now, this goes on simultaneously in my thinking.

S— Were you in anyway responsible for the premonition of the Amtrak disaster, that Ruth (Marlene's friend) was supposed to take?

E— The dear lady was in her car and she told Marlene that she had just purchased tickets to go to New York City. I looked at her and I said, (Speaking through Marlene) "Dear Ruth, you will not be on that train, because the train is going to crash and one of the cars is going to be burned out. There will be several deaths on the street," and Ruth said, "My God, I already have my ticket."

E— I said, "Go and change it, because you will not be on that train," and she did change it. The crash happened a few days later.

I— Did you save her life?

E— "No," because I said she would not be on that train and she could not be on that train although it was the right train. I also predicted the terrible crash that happened in Maryland the week before. I told Ruth there was going to be another major crash on the Amtrak line far north of here where there is much snow and ice, but it was that Amtrak train again." I did not realize it would be in Maryland. I did not yet fix on time, but when we did tell people of the Pan Am 103 crash, (the plane that crashed off the coast near New York City) believe me, we did save a life and that felt very good. I sense Judy (one of the visitors) thinking, "If you saved that life, is that part of her map-out. When this person told her friend that Pan Am flight 103 was going down and we gave the exact location, the day, and as close as possible to the time, she called her girlfriend in California and she immediately canceled. It did save a life, but the question from you, Judy, since you did bring up map-out, should be also, "was that part of her map-out?" The answer is clearly, yes. It was beholding to her to call and ask Eileen if it was going to occur in her life.

I— Jenny, you told me once that the past, the present and the future are all one?

E— For us "here."

I— Then you can actually tell me how to cure certain diseases?

E— Exactly, if I were a doctor. I am not a doctor. I have to pull in a doctor.

I— Can you pull in a doctor?

E— No I cannot. You have to be a doctor to speak to a doctor. You have to be a writer to speak to a writer. You have to be a pianist to speak to a pianist.

V— You said we are the bosses of our destiny.

E— You are the boss when it comes to your freedom of choice.

V— Say we go "home", so to speak. You said you learned a lot since you have been there. How did you learn that?

E— (Reflects for a moment) A very good question. Keep in mind, what I mean when I say that learning, taking place "here," is a part of your life, it is already the perfect life. There is no past, present and future. So, all I have to do is to feel for the life that I am in, the perfected form and I have all the answers.

V— Let's say a person is making a mess out of their life and when they do pass over they want to correct that. How do they go about doing that? They do not have a perfect life. Is there any guide that will help that person?

E— If James were here he would give you a lecture about his brother, the Rabbi Jeshua and his mother who was Miriam. You don't want James to lecture you about God. You better have me who can talk about the collected connected conscious. You perceive what it is that you want. If you were growing up belonging to the Judaic religion, your perceptions are filled with those feelings and you are comfortable with it. You come "home" with preconceived notions of what life here might or might not be. In the beginning your preconceived notions are for your vision. When you realize that you are creating it, and you do realize that "here", you then stop it, and you learn. We look at you, or better yet as the word look does not apply, we sense you. We watch your reality and we are amused. Then we say, "Oh my, I haven't yet experienced that. I am not perfect to meet my perfected self there. I have to be this or I have to do what this one is doing." You must be both man and woman. You must at all times have the worst and the best. You must have that in each life, so that you may live. You must also exemplify God, you must exemplify, no

God. There is not just one experience created by your thought. That, you must avoid.

V— Let's say that experience would be evil.

E— That is correct. The most gentlest soul can return as the greatest monster.

V— Would that be ideal?

E— (With no hesitation) Of course it would. Let us say during the Neanderthal time, pre-Judaism of course, that means pre-God but man did exist. During that time you were a very gentle soul but your society dictated that you eat fellow people as cannibals. That would be evil today. Would it not? But what was it then?

V— Then it was accepted.

E— So you see. You come into your society to fulfill what you deem is part of the map-out, not only for yourself, but for the society you have adapted your life to. Today, you would be considered a criminal, but during the Wild West days you had to have a gun to survive.

V— Let us say you are born into a society where you do not have to be a criminal. In that society, is it still good to be a monster?

E— (With emphasis) If you are born in that kind of society, which of course will never be, the term here that I have to say in a kind way, is get real. Get real and grasp on to my thinking and I apologize if I am not using the terminology to express it properly. If your world exemplifies love, regardless of the bad people, and you are a person longing for love, then give it and receive it. It will manifest goodness, regardless of which society you come from. But remember, what is goodness and love, is also relative to that society. You cannot separate it. A compassionate person will be compassionate. You can even be compassionate to a murderer. Look at your television. Look at those who have to die in the electric chair. Look at those outside with placards. Do you understand what I am saying? You can even be compassionate to your murderer.

V— Can you be compassionate to Adolph Hitler?

E— (Sadness appearing in Eileen's voice) you can't ask me a question like that because when I lived in France during World War II, I helped the children. I founded Tomorrow Magazine to help them. I published the magazine with my own money. I started it for the children so that I would have money and grants for the people who wanted to let their children go further on in the creative world, for arts, science, music and everything.

V— I once read someplace, where a question was asked either of you or Arthur Ford, (a deceased psychic) as to how we should prepare our-self in this life, so that when we do "go home", so to speak, it will be to help make that a very wonderful experience, and they mentioned music.

E— But it is not me. You have to understand that as different as you are as humans that's how different we are here, (Laughter in the room from the viewers). We are not of one thought but there is one thought that is constant and that one concept is love. That never changes.

S— How many books did you publish?

E— I believe it was eight books, but I don't recall now. I know four we published with my Creative Age Press and then another four I published with Putnam and Company. I wrote many papers and I also had a magazine. Then of course, there were other articles that were pertinent to the research. I also published under the name of "Little."(Research on Eileen proved her statements correct)

S— When you are not talking to us the way you are now, where are you and how do you perceive the physical world?

E— We "here", specifically, don't feel, but asked it in a way that you ask about colors. I work through vision; I always worked through vision in my mortal life. So it is easy for me "here" to fall into that thought of visualizing. Now when I visualize your world, my world, our world, I can pray for thoughts to come, but it is more like we don't do this. We just say it to our thinking. Just remember the word "thinking" applies because there is no brain here. There is mind. Mind is the creative force, the creative juices, so to speak. The mind continues on as this intelligence, and I perceive the world with the colors that I used to see, and it is of a memory of my existence. Now, that is not the only way. Another way is, because Marlene let us use her voice, we also can sense through her eyes, ears, mouth, chest, the throat, and her hands. That is why, she always jokingly tells you, that she can never live alone, she will never be alone.

S— Why were you attracted to Marlene?

E— It was not an attraction to her. Marlene used to belong to my life when we were both in Ireland, many centuries ago. I don't want to get into details right now, but it is because we knew each other, and we adored each other then. I adored her so much that I knew before I was even Eileen Garrett, that she would talk with me as I am talking to her, that is one of the mysteries that you will soon uncover.

V— You said at the last visit, that she was part of your soul.

E— (Nods in assent) That is correct, I am trying to tell you that this can only work if you visualize one nucleus, and only that one nucleus. If you want to call it master soul, I don't care.

S— How soon after you passed on did you try to make contact with Marlene?

E— I didn't actually wait, as James had already begun with her from the time that she was born and she became aware of him at seventeen, but she negated his existence. I would say that I began to attempt reaching her with my thinking, the latter part of the seventies, but James had been with her already. I was "here" in 1970 and I would say that it was, easily about 3 to 5 years afterwards, if not longer, I don't have the accurate date yet. I have to think of it and it will come. James had been with her then and there was a major problem speaking through her, because James was speaking Old English and it was a disaster. Then we spoke with her and I told her that since she is so thick in her ear, she will never hear me. She didn't know how to use her mouth for me. What I did was all the automatic writing, which is mine, and so much so that I wrote notes in her diary from 1976 until 1983, that my name is Eileen Jeanette Garrett, Eileen Jean. It couldn't have happened any other way, but I have news for you, it has been perfect.

S— When you were in your physical body, did you have any desire to contact someone after you passed on and become a control of a personality such as you are now?

E— I am not the control, James is the control and James and I are one, but the main aspect to the "boss" is greater than mine. Now it is my turn and I have the next ten years with it.

I— How did you get attached to James?

E— (Eagerly) We are from Marlene, Hemingway, Albigerit, Eschewold, Sir Thomas Hobbes, James, Miriam, Shimon, Andrew, and Caesar Aurilius, not Biberius. All are part of the same nucleus. I am trying to tell you that there are many of us from the master soul. Each one has to live a life. Sometimes we are on the earth plain together. Sometimes we are not. Until we all have experienced the whole entire spiral of all the lives, we cannot go back to the oneness of the nucleus.

I— Is there a given amount of souls in the world?

E— Yes.

I— Then how come if more people are born from year to year, where do we find the additional souls in reincarnation?

E— A fragment of a soul can exist. An aspect of a soul can exist. You are touching on territory that we are going to talk about, reincarnation, which I was absolutely against. I didn't believe in reincarnation, but look at me now! (With excitement)

I— So you are saying that a soul can divide itself into small parts, and there is no limit to how many there can be?

E— No, there are limits. I am just stating that the master main soul has many offshoots and each one of those belong to this "house", so to speak. Papa Hemingway is "here", James is "here", and I am "here". If we wanted to, we could pull in all those people.

V— Is that why some people, when you meet them, you are very attracted to them because they are part of your nucleus?

E— (matter of factly) Oh, you are very frightened by them. The attraction can be a plus or minus. Feeling people use the word soul mate often times. They misuse that because all it means was that you existed at the same time in a different life but you didn't necessarily have to love each other. You could have hated each other.

S— Is it possible that people who are born as twins or quadruplets or even more have some link?

E— (forcefully) Of course they do, absolutely.

S— And their ability to communicate?

E— (with stronger emphasis) Is even greater.

S— They seem to sense similar feelings.

E— Absolutely, or even if they are not twins. We are learning about people nowadays. I know that I used to do an examination with a couple and the couple had twins. One was adopted. And that is what they are studying now, but not only with twins. We have realized that people can have similar feelings and just be brothers and sisters, or brother and brother, or sister and sister that have been pulled apart.

S— I have been listening to some interesting talks given by people in the field of parapsychology and the current thinking is that the concept of mind cannot be localized in time and space, as we know it here.

E— Of course it can't. That is why, before I parted, I just touched upon that and I wanted to go so much farther with it. That is exactly why I am going to rewrite what I wrote, Spenser. I will be the proof of that, that the mind exists but not as you know it with the space-time continuum, but yet it has to be part of it.

S— How can we conceive of that?

E— (with awe) It is amazing. We need a scientist.

I— Jenny, do souls from earth travel to other planets and existences?

E— Let us put it this way. The answer is clearly yes. We do not stay where we are.

I— Do any souls come here from outer space?

E— Absolutely. (With no hesitation)

I— Are you telling me there are aliens on earth?

E— I am telling you, that you are the alien to your mommies and daddies, because all of you did not just appear.

V— We were on other planets at some time?

E— Yes.

V— In this life I have not traveled the way I would like to travel. I like to think that when I pass over I can suddenly go to Venice, the Orient and other places. Am I having a pipe dream?

E— No, you are not. Remember you have to deal with universal law that governs your life, the cosmos, as it exists. You have to deal in the dynamics of living. When you come "here" you no longer have to deal with the flesh. Thus you can go anywhere you choose. Literally to other planets also. You are an energy with intellect.

V— Let us say you reincarnate on this earth plain. What happens if Marlene is still alive and you will no longer be able to be her spoken voice?

E— That is not true. I, Eileen would remain Eileen while the other part of the master soul has been chosen from that life to have a different life.

V— So Eileen Garrett may not reincarnate?

E— I experience it through my master soul and thus I also can experience my future life. It does start with number one and it does go around and around and the spiral gets wider and wider. We then have completed everything there is to complete, unless of course, if we begin to manifest a new concept of life and the spiral begins again. Then we have to exemplify all the things that are necessary to that new form of life. By the way, ladies and gentlemen, you will experience a new form of life. (Smiling ruefully)

V— You say a new form of life?

E— There will be no hair on your body. You will have very thick skin. Your heads will be giant in size and your bodies will be teeny. You will look very similar to those that frighten you, called the aliens. This will take place before the sun goes out.

I— Jenny, if life is a learning state in which people are willing to learn, why does one person die at an early age and another will live to a ripe old age if they are both willing to learn?

E— There are lessons in each life. The man or the woman who had to enjoy the ripe old age, regardless of what manifested in their life, that was part of their process to grow old, to learn agedness. The little baby that died in the mother's womb or lived shortly afterward only had to exemplify a teeny bit of life, because it never experienced a birth, death or a child's death. That is it. The parents of those kinds of children also have a lesson to learn. They have to learn what it is to continue living, regardless of the pain that they suffered. The life that you choose is always exactly as it should be. Why? Because each life is filled with wisdom.

I— My first wife died at fifty-eight and I am still around. Why should she die at fifty-eight?

E— All she had to live was to be fifty-eight. She said that. That was her lesson. Nothing more. It is not a big mystery. It is not designed by God. It is not designed by a devil. (Intently) There is no devil either. I am sorry to disappoint you. And it is not designed by a boyfriend or a girlfriend. It is designed by you. You are the creator of your reality, before you come into your earth life.

V— This thought troubles me?

E— (thoughtfully) I cannot tell you why you are having trouble grappling with those thoughts. I can tell you that it is a choice. That is all I can tell you. Why would a human being choose to be poor when he or she could be rich? Why would a human being choose to be oppressed when they don't have to be oppressed? It is for the soul to learn its lesson.

V— Why would a human being select a cruel life? Is that a lesson?

E— (gravely) Of course it is. Think of the value of that lesson. Your society then, as a whole have raise their collective consciousness, because you can then say, "Look, that is a cruel being. You have admitted it then. Think of how brave it was for that human being in its spirit form, when it was "here," to say "OK", I will be the monster. Think about all the soldiers now and I am not talking about a battlefield, but the soldiers who take on the sickness of "Aids" to raise your consciousness, so that you lose prejudice. Don't you understand it? It is about love.

V— It has been stated we all have a lesson to learn. As we go through life, and we come to a crossroad, we can go this way or that way. How do we determine what lesson to learn?

E— (excitedly) no, no, the lesson is not the road that you take. The lesson is the map-out of the "must" accordance. Regardless of which road, A, B, C.D, E, F, G, it does not matter. It all has to go to "B", from "A" to "B." One to two, and anything in between. What you have, are freedom of choices to get there. If you have to climb a mountain, a wise man would say, "Oh well, let me see, the mountain has a plateau. You can take a helicopter to the mountain." A slower person might say, "You know, it is going to take me nine years to walk up the mountain." Do you understand me?

S— Most of the people here on this planet spend all their time thinking in terms of acquiring material possessions. Others are trying at least to survive, just to have enough food to survive from day to day. Aside from all these primary needs, what should we be striving for in our existence, in terms of helping us to progress in some way?

E— (in a lowered voice) Spiritually growing has very much to do with your mind set. Your emotions then come into play. Keep in mind that you don't have to go into poverty or take vows or be a priest or a nun to be aware. You must have a love in your heart and you must have compassion, even to your nasty enemies. That is hard to do.

V— They say that we are here for a certain amount of time. Let say we are murdered and our life is cut short. Is it even cut short against the map-out?

E— The map-out is my way of saying, the "fixed accordance," because the "fixed accordance" is in all your lives that you must take. You cannot get away from it. There are no accidents. Let us say, and Mr. Mordes asked this question one time about a brick falling upon his head. The brick fell on his head and caused him to die. I said to him with reference to your question, well, you did have to take the action when the brick did fall. You did not have to break your head apart. It could have fallen on your foot, if you had looked up. Now, you should say, "Well, if he died would that have been the accident?" The answer is yes. You see, he would have been called stupid by people for taking the brick on the head, and the one who got it on the foot would be answered, "Well, look how much common sense that person has." Ultimately it goes beyond that because truly, there are no accidents.

V— The natural question is the holocaust. Why?

E— (with sadness in her voice) There was a woman whose parents were part of the holocaust scenario and the rest of her family was wiped out. Also, she wanted me to hold her hand and to free her from the thoughts that she was connected to them. She so wanted to deny that she was the child of this family, but she couldn't free herself. She invented a story of being an adopted woman, so she could have peace of mind. Now, that is her map-out. I will answer your question this way. If people who committed the atrocities and were the oppressors, were to exemplify the task that they had to perform, as cruel as that sounds, and I don't mean to diminish what I am talking about, the victims had to exemplify the suffering. It all had to do with humanity, compassion of love. It had lost reasoning. It had to do with sanity. I had even the concept of mass hypnosis, self-hypnosis. So many valuable thoughts came from that horrific event. These people were again, the bravest soldiers of all, and yes, there are reasons why one would choose it. I have news for you. There are many souls who came "home" from the holocaust disaster that had already begun normal healthy lives as early as the 1950's. They just simply reincarnated. A lot of people who felt they so loved their nieces and cousins, returned as their mother or father. It is hard to conceptualize and to even justify that.

V— I always felt that the reason there was a holocaust was to return the land of Israel to the Jewish people.

E— What matters is, let me take you back in time, a bit. Those people, who were the victims, were also the Egyptians who beat upon the oppressed who were the Israelites. You see the role reversed. When you have mass society involved it is role reversal. There has been the connection to that thought, that the victims of the holocaust were the Egyptians who beat upon the murderers of the holocaust, who were then the Israelis. It is hard to think that way, isn't it? Think of that for a bit and you come a little closer to what it means to reincarnate, to realize what it is to love and to suffer, to love and to suffer. Think how unique and special each one of you is, each precious life is so unique and so special. Look at the wisdom in intellect, your creativity and the enormous amount of love that you have to allow to humankind to even begin. That is a different lesson.

I— So you say, "love your fellow man."

E— (confidently) I cannot say anything, but to love your fellow man.

V— Is anyone here (referring to those in the room) high enough in their lessons not to be reincarnated?

E— Many humans ask me that and the answer is, yes, you do have to be going into another life again. You realize that, depending upon who you are, you might only have to exemplify the birth, or might have to take on an airplane crash or a minor thing. It sounds minor but I know it's not. You have to understand, all of you must cherish your life. That is one of the reasons why it isn't always so wise to open up this way. Because then, you are not fulfilling that which you came here to fulfill, compassion and love. If you had a clue to being a monster in a past life, and in this life you are a rogue, then you understand that you will not complete the lesson for being the rogue. The whole idea is to be the rogue with wisdom, but the rogue you must be.

S— Can you tell me what the significance may be of having a recurring dream about something you have no recollection of in this life. Could it possibly refer to a past life?

E— Of course it can, or a future life. Or it could also, depending upon how good you are at filtering out the shaft from the wheat, and then you would understand there are things that you can comprehend about the symbolism, that might be pertinent even to this life. Of course, Spenser, it can be past, present, and future.

S— There was an experience of a young girl that I heard described on a TV program in which she kept getting this picture of a woman dressed in black holding a pair of scissors and stabbing her several times. She says she doesn't ever remember having that experience in this life and she was wondering, what the significance was having that particular dream all the time since it was so vivid. It seemed more vivid than her current life just to remember it.

E— (Casually) The hypnotherapists are able to delve into that kind of a program of the mind, and they would get so much information. The point is, one can overdose on all these philosophies too, and just simply accept what is. Often times, a repetitive dream is something that is coming from the subconscious and it refuses to let go because it is precognizant of something yet to occur, an incident that occurred in a past life. Most of the times, it is of a future occurrence, yet to occur. I would say that if you get one thing over and over it is precognizant.

S— Is it necessary to be in a situation where you are almost dying while you are very ill, in order to have an out of body experience?

E— No. I taught Marlene how to do this and she has instructed all her students to do O.B.E. (out of body experience) and astral projection. (Once a week Marlene teaches a class in metaphysics) It's very easy. It's just shifting yourself or allowing the energy to connect in a certain way in your body. When I was physical, I used to go through a spontaneous out of body experience. Usually when you are under stress or trauma, a lot of things will happen to the mind. Sometimes you are not aware that you went visiting other places by projecting that part of you there. That is astral travel. When you get out of your body and just hover above yourself, that is an out-of- body experience. I really mean that you are just projecting yourself outside of yourself. It is quite a sensation. It is somewhat like floating. All of you have been through it. Every human mind in existence has had it. You just don't remember.

I— Jenny, what method can I use to make you visible from the spiritual side without you entering Marlene's body?

E— You are talking about the ectoplasm. She and I are too connected now and I cannot ever separate from her. Be aware of that.

I— You said you have to enter her?

E— No, I wake up her mind to me. I am in her mind now. Understand that as time goes on she will have more and more of my thoughts and then we will really have fun. She is beginning to feel what it was like to be Eileen Garrett, and everyone else will begin to feel it along with her, as though they are all growing with her. I've got to ditch this accent. It is driving me coo-coo.

V— Is this possession?

E— (with conviction) No, it is not possession, but you have to understand that it is the mind allowing another mind with it's independent thinking to express itself. The problem that we are having is that I can't yet express myself and the lovely way I used to speak. I spoke well, didn't I Spenser? (Spenser knew Jennie Garrett before she died).

S— You spoke very well.

E— I did not have an accent like this. I articulated well.

I— How about as a young child in England. Did you have the accent?

E— I was not a young child in England. You know it was in Ireland. (I had attempted to catch her in a lie)

I— If you lived in Ireland, you would have had the accent.

E— Yes but it wasn't a cockney kind of thing. It was mellowed out so it had rich tones to it. I loved my voice.

I— Do you know when it is coming back?

E— I do, but it takes time. We have to work with the parathyroid gland and it is very delicate. As you know, we (referring to Eileen and James) had Marlene running to the doctor to do something with the thyroid problem. So now, we have to work with Marlene. That means letting me take it, and then using this voice box to articulate. James does his thing and he does it very well but I always did the writing. Now I am talking and I don't want to keep quiet.

I— Jenny, What will happen eventually? Will Marlene disappear and Jenny will be the complete person.

E— (with some indignation) Oh, don't say that. Marlene does not disappear. What happens is that she is actually in a very peaceful state of being, while I am animating her body. I have learned very well to use every part of her body. It is as though she was asleep, and I can even tell you what she is thinking about. Yet, she cannot tell you what I am going to say, but I can tell you what she is thinking of while we are talking.

V— It is like a split personality?

E— No, it is not split, we are separate entities.

V— What is she thinking about?

E— She loves to do the picture puzzles, the pieces going together. That is what she is thinking about while I talk to you.

S— Was there anything about your life, when you were in a physical body, that you don't want to think about, anything that you sort of repressed from your memory?

E— (reflects for a moment) When I was in mortal form, I did not know my mommy and daddy. My mum, as you know, committed suicide. My father went shortly afterwards. Of course, I was an orphan before I was two months old and those are things that do not matter "here."

S— But you did suffer a lot of trauma?

E— Yes I did.

S— Do you think that this might have contributed to your ability as a medium?

E— (in deep reflection and nostalgia) I always said I thought it did. I have always been very open about that and I would not have gone into the research if I didn't feel that it was worth probing. I was fortunate in the journey that I lived. Don't forget, I had Mr. McKinsey. (who researched Eileen) and his wife Barbara. He was the most magnificent man in the world who helped me when I was such a wreck, even though he and my husband Clive thought I was crazy. People were trying to put me in an institution or telling me to keep quiet. Mr. Ed Carpenter (researched Eileen) was the man who passionately examined what I was about and explained it to me and Mr. McKinsey. These are people I owe my whole frame of thought to. Remember, when I left Ireland I was a teenage child of fifteen.

I— Jenny, did you ever meet your father and mother when you crossed over?

E— Oh yes, my father was very handsome. I could see why my mother married him. She was beautiful.

V— Did your mother and father stay near you while you were living?

E— You know, I have to tell you that I used to pray for them to come to me. I had no little children near me until I was about twelve or thirteen and I didn't talk about it too much. After the incident with my aunt Leone, I didn't want to upset Aunt Martha anymore. (Eileen, at the age of five saw the spirit of her aunt Leone at the cemetery while the body was being buried.) She really was not a nice lady in my life and yet I felt my momma's presence.

I— You are now on the "other side." Are they still there with you?

E— Yes, I have to pull the thought in and when I do this I then can see them.

I— Can you do this with anyone?

E— Anyone from past, present or future. I can do it with any existence that is. Not everyone here has the ability, as they have not grasped how.

I— So when you speak with them from the "other side," since you have no physical body, how do they hear you?

E— We don't need voice.

I— Is it mind?

E— Yes, it is thought, complete thought.

I— Why is it that we can't take those who are blind and can't hear in this physical world and teach them that technique so they can use it here?

E— They can, but the brain has not yet been exemplified. It has not yet been examined to that point, but we can definitely tell you that the day is not too far away for that to occur.

I— So the blind will be able to see.

E— Most people, unless they no longer have the equipment. A regeneration of limbs is also coming.

S— What about spinal injuries? Will people be able to recover?

E— Absolutely, understand that technology is more advanced than mankind. Man has to catch up with the machines they built. They don't yet appreciate it.

S— What kind of world do you envision in the future in terms of our technology? What is going to happen?

E— You won't need your bodies, and you won't have to worry about overweight or underweight. Won't that be nice? What you will need are brilliant minds, and will need what you call your humanness. That is the vision to which technology will take you.

S— What about computers?

E— That is what we are thinking of.

V— What about those people who don't have as much intellect as others?

E— In the society of your future, they will have the intellect again. Even the lowest thought will be more brilliant than your geniuses of today.

It will be like the utopia that existed in Atlantis, except it will have people without their cumbersome bodies.

V— Will we be energy?

E— Yes, closer to energy, with equipment so you can still move. You will also have the ability to procreate the same way for pleasure too. It's going to be rough but the payoff will be brilliant.

S— Do you foresee any world war, which will involve many nations?

E— (vehemently) Oh yes, absolutely. I do know that there will be a world war three, world war four, world war five and a world war six.

I— So man will never learn.!

E— The wars will be without weapons, but they will take on cruel ways, since you will be dealing with a sophisticated and most intelligent society, which will be your society. Keep the thought in mind that you won't need things to kill the body, because if the body doesn't die, it might be more tormenting for it to live. I am just simply saying that there will be that type of a society, for a short duration that one or two in this room will choose to come through. You might say, what an idiot I am to come into a society where it would be better to be dead.

V— Jenny, when we cross over, can we then associate with anyone we think about?

E— Definitely darling, if you so believe. Let me put it this way. If you are a Roman Catholic, and you so believed in Christ, then you would have your Christ. If you are a Hebrew during the day, when the temple of Jerusalem was wiped out and you envisioned God coming close to you to save your life, that experience will be yours. If you were a Hebrew who was part of the early Christian philosophy that

Christ had spoken about, then you will not call him a Christian. You will call him my Rabbi, as James (the brother of Jesus) does. You would say, "My rabbi Yeshua, is the son of Joseph."

I— Did Jesus have brothers and sisters?

E— Yes, he did. You will have to talk to James, because James is the one who is now and has been for many years telling people about Jesus. He was the next younger brother of Jeshua.

S— What kind of calendar did they use in those days?

E— You tell me, I don't know.

V— Was it called a Jewish calendar?

E— It was not called Jewish. There was no such thing as Jewish people on this earth. These were proud Hebrews.

I— Jenny, are all the predictions of Nostradamus true?

E— My first book that I published was about Nostradamus. The answer is,"no."

I— Jenny, the first time you crossed over, you did not believe in reincarnation. Tell me how it felt to cross over and discover, "My God, I was wrong."

E— (with a deep sigh) Well I'll tell you, I had a peaceful death. I went to a convention in France. It was beautiful sitting in the park and I just simply went into a coma and left my body. That was it.

I— OK, you left your body. Continue on, what happened?

E— I stayed with my body where it was prepared and then I said, "My goodness. Look at this, I am now "here."

I— "Here" is where?

E— I am still trying to figure that one out. I don't know the word for "here." If you want to call it "Heaven," you may.

I— But is it a place like a city with houses?

E— I can conceptualize that picture, but I have to be honest. Being here today with my speaking through Marlene is wonderful because I sense the sights around her.

I— Can you see us?

E— I sense you.

V— Jenny, when you arrived on "the other side", was there someone to guide you?

E— My father. I was always programming my mind to meet him because he was spoken of in a terrible way. I wanted to meet this man, and I said to myself, that when I came "here", I would look for him.

Irv- How could you see him? You never met him before.

E— I know you don't have to meet people to know that they belong to you. You know these things. He came to me and indeed; he was the one who took me by my hand.

I— Where did he lead you?

E— He didn't lead me anywhere. I thought I was going to go into this big beautiful light and then I said, "Oh look, I still see people."

V— Which people did you see? People from the "other side"?

E— I saw my daughter, my granddaughter. I saw my foundation, I saw France, I saw things I did, and I so loved it.

V— You saw your past life?

E— Oh I did, and I enjoyed the life of Eileen very much.

I— Jenny, you speak French?

E— Yes, of course I do but I don't speak it now, though.

I— Why?

E— Because I told Marlene, that her voice box was used for Aramaic last night (James came through speaking in ancient Aramaic during Marlene's teaching class) and I am terrified that she is going to have a problem with the parathyroid. I was not really terrified, just exaggerating a feeling. What I am saying is that we are using too much of different dialogues through James, the inflections and the words are difficult enough for him to use. He spoke in Latin and Aramaic last night. Her throat is completely red inside.

I— Why?

E— Because it was four hours of James speaking. When we went into the foreign languages, he used a different aspect of her voice box. I am afraid to over use it.

S— What do you hope to do with Marlene in the days and weeks to come?

E— (with an enthusiastic tone) I need to use her voice to talk about my concepts and I also must become more of a verifiable proof of who we are. Not so much for the name of Garrett. You understand that? That is why we had a lid on it for so many years because we did not want to cause a big bru-ha-ha and throw her into testing which ultimately had to be either rejected or enhanced. The timing was not correct for her life. I can only use her life to do this with. I cannot even use my daughter or granddaughter. What I hope to do is bring forth pertinent information regarding reincarnation. I hope to somewhat regard myself as eventually reading into the scientific community to probe her as they did me and to allow their minds to examine it in this difficult time of Marlene's life. Oh God, she does have it hard. If the people who do research examine her the way I was examined, then I will be the proof of life continuance. I stated to you before that I am Eileen Garrett.

I— I accept that.

E— (with strong feelings) No, no, no, I am stating it, and I am Eileen Garrett. I did not sound like this Spenser, but I am "she", and I cannot always pull in the memory for finer points. Even to the last time when we spoke, talking about Hereward Carrington, (he researched her when she was alive) you asked me which one and I was saying. "Is it the double "r" or the "h.""? So I have to probe your mind and yet a thought from him was coming at me. So you understand, to release certain things, I cannot do it spontaneously.

S— Do you now remember who the person was that Hereward Carrington wrote about and the book which was published by the Parapsychology Foundation?

E— Don't forget, I was his subject for a long time. He was doing experiments and psychoanalytic behavior.

S— This particular medium I am thinking about was well known for the plasmic phenomena.

E— I am trying to remember if this was the one. She did shenanigans and was proven false. Is that the one you are talking about? I can't think of her name, but I am remembering. You see what happens, I too have to pull it in just by recall. It was a shame because she was really gifted.

S— Hereward Carrington wrote about her because he felt that she was a gifted woman.

E— You are correct and she did some false things that she didn't have to do.

I— You once came up with a hypothesis that your powers derived in part from the hypothalamus gland or the vestigial animal brain at the base of the skull. Does this still seem true to you from the "other side"?

E— Well, it does, but not for me. I am talking mainly for those of you who are doing this research. We do have to activate those portions in her body. The pineal gland too is played with; the thyroid, and parathyroid are involved. There are mediums that do trance work that can get away with that. Otherwise, it would be close to impossible for our minds to connect and use the vocal cords. Understand that we are still in research with this female. I would like for her to come upon some of this information on her own.

I— Do you believe that in some way you inherited some of your metaphysical powers from your grandmother and your uncle Leach Brannel? (I began to feed Eileen questions about her early childhood to verify her answers)

E— I know her name. She was recognized as the town herbologist. I suppose you would call her a healer in that lifetime, I did indeed. Having met her, I can tell you, it was upon all of us to be what we were. We followed suit.

I— Do you remember being taken to Tara Hill by Uncle Brannel?

E— Of course, you are talking about the ghost stories we used to hear. Keep in mind that the stories we were given in Ireland were very mythical. Of course I gobbled them all up. I enjoyed every little fable that I could hear and I also enjoyed going everywhere with Uncle Brannel. Of course, he often was not there for me. He told me the stories about the sacred rock and the tales about the implication of life, of past life. In those days, I was just simply told it was about ghosts and fairies. Yes, I believed in fairies and leprechauns.

V— Jenny, I read one of your books and what I can't understand, what are the "rats" and "meet" and the "Leo foil?"

E— It is the stories I heard as a child about the magical rock, fairies and ghosts.

V— Jenny, you once wrote that early in life you suffered from asthma, an inheritance that has never left you. Is the asthma still with you on the spiritual side?

E— You don't come here with a body.

V— So you have no sickness on that side?

E— Why would we want it? The mortal body had to respond to the lessons it had to learn. It is not for people to assume that when they are "here" that they can have those things. After all, that is a gift to you and to me and to others. Your term suffering is a present, a gift. Imagine that.

V— The presence of cancer is a gift?

E— Of course, it isn't meant to be sounding that you should take on cancer unless you wanted to. What it means is you learned from that suffering, and therefore, society gathered knowledge of how to combat it with research, which allowed the human body to reach a higher level of perfection. How can you do it if you don't create the illnesses? You need the illnesses to grow from. Many of you play soldiers by allowing yourself to have these illnesses so that you, yourself, will overcome them; the doctors and scientists will do research, and research and society at large will be elevated to support it. It is creating a near perfect world.

V— Jenny, did you pick asthma when you had it?

E— (with deep emphasis) Why not, I picked all my illnesses. I picked the heart. I picked the appendix. I picked husbands. I picked the loss of children. I picked fighting. I even picked my Aunt Martha. I picked my uncle. I picked Ireland. I picked my mum. I picked my father. I picked down to my very nose, fingertips and toes. I even picked Spenser.

V— Is emotion the bridge to out -of-body experience?

E— I often thought that it would take a dramatic event to allow that to occur or to have a wider opening to the connection to the psychic ability. Remember, we use cognitive and other thought here and it was Dr. Rhine (an ESP researcher) who separated them. I personally felt that the terminology applied to this specific area that we were involved with, falls under the parapsychology aspect of this work. It is all cognitive, precognitive, telepathic acting as one. Now, the thoughts I have here are very, very simple. A human mind can open up to this work regardless of what you fear. When you have a trauma to your body or mind, you begin to allow a shutdown of your conscious thinking to take place. In fact, you go back to the primitive thoughts that you needed for survival. There is also a very correct thought and safe memory of man, and in doing that, what you connect to are the instincts that you had when you were first alive in your beginning incarnation. You opened up because mankind was on that very, very strong level of using all of what we often call the sixth sense or what I like to think of as super-normal. None of this is really out of the ordinary, and to me it still isn't. It is all the senses heightened. Just imagine that you have antenna radar and it is all being fed in. How your mind assimilates it on that quick level of comprehension is the key factor, but always be on guard with your good common sense because without it, you are dead and you can be fooled.

I— Jenny, what is it like. I once had an out-of-body experience and my spirit rose four inches off the bed and I became so frightened I slipped back into my body.

E— Once you are able to lose the fear, what you are doing is releasing the thought that you are able to do it. All of you can do it. By the way, most of you do it in your dream state and you don't even know it. What happens is that when you feel yourself rising up, just think of the double of yourself that has the complete freedom to go where it wants. Some of you have weird pieces of thought that tells you that you are connected by a silver cord or that you are connected by a rope or by a magical light. Thought allows you to travel and allows your mind to expand and to open up to the great universe out there. Then use it. I can tell you that you don't have to put safety belts on. You can go anywhere. You belong with the life that you weave and you won't get lost. Nobody can absorb you into what they are doing. Understand that you should enjoy the astral and teleportation of mind. It is a wonderful thing to happen to your life, not because you will understand more, not because of the event of doing it, but because it can only enrich your life to realize that you don't always need the heaviness of body to open up to the greater part of you, which is universe. You all are connected; every atom of yours is "here." You are connected.

S— In the recent issue of the Journal of the American Society for Technical Research, they mentioned a test for a number of people to determine if there are certain psychological factors involved in people having so called out-of-body experiences. Based upon the answers I gave to these questions I should never have had any out-of-body experiences, or any kind of psychic experiences whatsoever, because my parents in no way influenced me to have such experiences. I therefore got no input at all from my parents. Yet the suggestion that is implied in this questionnaire is that the parents in some way psychologically drew you into having such experiences, either by encouraging you to engage in fantasy or imagination or possibly there might have been some trauma involved.

E— (without hesitation) Boredom. When little children are bored, they don't have to be abused. They don't have to be yelled at. It's just plain boredom that lets their mind wander.

S— So they don't need encouragement to use their imagination?

E— No, they don't need any of that. Yet it probably wouldn't fit the general norm for what they are doing again and the wonderful works that they are examining. Again it fails because it did not include the feeling of people connecting to people "here." You see, a lot of you take on an ability when you first come into your mortal lives. Every single person who is connected "here" today, and I am only speaking for those of you in this room, is allowed to go wherever they choose to go with regard to teleportation or astral projection. We would not be speaking to you about it, if it hasn't already taken place. Now you do have a group of people in your world that are very actively involved in teleportation. Those people have allowed themselves the experience and thus it becomes an easy journey for them. The best way to do this is simply to let go of your thoughts, and allow your mind to reach out. And you know the expression, reach out and touch some one. I am going to say reach out and simply have fun. Believe me ladies and gentlemen, you will. When your body gets lighter and you feel yourself being lifted above yourself just allow the experience of it to take place and also know that it means that you have the ability to go much further. It is wonderful. You are not using that which you are bound with. So Spenser, you are right. I would say, many times you were able in your mind, as a little chap to create the environment that would allow you to experiment. Many times you even thought about traveling without your thoughts and that too is very interesting. You don't have to go wandering with all the baggage that you have collected in your lifetime. Think of the adventure for mountain climbers.

S— Eileen, did you ever hear of the expression, "sleeping paralysis?"

E— Oh, of course we have. I have heard of it from a thought in my own thinking, and I oftentimes am aware that there is a paralysis abound.

S— Some psychologists tend to use that expression.

E— And it's a healthy one.

S— They use that expression to explain so called out-of-body experiences and UFO abduction experiences. I was wondering how you feel about that?

E— Spenser, I will tell you with regard to the comment about the paralysis, it is excellent. I will say it needs a lot of research and it should be exemplified, experimented and it should be done by psychiatrists. The researchers should use the pharmacological medicines to induce that stage. I feel that it is open and it must be done. How can I answer the UFO question? As far as abduction goes, I will tell you that I am completely aware of what has been going on in your universe. Your world, as it is, is imperfect, but we have it perfect "here." I will simply say that indeed those people who have the feelings that they have been abducted have been doing out-of-body experiences. They created the collective consciousness to examine what it was to be kidnapped by aliens. If taken on that level, they would be closer to the truth.

V— Two people did it together.

E— I don't care if it's a whole society, if it is taken on that level. We know somebody who personally swears that he and his friend do it almost every night and I can tell you although they claim to be an invited guests aboard the ship, I guarantee you that part is complete fantasy and illusional. I will tell you that the aliens that are with you are already part of your world. They are part of your system. They are part of you. You all came from them. I told you this before and I tell you this again. I just don't want to upset those of you who are caught up in your religiosity or your diatribes, which your thought creates after you die.

V— A number of months back you had been discussing something called nucleus. What is this nucleus?

E— The nucleus is a body alien, the nurturing for the harmony of mankind to evoke to where it was. It came from the aliens. What you call aliens were really your relatives. It was shabby at the beginning, of course, and it had to go by trial and error. Again we are busting bubbles about the creation of life. The big bang theory is true.

V— What was there before the big bang?

E— There were other universes. The entire universe, the one that you live on is connected to you. Everything in this universe, each and every one of you created. I know that is hard to conceptualize but understand even down to the likes and dislikes, your very atoms, your molecules, your very thoughts, your connection to what we are doing even now, you created, I created. We all created. We are all one. We are all part of the same universe whether we are here or there. It doesn't matter. We are essence of mind "here" that can go into the past and what you call present and future. Remember, the mind is composed of what I like to think is what your psychologists and psychiatrists have been teaching you, that your mind consists of the subconscious part, the conscious present, and the super conscious is the future. The subconscious is the collection of all data, which you can go into when you need to. Your conscious gives you what exists now. Your super conscious can attach to either the past, or go into the present to know what is going on about it, or go way into the future.

V— You said the aliens came here and created homosapiens. Can you give me an idea of about how long ago this happened?

E— Since the earth was evolved, a part of it was first begun with the vegetation. Before the vegetation you had the cataclysmic event that created everything. The aliens were at that time not there. I will not go into that now, but I will give you a quick overview. Understand, that when they came, they did not land. It was done by mind which you all were part of. The mind said it needed to adapt to a universe that would allow it a life. They needed to exemplify living in a form that they never had before. It has been going on for billions of years. The so-called aliens that you all think of now and that some of you freely want to connect with, have souls. The God you created in thought is even greater than that of mankind. It was given to you as a gift from them.

S— Aliens have been reported to go through solid matter.

E— With their minds, they can.

S— Allegedly, people who have been abducted have gone through the walls of their home to the ship.

E— By way of the mind, using teleportation. The collective consciousness of man is part of the collective consciousness of what you connect to as aliens. The collective consciousness of the alien thought is still part of you. You created it. You are separating your humanness from the alien and that is a tragedy. You are part of the same. Now the issue of God, the sweetness of God. The God connected consciousness is correct in assuming it is created by alien thought, but you are part of it. The power of creation to connect to a greater thought allows one to attain perfection. Do you think that perfection is going to be like some of the books you have read? In eighty life times, forty lifetimes, twenty lifetimes? Why don't you try one billion lifetimes?

S— Eileen, do you have any idea what the purpose is on the medical experience many people claim to have undergone as a result of being abducted by aliens?

E— I would hope that they are trying desperately to allow the science of what is going on, to go into the medical profession. Therefore, I would need to know whether or not they have done examinations of these beings and have found the chips placed in them where they maintain they are. Has there been proof yet of that?

S— Yes, there has been.

E— No Spenser, what you have gathered in worth is a situation, and it will come out soon, and please don't allow this to discourage you about the thought of aliens. I am going to tell you what was done. Several computer chips in different people have been put under their skin. Then they were removed. And the metal that was used indeed did come from your planet, Earth. You understand that people are so desperate to make a point that they will go to all extremes to prove it. That does not mean that you should not believe in it. I am giving you something greater. I am telling you, please continue to believe in it because there will be multitudes of frauds but if you get one that is giving you the truth, then wouldn't that be a blessing to mankind. Take it as a wonderful trip. Please understand that the aliens say thanks to those who want to connect to their thoughts. They don't even want you to call them aliens. Call them grandmas and grandpas because you are part of them. The God concept, was given to you by them, which was really your creation. Understand, mankind needed something to learn through many, many evaluations. I know that a new evolution is going to come in about 4000 years. You have plenty of time to come back and be miserable. What I am trying to tell you is, that until that event your bodies will change. Your heads will be rather large, and you will have more hair on your body. You won't need clothing, and the furnishings you use now will not be there. You will not look like you do now, but you will come with brains equipped to know what mankind used to look like. Then you will be on the road to such power and such perfectness. It will not be an easy society, but it will be a society that will have learned its lesson.

S— Howard (one of the people attending our meeting), will tell us about the seminar he attended recently in California and what he heard about the abductees.

V— There is a researcher in California named Dr. Roger Leir. He has been specializing recently in removing implants from people who claim that they have been implanted by aliens. All the people who made these claims actually were implanted, and many of the implants were different, but a lot of them were identical. One of the ones that I remembered was a cross on which the horizontal bar was magnetized in one way, either toward the North or the South and the other bar, the vertical bar was magnetized in the opposite direction. Now it is virtually impossible for us on this earth to magnetize objects in that manner. He took these objects to metallurgists who examined them and said we have no idea how this was done. It is absolutely impossible. Then there were other implants that were found. I believe the base was magnesium with bismuth bonded to it. He took them to many metallurgists and not a single one was able to understand how it could be done. They said according to our science it was impossible to bond these two elements together in the way in which it was bonded.

E— I do have an answer.

I— Where were the implants taken from, the third eye? (Believed to be located in the center of the forehead)

V— Yes, but one of them was in the big toe. Also an interesting thing about these implants, was that the one in the toe had certain nerve endings that grew from the flesh into the implant and that particular type of nerve ending was found only in the spine of a person where certain parts of the body project nerve endings into the spinal column.

E— You do have aliens among you and they are talking to many of you and they are coming to you in your consciousness and you can see yourself as you used to look like before you became mortal beings. They do look like they have shown themselves to you. They are your mothers and fathers. Your United States government has a hand full of them, and they did come here not in alien space ships but in fact ships that you used to drive yourself. They are not alien craft.

S— How do you know this information?

E— (eagerly) When one has to go back and you review your life of the ancient philosophers who used to teach it, it is not of your human man's soul. It is of the soul of what creation was from the nucleus. Beyond the nucleus was the form of the aliens. But you are that. You created that.

V— Will we ever go back to that?

E— Of course, you must.

V— In my incarnations?

E— You have so many yet to do. There are very few people on earth who don't have to be reincarnated as an alien or human again.

S— Many people have had near death experiences. I don't know of any of them who have ever mentioned remembering the kind of experiences that you are talking about.

E— By the way Spenser, you stand to be corrected. There are people out there now who are also connecting with their alien ancestry. Now, when you come "home", you are filled with what you have learned in your lifetime which is your bible, your schooling, and your mind is limited in your perception, because most of you do not come with a greater amount of awareness then what you allow to appear. Because of that, everything you connect to is of man, by man and for man. Even your very stars and moon. That is why most of your minds are evolved to perfection when you are "here." Most of you in your human body, your mortal self, have no way of understanding what I am telling you. It is your awareness to the vastness of your connective consciousness to the universe that makes the difference. Do you understand that?

V— Am I not the universe?

E— Of course you are, but not in the manner of humanness but at the very sweet simple level of knowing beyond the heart that mind connects to the universe. Wow, that is fantastic. I am connecting to what you are thinking. I know you are thirsting for me to say, God exists, a man made God exists. And there was this God that looked upon people and said "That shall be and so on and so forth." I leave that to James. I will not do that, but I do not see God "here." James would say, "Sh"! Don't yell. Just understand that Eileen is filled with her science and research, and she cannot accept these thoughts although her heart is filled with love. She cannot accept the God that we set to living. And we refuse to be part of her faith. That is what he would say.

V— The mind is not the same as brain. You are saying that the mind is the original, which we all have. The brain is the mortality when we are on earth.

E— (speaking very slowly and deliberately) Yes, of course. That one mind is the essence of the feeling of people. Think of this. You are aware when I am speaking, which is in mind. My correct thought is to

245

allow my thinking to think a thought to tell you what is occurring. When you think a thought, you connect to your thinking which allows a thought to be presented to me. Both you, the universe and I are now in a connected swirl of constant dynamics. Through the dynamics of the swirl, the connection of connected consciousness occurs. Isn't that easy? (A puzzled expression appeared on the face of those who were watching)

I— Jenny, did Moses see God?

E— Moses, indeed saw the burning bush but the bush wasn't burning. It was an illusion that God had to create for him, which the connected consciousness of man created so Moses would do what he had to do.

V— That was his life's plan?

E— Correct.

V— What about the parting of the sea?

E— The parting of the sea had more to do with the weather, James says. I can't tell you the truth as James will shut me off completely. (James, the brother of Jesus is in total charge on the "other side.") He is only giving you that much information.

I— Can James give me the information.

E— James can give you the information but he does not want me to give it in such terms because he feels I would be breaking too many hearts. I apologize.

V— If the brain is different from the mind, if you are dealing with people who are insane, is their mind still useful to humanity?

E— Absolutely, the reason that it is useful to humanity is because your connected consciousness becomes a heightened level of understanding that the illness shall not be part of mankind. We have to tell you the symptomology of that is just simply a man who went astray. The humanness of him being a chemical imbalance or a psychological torment that was created, is what all of you are to grow from. That is a soldier.

V— You say that when we are in this mind state, we have a chance to see our previous lives and take our next human life from whatever we have learned.

E— (with strong conviction) Absolutely.

V— To be perfect.

E— Not to be perfect in the living, but just to gather the suffering and love and to learn that love means truly how it fits in your mind.

V— So it is from the suffering and the misery you suffer that you learn and you choose the next life.

E— That is correct. You've got it. But remember, the key is to rise above it so that you learn to give in to it, in a way that you can, even to your enemies. Give him or her a hold on life. You don't have to hug and kiss him, but you have to make him feel good.

V— So, not only do we embrace the good, we also embrace the bad.

E— Absolutely, and in embracing the good means that it is also part of your life. Embracing the bad, the negativity, means the evolution of you.

V— In other words, if you are really angry at someone, apologize.

E— You must go to that person and apologize, even if they were wrong, because they have given you a gift. The gift was to grow from.

I— So, if someone kills your wife, you are supposed to embrace that person and kiss him.

E— No. You have love in your life that he will be punished. That is the lesson for mankind, not just for you. Not to be too selfish. That lesson in mankind would be to see that your judicial system is working. Apparently, it is not working out too well.

I— Suppose you kill him yourself.

E— (speaking with determination) That was your map-out, to finish off a debt with him or her, even to an animal.

I— But, then they may hang you for that.

E— That is okay. That was part of the deal. That was part of the growing and learning power of mankind. It is very upsetting. I understand that. That is why you created God. That is why you created religion; so that you can go to your churches and your temples, and elevate yourself, feel God consciousness or Buddha consciousness. Whatever you choose is fine. It soothes the soul because the soul gets so hurt, like death in its image of itself, every time it suffers. When a life commits suicide and wants to bow out, it has been arranged for it to bow out. When a safe falls on your friend's head and not on your head, the fall was what had to occur. Your friend did not have to get killed by a safe but your friend had to die that day.

I— Eileen, in your autobiography you state, "Even today I cannot draw a simple square without drawing its double to make it perfect." Does this still exist in the spirit world?

E— No, not at all. Over "here", you have to understand, we do have the symbols, but they mean zero to us. They are the symbols that we created in each life time, and again the symbols of the unified theory that Einstein was embarking upon was so great that when I trusted my thoughts to examine it, I began to realize that it was beyond my grasp to connect it to consciousness, but I did brush it into my thinking. Over "here" Einstein's unified theory is a brilliant connection to you and me. The psychiatrists of your world should examine it on the level that it can be used for people "here." You would find that the communication is going to be easy.

V— You were once asked, "What happens when you go to the "other side"?" I often wondered. Does time hang heavily on your work? Are there many things to do? Does time fly by? What do you do with yourselves?

E— (enthusiastically) You are so busy. Your minds are so busy when you come "home." It is one of the many thoughts that we create that we have no interest in time, as you know it. It is not a plot, of course, because everything is working in the dynamics of human thought. But to answer your question, your mind is able to connect, and I am putting it in the basic simplistic terms so you can comprehend it. Your mind is able to connect to your past living, your present living and to your future living. You become a quieter soul for easier thought. The soul is able to connect to all those lives and enjoy each of them.

V— Do we begin to live our past lives?

E— In a manner of speaking you do. You can choose anyone. You can exemplify anyone. You cannot undo it but you can create in your mind how you would have played it out if you had the knowledge that you have "here" to make it perfect. Once you realize that you can do that, you would be very bad as humans because every challenge, every step you take is that wonderful gift of growing.

V— Can you get into the soul that you want to exemplify and copy?

249

E— Yes, but you can only do it in mind form. You no longer want this body because the body was not perfect but remember, if that's the word, you want the body when it was perfect. Let us say you come into a life where you were born perfect. Most people will negate that and simply develop it to its perfection and go into it and see what it achieved through it's deformed state versus its perfected state, which might be the next life already.

I— So if you were born with one arm, you can compare it to your perfect state?

E— That is correct. One does not love the recollection of deformity but we do live with the love of perfectness. We are perfect "here." We are never bored. We are too busy. And goodness, I am not only working "here", I am working at my foundation. I am trying to reach Marvin Engel's (he worked as her editor in her publishing business) mind to correct a few things he wrote. I am trying to do other things. I am busy. And that is only as I remember my connected thoughts as Garrett.

I— Let us take Dean Martin who died. He was a singer. What does he do on the other side?

E— He is thinking when he relates to the Martin life. In an earlier life when he was a Rabbi, he was then doing something else, and by the way he was a Rabbi.

I— Dean Martin was a Rabbi?

E— Of course he was a Rabbi.

I— How far ago?

E— In his life just before this, he was a Russian Rabbi.

V— Eileen, in the new dimension, does the new mind exist as just an energy force?

E— It is not a new mind. When you first pass over, you are with the incomplete knowing of the many lives that you had. Therefore the attention is given to that which you just came with. In time an understanding comes to your thoughts of all those lives that you have had and are now having. And so you can have fun doing what you want. That is what you call your main nucleus, your soul essence, your big mommy and daddy. And you go beyond that, so that you have already reached that level of perfection "here." In other words, you are already experiencing the perfectness of the greatest thought you could have. Someone like a Hitler comes back "home" and his life is not even viewed as the monster that he was. In fact his life is viewed as the great lesson for mankind. Now, it is a horrendous thought to think about but until you reach that level of comprehension to understand that you created that monster, to allow that to occur so that you can grow from that. Even if it has the evilness to it of man, it has nothing to do with God, the God concept, Yeshua, Moses or Mohammed. It has zero to do with creation that you all kept on the side, to be pure and represented with purity of soul But I cannot go into it any further for we do have to end this session.

S— How do you obtain information about your past lives?

E— Often times, what occurs is that I just call in their souls. Their souls talk to me. Imagine this, our minds merge and I get the data from it, because the mind holds everything that is, and the word is applied to past, present and future. I don't deal in anything other than special time communication. You have to deal in the epistemology, ontology, and space-time-continuum past of your thinking. I do not.

I— So actually my soul is within me now. And you went into my soul to get my past lives. (While Marlene was in trance Eileen and James came through and gave me a "reading" of my past lives.)

E— I certainly wouldn't do that.

I— Then, how did you get my past lives?

E— You invited me to have a conversation and your soul spoke to me.

V— In other words, if I would say, "I am interested in finding out my past lives?"

E— I would say, "Sit here, your soul just said hello to me, the soul of a philosopher. That is your soul. In every incarnation that you had, you were a philosopher." So I would tell you, that is what your soul is telling me, or I may use the expression, I am sensing the following.

I— Do we return in other than human form?

E— You cannot come back other than the species that you were, including the aliens, because you are of that species. Now, you will learn that even down to the very symbols that you choose for your life. I chose and had three symbols. I also had other symbols but basically there were three. You all have your own symbols, ladies and gentleman. Allow these symbols to open up your mind so that your minds can connect to a greater, vaster awareness of universe. Connect to the universe so that you can grow and imagine all those (aliens) that you will be reaching. Gosh, I am so in love with growing. Please hold each other's mind in your heart and grow together. Adieu (session ends and Marlene returns)

6/96

EILEEN TALKS ABOUT HERSELF

S— Marlene, what have you learned from Eileen that you didn't know about before?

M— Some of the main points that stick out in my thoughts are having a clearer and a more focused mind with life in general. The ability to tell people about their own lives, a more thorough follow up on things where I may have held off in the past. I have learned to develop an intensity and passion beyond my scope of understanding of how to research. We must research, questioning, putting it down on paper, answering the questions, looking at it, turning it inside out and upside down, a thousand different ways. Also, examining it from the psychological aspect, from the science aspect, and seeing if it can or cannot be put into an equation related to what's around you. My intensity and passion for human kind has increased. My intensity sometimes is to be a little wild, although I was always extremely conservative. I have a new awareness of femininity and knowing that I have a force although I can't explain what that force is. I don't know what to call the controls, who claim to be with me. I just know that I accept this force most of the time but I question it all of the time. I have less confusion now as to what my work is all about and I am mostly reaching out to others in a way that I think is far superior to that which I have ever done before. I feel that this will increase in time, as this is just the tip of the iceberg. I am able to verbalize things on my own journey, which is my private thing, since the spiral is my symbol. We all know that the helix was Eileen's. I didn't know that. It is interesting to know, when I get my visions now, because I get part of hers and part of mine, and they just don't merge. Her helix is not my spiral. A lot of negativity, what humans might call negative thoughts, through my probing state, are torn apart and then built up to what this is all about. My students (she teaches a weekly course on parapsychology) are not aware of one tenth of my scrutiny into how I delve and work with this and I don't go around the way I used to by saying everything is B.S. I simply know now that it is B.S. so I have learned to be polite about it.

S— You mentioned the fact that you do not have the ability to hear spirit voices?

M— (Marlene reminiscences of her life as a psychic) I have never heard a voice in my entire life. I never claimed to hear any.

S— And yet you are able to hear Eileen.

M— I do hear her. I call it mental hearing. I don't hear words.

S— You hear the thoughts?

M— I hear the thoughts. I am not reading the thoughts. I even hear the thoughts now but they are not coming out in human voice. It is a total telepathic communication. I know for a fact that she is with me. She is even making me smile. I know for a fact, that she is saying to me, "Go for it, go do it. Let me tell them, let me talk." With that, all of a sudden, my temperature just elevates and I start to perspire. In the past I always used to be chilled to my bones whenever I did this work.

It would be like walking into a haunted house and feeling cold. For the last two or three times that we have been together my temperature has been going the other way, it has elevated and I break out in a sweat. I am in this intense heat right now and I feel it. This is just another manifestation physically that is taking place. It starts on my head and just trickles down over me as though I am being bathed with sunshine. When I come out of the trance, I am drenched with perspiration. James, (who comes through as the brother of Jesus) is able to cool me off, not Eileen. I don't need water before or after trance. I do not eat a thing before trance. I never hear, but I will know if it is male or female speaking through me. Since Eileen has been using me as a telephone wire, I, as Marlene, cannot be used that way. I guarantee you I wouldn't know your father, mother, sister or brother. In this state something happens.

S— Marlene, do you know ahead of time whether Eileen wants to talk about any particular subject.

M— Ask Eileen. I, in trance go to sleep and have no remembrance of what takes place in this condition. While I am resting, you will have your enjoyment in listening. Eileen and James will let you know if any strain is too much for my physical body. (The crowd sings Irish Eyes are Smiling, Marlene eyes close, and she sinks into a deep sleep and in about 30 seconds Eileen comes through. As Marlene's eyes close we notice that her eyeballs turn upward toward the top of her head and Eileen enters Marlene's body)

I— Hello Jenny (Eileen's middle name was Jeannette and she enjoyed being called Jenny). Nice to be with you again.

255

E— If I could only speak the way I want to, I would be most happy. I am trying very desperately to soften it so it would be a clear combination of Eileen and James. But it is difficult, at best, to remove this accent. It still is irritating to me. (Eileen could not speak in her normal voice since she was using Marlene's vocal chords)

R— It sounds fine to us.

E— But my dear Ruth, I spoke beautifully. I wish there was a tape available of me for you to hear.

R— Is there a tape available at the Parapsychology Foundation?

E— There is, and I wish you would get it.

S— I will try to find it Eileen. Did Marlene ever speak through you?

E— It is so frustrating to talk this way. Indeed, when I was a medium, this lady (Marlene) did speak through me.

R— Explain that?

E— Am I not talking through her? In truth you are mature enough to comprehend why there are so many intelligent females near this woman. By that I also include myself. I can reveal that there was somebody who I know that spoke through her and who was most popular during that time. If you look upon her face clearly, you will notice a resemblance, although we do not look alike. I will tell you that this female (Marlene) was part of the one who spoke through me and was very well known, and just know that a big, fancy story was written about her and we will leave it as that.

I— Jenny, give my regards to James (James is the keeper of the entrance to the "other side." He permits Eileen to come through and speak through Marlene).

E— Thank you. He is also "here." I cannot talk unless he gives me the o.k. I am constantly telling him, "If you don't mind, it is my turn." I like these Sundays because he does not come very often.

I— He spoke a long time when he gave a life reading for me. (Eileen and James gave me a past-life reading during a private session)

E— Yes he did. I too was part of that. He did not let me talk. It was my thinking of it that also brought it through. The regression was so fascinating that James insisted on taking over and speaking of all your previous lives. I have news for you; everything I told you was true. Excuse me James. All right, everything you told him was true. (James was speaking with Eileen from the "other side" and they tease each other). I prefer to think that I put it in my thinking to tell Mr. Mordes, that he was always in the healing field, especially when he took old metal and bound it to the body. That was in his two A.D. life. (I was a healer and a doctor according to my past life reading through Eileen and James)

S— Eileen, when you gave readings to people, what form did they take?

E— (speaking quietly while reminiscing) In my trance state, I was not conscious of that. I surrendered myself to Uvani and to Abdul Latif. (They were Eileen's guardians from the "other side"). Abdul would often times talk about health or perhaps some events of a traumatic nature that would occur. He was not like Cayce however. (Edgar Cayce was the famous psychic who died in 1945 and gave health readings and past life regressions to people). Abdul would not tell people what they should do or how to mix potions as Edgar Cayce did. That was not the Abdul way. He would tell them where they should seek help. He also respected the medical profession. He also believed in herbs, long before herbs became popular. He was an astronomer in the twelfth century and also a doctor. He also wrote and there was information that came through me when I was researched by Conan Doyle and Doyle's notes were more or less validated, but it was not validated through me. It was verified through Sir Arthur and also Mead and others. (They were psychic researchers.) You understand that. It was before I came into the picture. I became suspect in questioning my work believing always that it had to come from my subconscious because at that time there were very few intelligent and select people who were doing this work. I often wondered, whether I could have picked up information either telepathically or otherwise, and could Abdul be an invention of mine even though he was already established by speaking to others. Remember, when I lived he also spoke through a Mrs. Frances.

S— Did Uvani or Abdul at anytime give life readings or were they the same type of readings most people get?

E— No, they were both very different. Uvani came out in a much lighter way. He connected very easily through the telephone wire. When brought in, he would tell me oftentimes that I did hear, and not to forget. I was able to know before hand because it was an assumption of mine, and I believe a correct one at the time, that I heard Uvani speak. However, in the trance state I was able to do what Marlene can do. She can hear but cannot interfere and has no memory afterwards. Oftentimes Uvani (pronounced phonetically as oo-vahn-nee) would give the information about the person's dearly departed and what the problem may have been. We used to do the poltergeist investigations with Mr. Hewitt. We also did investigations in haunted places. These are not cases. I am not going to go into detail - I will only tell you that oftentimes Uvani came through with the information that set the pattern to examine it and make it all okay and better. When that occurred I often would say, "I wonder if it was not my own subconscious that was creating the Uvani personality and projecting it so I would feel as if I was doing mediumship. Of course now I know that was ridiculous."

Ladies and Gentlemen (to the audience gathered in Spenser's living room). "I exist. I am not part of her subconscious. But that is a different story." When Abdul came through, and this is not an insult to Uvani, you understand, it was on a much higher intellectual level. His words had a feeling for those who listened to him that it was more in accordance to sexual things, especially related to health problems. I would not say that it was a health reading. I would say that he just had no time to pussyfoot around with nonsense. He was very charming, brilliant and different.

V— Will Abdul come back?

E— Abdul will come back. He wants it to be a little more chaotic. His challenge is to be brilliant and make a dent in society.

I— When will the human species change?

E— The human species as you know it will decline and the total decay is not until 9507.

I— In the physical world, if a person is in a wheel chair his or her entire life and then passes over, does that person remain in this crippled condition?

E— No, we think of ourselves in perfectness "here", always. We can only be perfect.

S— I would mention that blind people who have had near-death experiences are able to see during the time they are outside their physical body. Eileen, do you remember anything about your near-death experience?

E— I can tell you frankly Spenser, I did not have Angels or harps or music or anything. I was dead and then I was alive and everybody asked me what happened and I said, "O.K., I am glad to be alive."

S— Do you remember going back and remembering everything that happened to you in your life as Eileen Garrett?

E— Completely - I did not attend my funeral. I was busy trying to figure out, was I really dead or was I 'here." It was very confusing to me because it was like I was in a comatose state. I just kind of slipped in and out and I couldn't shake my own body up.

S— Did you speak with the beings in the light?

E— Being in a light? I don't recall that. Am I a being in the light? I am energy, for goodness sake. Next month there will be another writer who has a fancy word for us. I am an intelligent energy form. This energy form can feed your life. I can also bring in, if this female (Marlene) would get out of my way, your loved ones. I am proud to do that work. We can all choose to be whoever, whenever and why.

I— Jenny, what do spirits do on the other side? How do you spend your time?

E— We don't have time.

I— Whatever you call it.

E— A typical untimed thought would be, I announce to my thinking that I am going to engender a program for that named purpose that I had in a life form as a mortal. Then I accept the program that I present to my "thinking" and I imagine that I am using it and prefer to talk about it. Once I prefer to talk about it; I then connect to it and can exemplify and exalt you. Did I just put you in a circle? (The people listening in Spenser's living room are totally puzzled)

Audience— Yes

E— You see ladies and gentlemen, very few of you are truly capable of comprehending me. It is like this. When I put myself aside, my thinking aside, and Marlene comes back to you, during the last five minutes to five seconds, when she comes out, she will have the exact same thing that I had when I came "here" as Garrett. She will recall in a matter of those two seconds, five seconds or five minutes everything that was said by me to you. And then it is like a curtain; it comes down because her conscious mind can no longer endure it. I "here" create a thought. Thus I create what it is I have to bring forth to you, for the time that you are with me. In doing so, I stir your thinking to stimulate your thoughts about who I am. In doing that, I then create the program so that I can report to you as to what I am doing. Did I simplify it? (The faces of each person in the room showed total consternation.)

I— Do people age on the "other side?"

E— (emphatically) Never

I— Do they progress?

E— Absolutely

I— Do they get wiser?

E— We really are in thought what every human being will have when they come "here." You know that you are experiencing all that you ever can be once you are "here", even though you can fragment part of you, like I had to do in order to speak through Marlene. You understand that the wisdom "here" of course is difficult when one begins to believe that they are indeed "here." It is not so simple. That is why you have ghost phenomena. That is why you have manifestations. That is why oftentimes they become a little silly "here." We are with our personality intact; with our intelligence intact, except we have the added advantage of knowing almost all of our lives. Of course we are wise. Do you want to speak to a moron?

I— Since you know the past, present and future, do you happen to be wiser?

E— No, all it means is that I am more knowledgeable.

I— Do you retain knowledge from the "other side" that you can use when you are reborn?

E— Very seldom, unless you open up in such a way that we can connect and feed it back to you so that again you are predetermined as to who you are. Some of you call that predestiny. Then you are destined to fill the predetermined events in your life. There are no coincidences. The conversation that Val and Jane and Pat had with this female (Marlene) earlier, (Visitor's questions that were asked of Marlene). I want you to know, were my thoughts that I was giving to her and that is why she sounded so eloquent. I was a bit amazed. It sounded good. It was quite true.

V— We have no choices in our lives?

E— (impatiently) You always have freedom of choice. It is the one thing that is always there. But if you choose a life to be a nun, you have freedom of choice to choose the kind of order that you wish to belong to, the kind of people you choose to help and the kind of obstacles you choose to overcome for the lesson to complete as a nun. You had no choice not to be that nun. The freedom of choice is how you go about in your nunhood and how you rose above the heavy obstacles. Mind you, it does not work that way if you are a very simple imbecile. That life had no mind because he chose that particular path to experience the imbecile feeling and succeeded in doing so.

S— I received a communication through a medium, from a person who has passed on. She told me that she was busier on the "other side" than she has ever been when she was in her physical body. She also said that the picture she gets of life and reality is so awesome where she is that it is completely incomprehensible to us from our point of view. Would you like to comment on that?

E— (forcefully) I would absolutely agree. I would not even think of telling you otherwise. That is true.

S— What does she mean when she says she is busier than ever before?

E— Because she is aware of her many different lives and the potential of mankind. You see, when you are "here", you really then begin to comprehend why you have to live in mortal form. So when you understand that, you really do create your reality, thought "here" collectively creates your world. The magnificence of color, of the humanness of sound, the heart feelings of your emotions are magnified beyond measure "here." The taste of the remembrances of the sweet moments, even that which we can do, and it is so real in our world "here", where yours is bland in comparison. To understand that you are embraced by an energy "here" that is pure love is incomprehensible to your mind because of your humanness. But I tell you all that pure love is "here" and I am not speaking in biblical terms. Each and every one of you has this power, this energy, this force, none greater than the other, none smarter than the other. Each and every one of you has it, and because of that, it is a guarantee that when you come "home" you will truly enjoy it.

V— Then why do these spirits choose to come back?

E— Because you also understand, that we, the souls, grow from the lessons you had to endure and it magnifies the game playing of when you have to live. It is what we call like "playtime." As hurting as it is, it is "playtime."

V— Can we experience any of that love here?

E— (without hesitation) No, when you meditate or use prayers or use whatever you feel you have to use to connect to this power, what occurs is a glimpse into who you are and just a teeny bit of the awesomeness of who "we" are, and the tremendous amount of energy from "here" that you will get when you come "home." The gift is so great that when you all come "here", you are going to say, "I will enjoy that life. It does not compare to my life on earth": You will have complete memory but you may not have memory of the little details or the dates.

V— Are there holy people alive who, when I see them, have this joy on their faces?

E— You are talking of mortals that can have it upon their continence. That is only pale. It is so much more magnified "here" I cannot describe it. It is not a joy that shows on a face. It is not of flesh. Can you imagine an energy smiling at you? Can you imagine a Christmas ball that all of a sudden becomes alive and starts to sing, "Merry Christmas."? Take that and magnify it even greater. Can you imagine a snowflake that touches your thoughts and you love the sensation of the coolness of it. Can you imagine the sun baking down and you remember what it felt like on a beach except you don't have the body but you can remember the feeling. It is of the intellect, the emotions the wisdom and as you said, "I prefer the knowledge of knowing." That makes it "here" greater than any place you can ever think of. It is also for those who have had N.D.E. (near death experiences). For those who have transcended their physicalness and have come back "here" for a very brief moment of their time, they get a glimpse of this enormous feeling of love and comfort, as if you are now feeling God. In fact it is not God. You are all so powerful that what you are feeling is your own souls in total. For you are just a fragment of who you are, just a teeny fragment.

I— Jenny, what would you hope that people consider when they approach the paranormal?

E— That they had healthy skepticism, of course. That they would not exam it from a limited point of view. Examine and research the information given by extending it to even those that don't seem able to do it. That means by putting themselves in the same circumstances to duplicate it. They have been too busy testing those who claim to have power or gifts. They have been denying themselves the fact that they, themselves, can do these things. And once they have bitten it and have tasted that they themselves are a part of this enormous power, they might then begin to open up to further examination upon people who are more credentialed and qualified to do it.

I— What makes you a conduit for these communications and I am not?

E— Because we have always done it in every life, that is why.

I— Then go back to the first life. What made you the one to do it?

E— My soul demanded it of me to grow this way; and I obeyed my souls journey into it.

V— Eileen, do we have guardian angels?

E— (speaking intently) Thinking in that vain, what you have indeed, if all of you would open up to it, are beings near you, energies near you, that come to you in time of hurt and sorrow and some others pull away during that time. Those that latch on to you during your time of certain sorrow, if they were part of your life, oftentimes hope you would hear them tell you how not to suffer. Now, there is a thought here about a master soul, an over soul, a guardian angel soul, something near you greater than your own presence that is gently guiding you and is somehow connected to you to help you.

V— Why can't I hear or feel this soul?

E— I will tell you that when you are able to open up, then one day you will begin to sense them.

I— Jenny, if physical death is just a transition to the "other side", can we learn enough from you to build a working hypothesis, a foundation from which further scientific investigation into life after death could proceed?

E— I understand your question. Thank you. Not only can I produce that, but I would like to develop a hypothesis exactly like that. When will you begin?

I— Right now.

E— No, not with these people. This has to be done without interference of the mind. It must be done with minds who are able to comprehend anything I tell you. And in order to do that, you are going to have to learn to tell this woman (Marlene) to let me have my voice. The most important thing now is that I need my voice because when I have my voice I will begin to recall me as me.. It is difficult. I am strangling her throat to talk to you.

I— You told me that you are speaking too far down in her throat?

E— It is impossible. Then when I go too high, I am singing like a soprano. That is terrible.

I— Where do you want it to stop?

E— I want my old voice back and maybe if she has a taste of who I sounded like she would begin to allow me my own way of speaking.

I— She says that she has no control over you.

E— She doesn't, but her vocal cords are being used by a British sounding man called James (he says he is the brother of Jesus) who is not British but that is the only voice he can use through her, and to show a distinction between us I have to use the brogue from Ireland to get on, and it is very difficult. Marlene has to hear my voice and once her consciousness is willing to hear it, maybe I can work on the vocal cords to duplicate it for me. All I need are the vowels.

I— If I can find a tape with your voice, do I play it for Marlene?

E— I have to hear it. I have to remember that my voice was a very powerful voice and gentle at the same time. I am using a woman who is larger than me although she will tell you that I was chubbier than her. But she is much bigger than I was. And believe it or not, I am feeling the physicalness and I have to play with the parathyroid here. So it is not easy to do. There are a lot of things you are not aware of. For those of you who do mediumship work, it is the mechanical changes that go through your body that makes us ready to speak through you. You would not feel comfortable knowing some of the things we do to you. I am referring to the people we speak through.

E— There is a man by the name of Vursel. He worked for me. I believe he is still alive. I may be incorrect in the spelling but it sounds like that. I don't recall his first name. This man was a brilliant writer and when I no longer could support my adventure in my New Age Press, I pushed him on. That is what I remember. If there is a recording of my voice, Alan Angoff (worked with Eileen) might have, it or my secretary. I need to remember where I placed the emphasis on words. To me words are extremely important. When I use Marlene's voice it almost gets to where it should be and then I have to go back down because I will cause her to cough severely. She has a very tiny opening here. (pointing to her throat). Tiny, abnormally so, when I start to talk. By the way, Abdul is "here" today with you. What occurs is that it almost feels as if I am going into a trance state of a trancer.

V— Let us hear Abdul.

E— No, we do not put ourselves on show like this. We are never the monkeys.

S— There seems to be some evidence at the present time that alien life forms are trying in some way to create a hybrid species with us.

E— Keep in mind that every time I speak about aliens you cannot accept the fact that the aliens are your mommies and daddies. Truly they are. If you understand, what I am saying is that when you come "home," "home" is not a planet. "Home" is not your mother earth. "Home" is not this galaxy. "Home" is like a star in the sky and beyond that. Every intelligent presence exists where I am, from the very inception of thought., Yes, there are aliens among you, not really aliens, but they are your relatives. They are people who look like you.

S— Why do people have these abduction type experiences?

E— Why they have N.D. experiences (near death) is to bring about, and to ready all of you, to know that your future look of what you are going to be is going to revert back to who you really were. These creatures that were hairless with bigger heads and shorter and some bigger bodies than you, will mostly be comprised of hair. You will need all this hair. Your sun is slowly dying. You must be prepared for the kind of skin you will have. Such a thing that you call beauty will just be a trace memory, because you will all look very similar. You won't need glasses, believe me.

S— Will man anytime in the future be physically capable through probably some scientific achievement to actually go to a different planet?

E— You know, Edgar Mitchell (the astronaut) had a interesting thought on that and I would agree with him. We will definitely go to other planets. When Mitchell was in cahoots with all the investigation of all this, it was very brave of him, for he himself had the experience and he knew that there was much more to it.

S— Are you in anyway able to speak with Edgar Cayce on a regular basis?

E— I certainly can. He is part of the same nucleus that I come from. If I sound like a snob it is because I feel that way.

I— Jenny, do deceased loved ones play a role in our day-to-day life and if they do what is it?

E— Some do and some don't. It depends upon what your life was like. If you are a man who was promiscuous, your deceased loved one, if it is

269

your ex-wife, indeed, would want no more to do with you. We have no vengeance "here." We have no passion to hurt. We only have passion to give love and guidance. I can tell you, if you are trying to struggle through to get an answer, to help another person who may have lost somebody and is in pain, then your loved one would be around you to give you hope and kisses to remember the goodness of that which you shared.

I— Why do some spirits from the other side communicate and not others?

E— (speaking with positive emphasis) All spirits are able to communicate. All.

S— Why do we hear some and not others?

E— You are the obstacles. Through this one woman (Marlene) you hear from James and Eileen or who we purport to be. Can you imagine if there were a million more like this lady (Marlene). It would still not be enough for all of those "here" who wish to speak with you.

V— Are spirits able to see the pain and suffering of the family left behind from day-to-day?

E— One hundred percent, yes.

I— Jenny, you mentioned the fact that when we pass over we go "home."

E— This is "home."

I— Where is it that we go?

E— You are an energy form. You can go anywhere you want to.

I— Then "home" is the entire universe?

E— Yes.

I— That takes in a lot of territory.

E— We don't think in terms of territory. You are thinking in terms of your space, time continuum thought. This has nothing to do with space, time continuum.

V— Eileen, you mentioned that you and Edgar Cayce were part of the same nucleus. How many nucleuses' are there?

E— It started with four that came from what you would call aliens. From the four it produced a few more and it became ten. North, south, east and west. From each ten it stayed. Each ten had to say as it collected its thoughts together, what can we do to have a life form. I won't go beyond that today. I will only tell you that the nucleus can have as many as two hundred and fifty different forms. From one nucleus it breaks off into what you call the soul. So if you imagine a soul, then below it another and another below that, I believe you had terminology that was bandied about, master soul, oversoul, and so forth, all are ridiculous things. From the time you are "here" you automatically are perfection. You are perfection because there isn't anyone existing "here" that isn't perfection. In my world, perfection is always eternal. Don't rush "home." You still have to suffer a bit.

S— Eileen, when Marlene gives a reading to a person, is she actually hearing her thoughts?

E— There are many times I help her and there are often times she is capable of doing it on her own. Quite frankly that is it.

S— Can you see the auras around people?

E— Of course, that is baby work. I can see the auras of the people in this room. (the room where Marlene is in trance). I know that they shade differently and then again Spenser, remember I would go back to how I used to do it, which is quite a bit different than this lady (Marlene) does it. (Spenser had met Eileen Garrett when she was alive.) I must say that she is so accurate in her sensing of auras. I interpreted certain sensing of color to mean certain illnesses in parts of bodies that were ill. I understood then that I had to send a prayer of healthiness to that location. That is common work for most healers today. Aura readings are the easiest thing to understand.

I— Jenny, once we cross over to the spirit world, do we retain the same relationships we had with those who are in the physical world?

E— No, it changes. Lesson learned, lesson over.

I— And yet I have read cases in reincarnation through past life regression where two people existed in their previous life time together as man and wife and they are man and wife in the present life time.

E— That was their choice. It was never a thing that they had to do and it is very often that way. It is a simple choice. We cannot make it any plainer than that. Consider this, if you choose to come back as man and wife again, whether you so much loved or whether you so much hated each other, all you are incurring is more debts to your thoughts and your soul. I should not have given that to you because when you come "here" you are going to remember I told you that. That is the key factor in growing towards perfection. Nobody has to ever return to the physical.

I— But, if two people love each other and want to be with each other again, why wouldn't they, when they cross over, find each other?

E— That is different. If you are saying that they loved each other so much that the lesson was not completed because they were not satiated with each other, then indeed they can have a part of a life in a new life. Not without struggle or some sort of thing that would make that life a challenge. Otherwise you would not want to go back. The point of living is to experience, not to be bored.

S— When you were in your physical body, how did you view homosexual individuals? What did you think about that practice?

E— (speaking thoughtfully) I felt that God put creatures on our earth for all of us to love. I felt that there were certain things involved with people that might have been abhorrent to many. But, when I was looking at a life I also examined who they were beyond their physical existence. So, because someone acted out a homosexual role it really did not matter. I did not go around condoning it, but at the same time I did not think of it in terms of being right or wrong. It was a lesson, and as you know, I knew many who were my friends.

V— Why don't we see Marlene's eyes while in trance?

E— I can open her eyes except that the eyeballs go up into the head because this way I am taking over the whole top here. I can do it so her eyes will open, would you like that? O.K., maybe you will see the glint in my eyes. Maybe you will see that soul that Marlene and I are a part of, eternally. I will do that. That is a very sweet thing to ask of me. And this way her eyes won't glue together with the makeup. (Eyes open for several seconds with the white of the eyeballs showing).

R— Eileen, does your energy expand or at times dissipate?

E— Our energy is energy. We are not an energy dot and then become an energy ball. We are always like this. We are consistent. We will come to you if you ask. But, for those of you who believe in Jesus Christ, he was not a redhead and he did not have baby blue eyes. They were violet.

I— Jenny, from what you know from the "other side", how should we better prepare ourselves in this life for the inevitability of our physical death?

E— It is much wiser not to ask that. It is wiser for you when you are "here" to say, "How can I prepare myself to have the best life ever?' Because we have the benefit of not having to feel the physical part of everybody's life, you must know there is no way of preparing yourself to come "home."

I— What does the other side say about our funeral practices, our death rituals and rites?

E— (bursts out laughing) You are going to be embarrassed. Save your money. Go have a good old-fashioned Irish wake. Dance and sing and know the joy. Although I can't validate it, and I regret I cannot, to know that life continues, even though we continue as an intellectual thought, an energy form is a great joy. You must all understand that we live and live and live. I can't tell you not to, but I will just tell you that we know that you spend a lot of money for those of us who come "here." For some of us it feels good because there was money enough to do it. But, when there is not money enough and you gather your pennies to make a big bang over death, that is stupid. Think about that. Hold a party and live. But, then again, that is my influence from the island (Ireland).

I— When people are afraid of death, are afraid to leave children and loved ones, does death affect them when they cross over?

E— No. Any fear you have of death is quickly negated once you are "here."

I— I was thinking of the woman, Jennie Cochell who came hunting for her eight children that were left behind when she died in a previous life in 1938, because when she died, she was worried about them.

E— There is a thought that has to be raised here. It is not so much that Jennie was that woman, but in fact that Jennie is what many "here" would call an open channel. And I am only offering this thought as a proposition that the essence, the intelligence of that spirit had to come back to show and help to validate the Bible. Just open yourself up to it. Everybody is very eager to talk in terms of past lives. In fact, it may have been a beautiful communication taking place.

V— Just in the essence of prayer, what is the validity in prayer avoiding the religious aspects of it?

E— Prayer is positive energy that works. When you have somebody who is very ill your prayers do reach that soul and the soul looks over the body that it is in and it knows and understands that it is not going to live. So, therefore, what you are giving is a present to the soul because the soul then takes it and feels your love. The soul takes your prayer and nurtures the body along knowing that the amount of suffering is going to be lessened because it will live. But, it already knows whether it will live or not. So for those who are not going to live, praying is still excellent because the soul is rewarded by that gift. For those who are going to live, praying is excellent because the soul then takes the gift and nurtures it to a body that will live. It's a win either way.

V— With regard to the praying, how about those praying for wealth, affluence, values?

E— One of the things that people must be concerned about is that they feel guilty when they pray in a manner for such things. You are human beings and you cannot be selfless. You must also be selfish so that you live a quality of life. You should not gather guilt for wanting prosperity for yourself and your neighbor. For after all, in the mention of praying, you are following, according to James law, and therefore when you give out "good", it should come back to you too. So, you may pray for prosperity, for love, and that is a truth.

I— Jennie, do animals have souls?

E— If you take it from the biblical point of view, God created everything and man was supposed to be above his animal kingdom for the lesson of learning. You are asking me if an animal has a soul equivalent to what soul is meant in the context of who we are, the answer is yes. But, if you are asking me if animals have a soul relating to a God or any kind of thought about that, the answer is no.

I— You are telling me that when I pass over, if I had an animal as a friend that died before me, that animal is waiting for me?

E— (with deep emphasis) Absolutely, yes, even down to your palmetto flying bugs. But, when you are "here" you have to feed it to your thoughts. I had a collie. I thought about my collie, fed it to my thoughts and my collie came to me.

V— Do those on the other side have all the answers, especially for our lives and our personal problems?

E— That is the way of saying to me, I know it all. I told you we have knowledge, but we don't often feed it to ourselves or to you, because to plan it out is more important than anything else. Planning your life is the key to living.

S— Eileen, shouldn't we take responsibility for the direction of our lives rather than to depend upon others or spirit guides?

E— (with a sigh of exasperation) You know how I feel about that. I also must tell you that I would find it insulting to think that anyone would take something that even I have said; to take my thoughts and base their lives upon what I have said. I feel that an individual must always plan their life, be accountable for what they do, recognize their errors, and then in a lighter way have a good and better life.

I— Jenny, are there many worlds and many dimensions?

E— I don't use the term dimension. I will tell you, yes, there are many worlds.

S— We would like to hear from James if there is anything he wants to say.

E— Then I will say it has been my pleasure to be with you today and hopefully I will get most of my voice back and I think you got a glimpse of it before.

I— Your voice sounds like it is coming back. We are trying to get a tape of your voice.

E— I hope so. I just wanted you to know the richness of me, not that Marlene does not have a rich voice, it is just that James has controlled it so long and it works for him and not too well for me. Remember, we are all part of each other. The essence of who you are, what you are, where you go, who you will be is within you right now. Goodbye for now.

(Eileen leaves and in five seconds James speaks)

(James takes over the vocal chords of Marlene as Eileen fades into the background. She can still hear the conversation with James and can intercede anytime she wishes.)

J— I will speak to you of Jesus as a boy, a boy who grew into mighty deeds of love. When I speak to you about Jesus, I am also telling you that he was my brother. (James is speaking in a deep male voice whereas Eileen spoke in a rich female voice with an Irish brogue). As a brother to your Lord or your Rabbi or whatever term you choose to equate to him, I am speaking as one who grew with him, family alike. I will also tell you that we still feel the impression of a lot of you in this room. When a human being presents itself, we taste their living. When you want me to give you what you want to hear then I am going to leave. I refuse to give that which isn't true.

I— I am willing to accept what you say as the truth.

J— My brother, Jeshua, was a messiah. No less, no greater than other anointed messiahs, among whom were Solomon, David and Paul. The difference between Jeshua and those before him was that he brought the word of the loving God to all who came to hear him. He did not exclude the dirty ones or the unholy ones. He made sure the people who were tested for that work were indeed capable of presenting it. Any questions?

I— No questions. We just wanted to be with you for a while James.

J— I am oftentimes aware that you want to say things to me. I tell you again and again that the way to feel Jeshua is through me, his only living life brother who is speaking in this world of yours at the present time. I, James, created the first house of worship in the name of my brother, Jeshua. Paul and I did not agree. I, James, was dead before the work of my brother got around the world. But, I, James, know that Paul bastardized everything that we did in Qumran. I, James, speak boldly and proudly and eternally in the name of Jeshua, the only brother of God's son I have ever known. Yahna, Yahna, Yahna, air ee abt, ah-day-ah (phonetically), adieu and goodbye and we love all of you.

I— We will see you again James?

J— You will hear me again. (James leaves)

S— He always likes to talk about his brother.

I— We should ask him questions that don't cover his brother.

R— His only task in this world is to bring forth the message of his brother Jeshua. He will only answer questions about his brother, the holy family, Jerusalem, and the Bible.

I— I will have to go to the Bible and pull out all the questions that I have to ask him.

R— He will give you one answer for everything in the Bible, it is all garbage.

I— The Bible was written by man and man can make up his own stories and he has.

V— Then what is the truth?

(Suddenly a voice speaks from the mouth of Marlene who has been quietly sitting in her chair, in a deep trance with her eyes closed)

VO— Hi, (It sounds like a young woman's voice of about 20 to 25 years. The voice sounds completely different than Eileen, James or Marlene's voice)

I— Who are you? What is your name?

VO— I think I am, Gena (she laughs), I overdosed. What am I doing here?

I— What is your last name?

VO— Caprilli (everyone is laughing as this has never happened before)

I— You are Gena Caprilli? You came through as Gena Caprilli.

279

VO— Oh, that's neat.

I— When did you leave the earth plain, Gena?

G— Awe, man. I am not sure.

I— Gena, at this moment where are you?

G— I don't know (answers with total surprise in her voice). I don't know who you are.

I— Where were you before? Where did you live?

G— It's too much. Don't ask me so much. (The crowd and the questioning quiet down). G— Where am I? Who are you?

R— You are in the state of Florida in an area called Lake Worth. You are visiting a group of people. You are using the body of the medium known as Marlene.

G— In 1979 I overdosed. I was a heroin user.

I— Where did you live?

G— New York, man where the hell else.

I— Give me your address.

G— 1422 E. 34th Street. What am I doing here?

(She is completely surprised at where she is and who we are)

I— We will find out. We are your friends. You are safe here. (Suddenly Gena disappears and we are unable to contact her any more. (I was able to verify that Gena Caprille had died in 1979 and lived on 34th St.) James returns and speaks in his deep male voice).

J— I want you all to know that there was a gap and I apologize but we will not let that occur again. Eileen wanted to continue and as her thought to talk occurred, I was receding and the sweetest, sweetest little girl came flying past and got stuck between us. It was sort of like turning the dials the wrong way. We apologize.

I— It is all right James. We enjoyed the moment.

R— That sweet little girl didn't know where she was either.

J— It shows you, it is not easy all the time, is it?

R— No, it isn't.

J— Goodbye, people. (James leaves)

I— That was interesting and unexpected. Marlene should be coming back now.

(Marlene returns and slowly opens her eyes)

M— I am back.

I— Do you remember anything that was said?

M— I sense that James was talking, but I don't have the vaguest idea as to what he said. I do feel warmer than usual, but it is internal.

I— Are you thirsty? You have been talking for two hours.

M— I am not thirsty, but I feel very rested. I feel terrific. I had a wonderful nap.

(End of tape)

7/96

THE PHYSICAL LIFE OF EILEEN AND JAMES AS TOLD FROM THE "OTHER SIDE"

S— Marlene, when did the personalities start to speak through you?

M— Early in the seventies. I have the capacity to sense what you people call ghosts. I have thousands of stories on ghosts, and just assumed, when I was a little girl, that everyone had this capability, I without knowing that people didn't. Therefore it was never really discussed. As I became older I taught yoga, went into the Eastern Philosophies, though I didn't study it deeply. I know I had a knack for teaching and I wanted to teach something that would bring pain and tension relief to people. I married young and had a family. One day, early in the seventies, I was minding my own business, my mother-in-law had recently passed away, a ghost essence, not spirit, which looks just like we do sat on a chair of hers that I brought into my house while I was liquidating all her furniture. I loved this woman dearly, a wonderful relationship which I had with my mother-in-law. She was sitting there and my younger daughter, who was 5 years old at the time turned around and said, "there is Nana." Just then my mother-in-law started to fade away. Several weeks later there were two strangers sitting in my home. One of the strangers said to me, "I am going to be with you for the rest of your life." I often have chased so called entities out of my house. I must have an open door with a sign that says, "You are welcome to visit." Finally, the bottom-line is that these two same entities came to me later. They did not look exactly the same as they did, the male and female, when I first saw them. They said that I belonged to them and they intended to stay with me and then suddenly they evaporated. A couple of weeks after that, while meditating with the pyramid meditation technique, I had myself focused into the pyramid in the northeast corner where I like to vision myself and something happened. I am lying down on the couch and there is prickling all over me and I yell, "cut it out, cut it out. Stop fooling around." That night when I went to sleep, I was thrown out of my bed by unseen hands, wound up on the floor and about a thousand pins and needles like an electric current went through my body. I thought I had a heart attack. What I immediately did, for the third time in my life is that I slipped out of my body and rose to the top of the room. I am looking down at myself getting these electrical shocks, but I just kept rising. I couldn't get back into my body. I kept going higher and higher and suddenly a hidden hand pressed on my right shoulder and pushed me back into my body and I was suffering with pain, clutching my chest, and since that time I have had a series of unaccountable dramatic occurrences.

V— What caused that out of body experience?

M— The out-of-body experience is the nice part. What it is, is that sometimes when you are doing it automatically, it is because you haven't learned how to control it. Once you control it, you can reap the benefit of where you want to go by directing it. My theory is that all human beings have out-of-body experiences, but they are not aware of it. Eileen and James at this moment are giving me the thermometer. I feel the heat. I have to go "under." I can't talk anymore

(Marlene goes "under." There are little subtle things to be observed such as her body beginning to sweat. Marlene slips into a trance and James comes through and speaks)

J— I am going to be here first today. (Eileen usually is the first to come through.) My name is James Ben Joseph.

I— James, it is nice to hear from you again.

J— I must help this woman (Marlene) so excuse me (it becomes quiet for 30 seconds)

J— Yes, Ruth, it is a case of love again. She does have the broken shoulder and we are healing her. (Marlene had torn the shoulder rotor cuff in a fall several weeks before). She cannot move her arm to the side and we are knitting it together. For those here, I am the brother of Jeshua (Jesus). I was the creator of the first set of early known records of my brother Jeshua. Jeshua was brought up with me, and thoughts of my life and his I can bring forth and write down. Many of my notes will be uncovered in the lower part of the caves of Qumran in the near future. Do you have a question for me?

I— I came across an article which said, "Legend has it that Jesus spent his middle years studying in Egypt, India and Tibet. According to the Hathors, interdemensional beings considered to be masters of sound and love, Jesus visited several mystery schools in Egypt including the Temple of Isis. As part of his training he was sent to the Temple of Hathor. There he received esoteric information prior to his return to the holy land. Is this true as far as you know?

284

J— I will answer it if you answer a question for me.

I— What is it?

J— Where did you get that from?

I— It was an article in a magazine I came across.

J— Identify the magazine.

I— It doesn't mention the magazine. I just tore it out and thought I would ask you about it.

J— I would tell you that my brother's training was more with the Egyptians than it was with the Essenes. We taught him about the Kabbalah, astronomy, and numerology, which we invented. We also invented the Kabbalah because all parts of the esoteric learning that came, came from God, and we were his direct descendants. My brother learned from the Essenes, and from the ancient Egyptians.

S— James, you identify yourself as being related to Jeshua. Could you tell me whether or not you have lived any other lives?

J— Certainly I did.

S— Can you tell me a little bit about those other lives?

J— I was a devoted Roman Catholic priest. My name was Ignatius. Then we were able to have friendly feelings toward females so I certainly did. And I was not Ignatius, the Pope, although I did know him. I just was Ignatius. I belonged to the Order of The Brothers of God. Of course, in those days we simply called them God brothers. We were early Christians. I was also known as Father Michael Ohanna Oleara, quite Irish. That life was an insignificant life.

R— What country?

J— I would have to tell you it was England.

R— What year?

J— Ruth, I didn't want to speak on that. I would say it was the early part of your nineteenth century.

I— You said that Paul bastardized Jesus' story about his life. Is that correct?

J— (deeply agitated) That is one hundred percent correct and I have thoughts still on that. Allow me to feel my anguish. Christianity, as you know it today, is not what my brother preached. My brother was a Hebrew first and being of that religious order he certainly followed the law. The law was your Ten Commandments. I will also tell you that being an old hand at love, my brother never said that he was the Son of God. The Hebrews never served men. They never produced a deity, so that people would love them. We were not interested in numbers. We were interested in truth. My brother could not take what people spoke so he went among them and he said, "I will shape the minds of the ill, the maimed, the unholy and the unclean." I will bring them God and in his devotion to the law and to his God he was deemed seditious. Paul wanted to sell a deity. He was having difficulty selling the law. Most interested people were anxious over why Paul wanted to see them as Hebrews. The Hebrews were not loved. Paul took on this work when he had to stay with the Essenes where I dwelled and I had the first temple of my brother Jeshua built. Paul stayed with us for the required three years and he went on to proselytize my brother's words. When he came across people not wanting to adhere to the law, he invented a new God. He made my brother famous and popular and then he even put a face on God. We called him back. Paul came back to Qumran. We punished him and he had to again realize you do not sell a right arm of God. You do not put a name, face or paint God. For that is our way. In the long run look where we are today. We have silly Bibles filled with nonsense.

I— Since you have the truth, if you were to tell the entire story of your brother Jeshua- - - - - -.

J— I wrote it down. It is being uncovered in the Dead Sea Scrolls. A new location with a new team of Israeli, Arab, English and multi-national archeologists will uncover the rest of my written work and everyone will know that I, James, indeed wrote about Jeshua.

I— When will it be discovered?

J— Before the year 2003. It first must develop in the minds of people. Even those among you who claim that they have the House of David in their heart, I can't stress that more.

I— Did Jesus die on the cross?

J— My brother did not die on the cross. He was taken down off the cross by Josephus and John and brought to the Essenes who applied special herbs and brought him back to quite a healthy life. We ushered him off to India.

I— How long after that did he really die?

J— He died at approximately the age of fifty one, or there about. We didn't keep years like yours. We can't remember the mathematics of the calendar then, but we had a different way of numbering our days and we then had a Aramaic calendar, which would be appropriate to yours.

V— Did he ever get married or have children?

J— Oh, for goodness sakes, of course, never. The Essenes were broken up into two sects. Some of you will read that we were a multi-type of order. That would be correct, but it depended upon whose work you read. I can tell you both are incorrect. In fact, Qumran was divided into sections and we had families and we also had the monk type of living, which was celibate, and we chose freely. It did not mean that we could not have families once we decided to. We felt that families would interfere with the focus of our knowing of God. We wanted to be as accurate in writing down our information as we could without being taken for a pimple head. I know that wasn't funny, but that is how it felt. Women, by the way, were not treated as rude as some of the women of today. We respected the females for they were our mothers.

V— Was Jesus born through the Immaculate Conception?

J— The Immaculate Conception was invented by Paul. My mother was a healthy woman. My mother Miriam had eight children, four sons and four daughters. Don't ask me for the names today. My brother indeed was a healthy man and I can tell you Martha was not eighty when she gave birth to John. It was closer to twenty-two.

S— That explodes a lot of mystery.

J— I should hope so. The Immaculate Conception was invented by, of course, Paul to produce the thought that here was a God greater than all other Gods. In fact, if he didn't do that he would only have a derelict new sect of the Hebrew people. So, you realize that those we took into the religious order of the Hebrew faith, knew that they had to stay with us for three years and purge themselves daily, similar to the baptism. Three times a day you had to bathe. You had to pray about five, very similar to the Moslems. So Paul bastardized the law to soothe the Hebrews and he insisted that he heard Jesus on the road to Damascus. That truly is a cockamamie story. Your Bible is filled with nuts. I can challenge it at anytime.

I— The world will change after they discover your writings?

J— The world had already changed with or without my writings. The world will change because the Vatican which is really a temple, a big shul (synagogue), will begin to honor and respect Jesus for who he really was, a Hebrew, a Rabbi, a man of distinction, an honoree set apart and put forth by Hebrew love. There is no such thing as Christian religion. That was invented by Paul. Paul's religion should be called Paulines. So those of you who make the little cross on your forehead and on your pupick (belly button), think again.

V— You said that the Bible is a bunch of cockamamie writing. Are you talking about the new Bible or the old?

J— Both Bibles have exaggerated historical events to slant it in Paul's direction. The new Bible is totally fallacious. The old Bible is about eighty percent false. My goodness, I have broken your heart (speaking to the entire group). That is, of course, the people who were commissioned to do the writing understood the impact it would have on future people. Many of the things you read about, like parting of the Dead Sea, I would say that the Dead Sea did part, but it had more to do with the universe being lined up with the stars and the moon and the tide, not because it was a feat by Moses. But, I will tell you if you take into consideration that indeed Moses was talking with God, I cannot say that he exactly saw God. None of us see God, not even you when you come "home."

I— I believe he spoke with God.

J— We all believe he did, so do you. Indeed he did. But, if you were to get down on your hands and knees and speak to God and if God chooses to answer you then the straight jacket will be ready.

V— What about dietary laws in the olden days?

J— That is extremely important and that is why the Ten Commandments were given. That is why God did speak to Moses. There were many more. My father Josephus is "here" and wants to talk to you. (He spoke in the ancient Latin tongue, but had difficulty using the vocal cords of Marlene and we could not understand him. He spoke for approximately one minute. The voice seemed deeper than James.)

J— My father tried hard, but the closest he could come to speaking correctly is confused Latin. We tried. Thank you, father.

I— In Latin?

J— It was a mixed bag of Aramaic, Hebrew and Latin. All together, he tried hard. It was not easy, but his message was clear to me. He said to remember him as a Hebrew. He chooses not to be associated with the present philosophies of Christendom. He said he was a proud Hebrew and he will be a Hebrew for eternity. On the other hand, don't dicker with my father.

V— Why were all these lies written about Jesus, which created hatred throughout the centuries and was against other people and we still have the problems today. There is no love.

J— It has little to do with Jesus and Christians and of course Hebrews. It has to do with human lessons, learning lessons in life that you create for yourselves. Think about it this way. The soul goes to perfection, always, and in order for it to be challenged in a life it must create a connection to it's purpose. But, it has more to do with the acceptance of God. So, when the Hebrews had their one God, and then the Christians came back, they could not incorporate the Hebrews into their way of thinking. In fact they distanced themselves and had to say that Christ was for them. Christ was never for anyone other than being a faith of God, which they invented.

R— Many people that I have come across, the Jewish people—- ———.

J— (speaking with authority) We have told you as we have taught many others that the old Hebrew was the only language that was used then, and the reason it was used was because they were a Nomadic Arabian tribe, no different than any other Semitic group of people who crossed over the River Hebron. That was all that Hebrew meant. So those people who bounded together and crossed over the Hebron were called Hebrews, no different than other people from other places. Never be confused with their Semitic coloring, or realizing that Hebrew was the only words associated then, with the world that you think is Jewish. Jewish and Hebrew are two very different things. Now I am leaving you to permit Eileen to come through.

I— James, it has been a pleasure being with you. We look forward to visiting with you again.

(It is quiet for approximately thirty seconds and Eileen begins to speak in her Irish brogue)

E— I am already here.

V— Welcome, Eileen.

S— Eileen, can you remember anything about your mother and father and about your marriage?

E— Well, it has been said that my mother committed suicide by walking into the water and that my father committed suicide shortly after. Due to the family privacy I believe I should leave it alone and not divulge at this point in time what happened to my parents. It is because my mother did perish with a broken heart. To tell you how she perished, you can look it up in the records in Ireland and you will have the answer. If I know the answer and tell you why she did die, you have to understand that it is protection for the family still living. So I cannot break what I wrote in a book whether it was truth or not. I don't want anyone to know. I was married several times and Clive was my first husband. He was an architect and he thought I was crazy. He insisted that I stop doing what I did. I married him when I lost three sons previously, but my daughter continued to live. I divorced him because of our differences. But, we did not divorce in a hostile mood. I was never rude, but I had a reason for that marriage. I went from the frying pan into a bigger frying pan. It wasn't quite the fire. I then married a young soldier and this is already written about so me telling you is repeating what you have read.

S— There are things that you can tell me that are not in the book.

E— The young man did pass on. Of course I knew that he didn't have long to live. He died as I saw it in a vision that was given to me. Indeed, I wrote about it because it was quite important and then after that, keep in mind, I had a hospice for soldiers. I also had a café and I was quite a businessperson.

S— How do you feel about astrology?

E— I think it is very nice that people would sit down and calculate the birth date, so on and so forth. I had no feeling one-way or the other. For me it is an instrument there for one to grow with and eventually leave and not become dependent upon. I would feel the same way about Tarot cards and about any faculty out there that relates to the awareness level of a psychic. I believe that the human being must use the telepathic, clairvoyant and clairaudient methods. They must become totally sentient and I believe the best instrument is themselves, but for those people who do use the cards and other things to focus in on I think it is wonderful.

I— Jenny, when did the first UFO land that we can all know about?

E— The government can no longer deny it, from Astronaut Mitchell to even beyond that.

I— But you do have UFO's that have landed in other countries.

E— You call them UFO's, but in fact they are really a bunch of your mommies and daddies, your great, great, great grandparents, in flying machines who have come back to see how their children are now doing.

V— Do they look like us?

E— No, they had to acclimate to the society that they were in, but you are indeed their descendants.

V— If scientists put their genes under a microscope would they be the same genes?

E— Yes, they would be very close, just about. The DNA would not be correct, but the genes would be very similar.

I— Where do they come from?

E— From other galaxies and other places.

I— How can they traverse this great distance?

E— They are brilliant. They are much closer to the perfected soul.

V— Was this before ancient Stone Age man?

E— My gosh, yes. Macrobiotics examines it better. I would rather that a scientist would come in to describe that. I don't have one handy now.

I— Jennie, are there schools for learning on the spiritual side?

E— It isn't like a school that you go to. Consider this, you have your thoughts and in your thoughts you have the capacity to create anything you choose to. When your thought links up with other energies around you, we call that the connected thought. When the thought links up internally of its own thinking, we call that the connected collective consciousness of thinking. Do I still have you with me? Then when the connected, collective consciousness of the one links up with the collective consciousness of those near them, they create a reality that you created because you are part of that too, and you created the vision. Your power of creating produced what you needed in lessons to make a soul become perfect. Keep in mind, that while a soul is experiencing its most horrendous living through the body, by choice it also is living perfection. Isn't that amazing. You can never be an idiot if you are "here." You can be one who does not choose to recall, but you cannot be stupid. You can never be evil if you are "here." You can be one who chooses to remain in a warped sense of values of remembering, but you cannot be evil. We dwell in love. James showed you that the highest form of love is healing totally. Beyond that, is perfection by curing. Now each and every one of you has the capacity to have this enormous love and this enormous feeling toward each other. That is the growth of the soul. Many of you have spoken of love, but do not practice it. Many of you are very kind, but yet you hurt yourselves. Many of you are very selfish yet you are very loving. So you see what you bring to your life are multitude of situations that you have to learn from. Not one among you is yet capable in your human mortal life to exhibit unconditional love because of the conditions that affect your life or when your family is put into a threatening situation. Unconditional love would mean, regardless of what is dished out to you and your family, you can still love your enemies totally and none of you are capable of that. In your philosophical wonderings you have achieved it, but you cannot yet do it. We do not sit "here" in judgment of that. It is understood that you are human beings. You have to grow. I had to grow too. If I didn't like anybody, I spoke up. (the audience felt inspired and awed by Eileen's philosophy)

I— Jennie, do persons crossing over to the spiritual world find their mother and father?

E— Of course, if that is what they want to do. Keep this in mind, first, that if a person comes "here" and does not want to find a mommy and daddy, they do not. It is what you want when you are "here." The simplification of it has been written about by wonderful mediums who had received information and part of the information was from "here" to those people, and we would agree with it. Imagine yourself as an intelligent energy and all you have to do is think a thought and you create the reality magnified billions of times greater than what you call your five senses.

V— Suppose you cross over and you want to see someone who does not want to see you?

E— You can still see that one: even if they choose not to have you near them. You can project your feelings towards them, which would then create the purest love. You see that seldom happens, because even my Aunt Martha (she raised Eileen as a child) and I do love each other.

S— Suppose your mother and father, who you might want to see, have already reincarnated.

E— That doesn't matter because the conception of reincarnation means that you then enter another incarnation and the soul is being nurtured to grow for that life. Remember, I used to talk about "fragmented." Some of you here likely have heard me use the topic over and over again. Understand that I am a fragment of my soul and I am able to come here as part of Eileen Garrett's consciousness. Not all, and that is why it is often difficult for me to pull in the kind of better work I did when in my body. I sometimes have difficulty pulling it into the level that I am accustomed to.

I— Jenny, if a person in this lifetime commits suicide and crosses over, does he or she go to a special place to change?

E— (with no hesitation) I know you have probably thought of that or read it or fabricated it. The answer is that it is ludicrous. There is no such thing as punishment headquarters "here." There is no devil 'here." There are no angels flying around with wings "here." There is no "Gabriel blowing a horn", "here." All we have to offer "here", your "home", is your soul. What we offer to that soul is pure love. And out of the pure love you have the power to create a society of human beings that is greater than anything you can ever imagine; or you have the power to go and destroy your world with your thoughts that are not cleansed. When we talk of the unholy or the dirty, we talk about the souls that weep because the lives they lived were not able to rise above their problems, so they have to come back again and again to regain that part of their development. They can rise above it from that lesson only. I am not talking about the total soul of perfection. I am talking of the challenge of living.

I— Are you saying that everyone on your side loves each other?

E— I would say even Hitler, and don't be upset, Genghis Kahn, Napoleon, despots, the most despised people from your history books have chosen that world to teach mankind lessons so that you have learned the difference between good and bad, evil and sweet.

V— Eileen, if someone here wants to go toward unconditional love is there a way to facilitate that?

E— Yes. The answer to that is that no human mortal can be perfect. But the soul becomes nurtured daily. When you blink an eye the soul is already giving forth a love. Now, in the blink of an eye when that love is brought out, all you have to do is to know that you are a cherished love "here." As you are cherishing people and power to learn of this unconditional love, you are realizing that your soul is growing and freeing itself. But you are still mortal and your thoughts are of unconditional love and yet you cannot act upon it because if someone hurts the one you love, you would get angry and, rightfully so.

S— Would you say that a person like Mother Theresa had unconditional love?

E— Absolutely, only in philosophy and in many of her good deeds that she did for mankind. Her power was love and a greater part of her was unconditional love. Think of how brave she was to go among those with Aids before anyone did. And think about all the good work she did.

I— Jenny, through what spot on Marlene's body do you enter?

E— I do not enter the body the way you think. It has more to do with putting aside the consciousness. Over "here" it is not an entrance through the top of the head, but the solar plexus is the door for me to come in. Also, the forehead or the third eye.

I— Are we all telepathic?

E— I once told my students that you are all telepathic. Now use it. You have that power and gift. What greater gift can you have? Everyone in this room is a telepath, too.

S— Eileen, are you aware of everything that is in Marlene's mind?

E— No, oftentimes I don't know if it is something we are hearing on her television or if the human being is actually in the room. She will quickly remind me that it is only a show or a thought that is going through her mind. Concerning unconditional love, this female here (Marlene) has a good enough value of life to understand that unconditional love can never happen to a mortal.

I— Is that because the ego comes in?

E— Yes, but beyond that, you have to protect those you love. Once the word, other than love is there, it is no longer unconditional. For instance, protect becomes the important word.

S— Is it possible for a person to have the experience of seeing oneness in everything, seeing God in every person that they come into contact with?

E— Yes, but that does not make them unconditionally loving. What it makes them is comprehending and gathering the information from their belief system that they have to endure even though they may disagree. That is a belief. The eastern philosophies enjoy that.

I— Jenny, what do you think is the most important area that parapsychologists might work in today?

E— If you want to understand what we are, you have to know me and who I am. When I respond and say I am Garrett, you have to say, "How do I know you are Garrett and not Bertha or anyone else? I am teaching you how to ask questions and then after I give you that kind of thought, you have to say, well, Bertha, how do I know you are Bertha and not Garrett. It becomes a vicious circle sometimes, but I will then say to you that Bertha is upset because Bertha is now in this room (the room where we are holding our meeting and she is an entity from the spirit world). I am so sorry Bertha. But, I will tell you that the thought pattern is to remember who we are. When you remember who we are, we begin to understand how it was when we were human. Then we begin to formulate our thoughts to connect to yours. When we know that you are thinking, we then connect to your thinking and thus we create the communication. But, it happens instantly.

I— Jenny, do religious denominations and dogmas have any meaning on the other side?

E— What it really amounts to is that the different religions have caused a lot of anguish among so many different people and it has begun to wear thin even "here." The religions that you know today will be non-existent in about 700 years.

I— What happens when people cross over with these religions?

E— Most religions will merge and you will begin to have a technological society that will have no use for religion. The scientists will be able to program minds to think in a way that will produce more time for humanoids of that time to grow and enjoy life. Procreation will become an interesting thing of the past.

V— We are not going to procreate at all?

E— Not how you do. Women will say "thank you." There is a female God at last.

S— Do you see the time when robots will do all of the housework?

E— Yes, definitely without a doubt. You can count on that, but I would not put my money in that yet.

S— Will it be done by voice command?

E— Yes, definitely. They have already begun that, but it will go even much further. Imagine talking to a car and saying turn left, turn right or now fill me up with gas. That will happen too.

V— Will all disease be conquered?

E— (speaking forcefully) Definitely, people will not have to regenerate parts of their body because the scientist will be able to mass produce parts of them that will fit. You will have what you call "heads" and your "heads" will have to grow bigger to accommodate the better portion of your minds that you will use. Some of you will choose fat bodies so you can say, "Oh, let me see what it was like to be heavy."

V— In that case, we will not die and we will not go "home."

E— There will be disease of the brain. Yes, you will die. You see, society will have its way of taking you "here", but longevity will be much greater, and of course, procreation will be less and less.

S— Can you speak about ecology and pollution of the earth?

E— I worry so, even as we are talking now. My worry doesn't mean that I worry as a mortal, but because of certain insights that I have. You know what a passion I had for this beautiful earth and how I worried often, and I still am worrying about the death of the planet. You are ruining your earth. You are polluting it with everything that you do. You have created a terrible, terrible atmosphere. Most of you will have to wear masks in your futures. There will come a time when you will not even be able to go outdoors because the pollution will be so bad.

I— It is happening in Los Angeles now.

E— Yes, but I don't see them wearing masks. We are talking about a time when the earth will cry for help and your scientists will be able to heal it, but at a very heavy price.

V— Can you tell me what life is like on the other side?

E— (reflects for a moment) Imagine, as you are sitting in this room today, that you are reflecting upon a happy moment. All you do is think that thought instantly, without the cumbersome body, but if you want to remember your body, you may. You are instantly playing out a role, which in a lifetime is very real. What you have "here" is the power of creation. So, in a sense, those of you who say you are God, indeed you are, but not as mortals. But, indeed you are God, especially "here." Everything and anything you ever wanted to do, you can do. There is only love "here." Love conquers everything. We are creatures of habit. Oftentimes, in several lifetimes you would have had the same habits and you would be amused to notice what your habits are. We are free to choose who our moms and our pops will be, free to choose who your lovers are going to be and you play it out "here" before you become a mortal. You are free "here." You have total free choice and you teach yourself to think and the soul is just blowing itself up bigger and bigger. It is beautiful, filled with love. If any of you ever get a message from anyone in this "here place", that I passionately and sweetly call "home", and they tell you that they are miserable, you know you are not getting the message from "here." That is impossible. However, you may get a message of concern for your lives.

S— Do we know in advance whether the body we are going to inhabit will have a genetic disposition suitable to what we desire?

E— (emphatically) Absolutely. Most times you choose it before hand.

S— Why?

E— You choose it for the lesson either to become an experiment or to die in that life so that more people will grow and learn from that. We call those people heroes. I have termed it the phrase, "all those who have Aids are your searchers fighting World War III." They are the equivalent of men and women in battle in World War III. For they have taken this upon their lives completely, to show you, to raise your consciousness for you to fight, to get rid of that disease, regardless of who they were in this lifetime.

I— Jenny, in World War III, who is the enemy?

E— It is a global war that will be undeclared, mostly over territory in the middle east of Europe.

I— Will aliens ever come in and try to take over?

E— They are already among you. They don't have to take over. They are your great grandparents.

V— (quizzically) Am I another alien?

E— (forcefully) You certainly are. All of you are. Your ancestry is alien.

I— Jenny, while in the physical world, did you ever teleport any object?

E— I tried to do that, but couldn't. What I was able to do was teleport myself. We used to call it teleportation, which is called astral projection today. I did have success in some experiments in New York to reach Newfoundland and also in California. We did some experiments from there. We had some success with it, but we didn't know why it happened, and again I kind of felt that telepathy played a major role in this,.

V— Does music play any kind of role in the afterlife?

E— Yes, especially to musical people it plays a major role. If you get a soul that feels that it doesn't need to hear it, then it doesn't bother to think it, but it plays a role, no greater or less then the concept of God.

S— What kind of sounds would you hear on the other side?

E— Well, you hear horns and flutes and all sounds, but you have to understand that you must think of the century. If I want to tune in, I don't have to listen to an entire band. I can hear a single bagpipe that I love. Or I can hear a Glen Miller tune, a Chopin piece or any music.

I— Jenny, you were complaining about your voice not in the right spot?

E— It still is not. It is not like where I want it to be. I would have enjoyed hearing what I sounded like, so that she might be able to emulate it and release that part of the vocal cords that is necessary so that I might begin to sound like what I used to.(up to this point in the years that I spoke to Eileen, she would complain that her voice never sounded like when she talked while in the physical body. One day I discovered that there was an audiotape of a lecture she had given to a church in Connecticut. I was able to secure a copy of the tape, which I played at the next meeting for Eileen and from that moment her voice began to improve.

S— When you first spoke through Marlene, did you have difficulty speaking through her vocal cords?

E— Yes, not difficult, but what James had to do was manipulate her vocal cords so that it would feel masculine for him and feminine to me, otherwise it stays in the masculine voice side and I resent that. But, I will tell you we intend to put her out much deeper coming up soon and although you will not be witness to it, we will get you tape recordings.

E— I leave you with these words. Please do not weep for us, because really you are weeping for yourselves. Just know we are near you and when you cry for us, we rush to you . You can't believe how we rush near you and kiss your cheeks and your face and the top of your head. We love you. We do love unconditionally.

S— Did you ever suffer from any kind of stress?

E— Don't be silly. Being married to Clive's body was stress. Stress like you can't believe. Do you know what it was to be married to that mind? It was difficult. The way Marlene has it now she has it ten times worse. But I wouldn't say much more of that. That personal life I had with Clive, was romanticized by the pen. In fact it was hard and emotionally draining. I believe I told you the last time, that I went from the frying pan to a bigger frying pan.

S— Were you physically abused by anyone?

E— No, of course not. Mentally, yes. Emotionally, yes. But never physically.

S— Did anybody that you met ever call you a faker, or a liar?

E— (Reacts boisterously) Absolutely, by my Aunt Martha (She raised her from childhood since Eileen's parents had died from suicide). I learned early on what it was to be treated terribly by that female. I was accused of lying when I knew what I saw. I could not tell her. I'd point. You know what it is. It made me commit a murder (killed a duckling when she was three years old.) I told her about someone coming to visit me with the baby and I got so upset, and again I was punished and put in my room (Her Aunt Martha thought she was lying). Then, of course, the nurse came when my other auntie and (Eileen's other aunt died in childbirth.) the baby died, and my Aunt Martha forbid me to say such things for fear it would become a reality. They were expressed with much more hurt by her. It was almost as if I was a curse. I was so badly treated and I was heartbroken. I knew she had some prize ducklings and I took care of them, but I regretted very much killing one.

(Eileen leaves and Marlene returns)

9/96

MARLENE STEWART TALKS ABOUT
EILEEN GARRETT

S— Marlene, a person who has been listening to the tapes wants to know what you have read concerning the life of Eileen Garrett. What books have you read, and what material have you come across? When did you read this, was it recently or a long time ago. Was it over a period of years and how much of this do you remember? Please enlighten us.

M— I will enlighten you. I will supply the dates, the day, the hour and I will go so far as to tell you why I started reading it. I never read a thing about Eileen Garrett until it was appropriate to find out.

S— So, before you met us (the researchers) what had you read?

M— I had one book that Ruth (one of the researchers) had loaned me because too many things were occurring in the course of conversation and it is all linked to Eileen Jeanette Garrett. In automatic writing, over twenty years ago, I would get information from one called Eileen, who kept repeating the name Eileen, Eileen, Eileen and then she would get frustrated and say, "call me Jenny." The most astounding thing was confirmed by the one who purports to be this fantastic lady. I was starving for concrete information about her. I wanted to do everything, so much so that as you and Irv know, last year Ruth and I had the wonderful privilege of going to the Eileen

Garrett Foundation in New York and I had an extraordinary experience. I met this wonderful lady who was secretary to the foundation and I was delighted in her unbiased, unprejudiced attitude toward me. She did not accept nor deny me and I am sure that there are people who walk off the street and say; by the way I was in communication with such and such. She treated me with respect and I had a very interesting experience there and she gave me a few pieces of information that I asked to copy as per Eileen Garrett's command. (Eileen Garrett would come through Marlene and tell her what to do.) I have them at home and they will remain with me since I still don't know what to do with them.

S— I don't know whether you want to tell the people here about that very fascinating story of the horses.

M— Three weeks ago, I was giving "readings." I had one day set aside where I do person-to-person readings. This lovely lady came to me and in the course of giving her a "reading," I told her that she had two very sick horses. After validation was made, I met her again two weeks later in the same place where I had been giving "readings". She said, "Marlene, I am at my wits end. Is there anything you can do for my horses?" Now keep in mind that this woman has acupuncturists for her horses, and masseurs, and doctors who are take care of her thoroughbred pologround type horses. We got to talking and I say "Well, if you are interested, I know somebody who has golden hands and she is a lovely lady and I cannot go beyond telling you that this woman can cure your horses, if you understand what a "healing" is. She may have an effect on your horse even if it is just to quiet the animal enough so that the body can generate some healing for itself.

307

She said, "I will try anything." Ruth, (the healer) and I are used to feeling like the bottom of the barrel when people are desperate and say, "Help." I said to Ruth," Would` you like to do some healing on horses?" "Yes, she said, and so I took her to the woman's home in Florida. We were on a lovely farm and out comes horse number one named B. C. I don't think we should tell the horses name because these are horses that you would know. BC was injured and needed the "touch." I don't like to interfere with what Ruth is doing and she does not like to interfere with what I am doing, so I walked out of this lovely barn, so clean that you could eat off the floors, Ruth was doing her thing and the horse was so fantastically relaxed that it closed its eyes and began to go to sleep. The entire barn came to a complete hush. Even the dogs there were quiet. Ruth did her fifteen minutes of dedication, love and "healing" and everything went perfectly well. Then comes the horse of horses. Out comes this frisky, nasty, biting, ferocious, monster. Now Ruth is no tiny person. The horse came out and made her look comparatively small. The horse was so tall and I know that what was going through Ruth 's mind was, "How was this horse going to allow me to touch him." It was aiming to bite her. I thought that at this time it would be best if I left. I rushed out of the barn and took a walk. I am about forty feet away and I know Ruth is having a difficult time. I am out of the barn about ten minutes and I hear my name. Now I do not have clairvoyance, what I term as mental hearing. A masculine voice is calling, "Marlene." I ignored it. Then, I hear my name again, Marlene, and so I ignore it again. Then I hear, "Marlene, get in the barn." With that, I start running. Ruth does not know this for she is trying her best to calm the horse down to give it a healing. I run into the barn thinking that the horse had injured Ruth. As I run into the barn, she is approximately twenty feet ahead of me, and she does not turn her head from the horse's eyes, and as I look up, the horse's eyes are following me. I go to where the owner is sitting and I am talking to her and I said, "Did somebody call me? She said "No." Then somebody in the barn yelled out quite clearly, "Marlene, My name is Sam." I am the only one who hears it. I am now looking at the owner who by this time probably needs cold compresses. She came to me for help. And I bring in a healer for horses, which is definitely a no-no. And now I am hearing voices. You can imagine the scenario. This lovely lady says, "There is no Sam here," and I am getting a little frantic. The male horse says to me, "I am addressing you," and proceeds to say, "My name is Sam, not Mec." (a very famous name I cannot give you)." I speak to the owner of the horse and in a rapid-fire exchange, as I am getting information from the horse, I give it to the owner and she is validating it for the next fifteen minutes in which Ruth is unaware, and almost exasperated. She is trying to calm down the beast of all beasts while he is talking to me. The horse is communicating with me telepathically, telling me why he will not heal, and refuses to heal because he was moved two days before from a stall that he normally had. He will not heal unless he is next to his sweetheart. I am telling this to the owner who says, "He is absolutely right. He was moved two days ago because he was using his injured foot to break down the stall to get to his lady love in the stall next to him." Then Sam says, "Don't you dare retire me to Virginia", which I repeated to the owner, and she says, "He is absolutely right. I was going to sign the papers to send him to

309

Virginia." Then Sam tells me all kinds of things, what he has to have, how he is supposed to eat, where he should defecate, everything personal. When he was finished with me, and I could not make this up if I tried, he dispensed with me as if I didn't exist, and looks down at Ruth. She is unaware that I am in the back doing this, and he says to me, "Look at me." I kind of meekly look at the horse. The horse actually winked to me and says, "I will allow this creature now to touch me." With that, as my eyes looked at him, his winking towards me stopped, and her hands were finally able to go up. He bowed his head down to allow her to heal. That was it. The owner said, "What can we do for you?" We explained that we never charge for a healing. And that it is a sacred thing. I jokingly said to her, "I have a passion and it happens to be with pigs. Next time you invite us, how about renting a pig." She said don't go away. Hazel is here. I run back toward her and there is Hazel, a Vietnamese black pot bellied pig sitting down. I go over to Hazel and I am about to touch her and Hazel says to me "don't touch my back, I have a spur." I looked down and there was a spur. I said, "Can I touch your head?" And Hazel says to me "very lightly," and I did. As I am leaving I hear her laughing. It is interpreted in my mind as ha, ha, ha. Then Hazel said, "Thank you, have a nice day." Ruth and I were flying high that day. Yesterday we went to a home where there was a beautiful big Doberman and a cat named Samantha. They both needed a healing. The Doberman says to me, "Call me Jake, Ean Jake," and I did. He is telling me about the dog before him, a poodle who had died in the house and whose ghost remained to be near the owner. He tells me a few things about his diet that she used to feed him, stuff that she does not give him anymore.

310

Then he went to Ruth. And Ruth did her "healing." Then the cat starts talking and she dismissed me like the thoroughbred horse, "Have no time for you. This is what I want. I am rather chilly. Keep it warmer here."

M— The healing took place. We don't know how it translates. We knew that magic had taken place. I should tell you that about four years ago Ruth visited me in New York and there is a place called "The Magical Child." It is on 19th Street between 5th and 6th. The man who owned it was a man named Herman Slater. He used to have oddball things going on in that shop. A lovely little fun shop to go into, especially if you are interested in educating yourself. And he had a lot of books that you couldn't get anywhere else. And somewhere in the store I hear my name being called. It said "Marlene, come to the back," My name is Sadie." I go to the back of the store; standing there is a woman who looks like Elvira the witch. I look at her and I assume she called me and I asked her and she said "No." She points down and there is Sadie, a beautiful cat. I said "hi, Sadie." The cat's name was Sadie and was telling me, "hello."

S— Have you had a lot of other experiences with animals?

M— I communicate with birds daily. I happen to have a passion for doves and when one dove comes on my land, I tell it to bring two or three to see if it is working. So I wait about five minutes until I am ready to leave and they bring them.

S— Since we are pretty certain that animals don't understand the English language how do you interpret what is going on?

M— I'm still investigating it since it is constantly happening to me.

S— You know, of course that there are other people who are able to communicate with animals. This has been recorded in the literature and also on sightings.

M— I believe it completely and it is absolutely wonderful. But from my own personal experience, the animals do not speak a language. I think the animal sends out a thought and then my thought is able to connect to it, that which Eileen Garrett would call the connected collective consciousness.

S— In other words your mind is tuned in and interprets it.

M— I suspect that it is on a telepathic level.

S— How do you account for the name of Sam?

M— How do I know? I don't know. Why ask me that. Why not Jake? Why Ian?

I— Did the horse have a name by the owner?

M— Of course, I am not permitted to give you the official name. Yes, these are thoroughbred horses. I am saving her identity. It would not be polite to divulge this. The horse told me not to call him by the name given by the owner. He said, "Call me Sam." He did discuss the Bible. He said in the pastures we have manure.

S— For those of you who may find this a little hard to believe, there is a lot of material in the literature about amazing animals that are able to do all kind of remarkable things. My old friend Murray Bernstein had a very extraordinary experience with "Lady Wonder." She was written up in the literature that some animals can do mathematical calculations. It was thought at first that the owner of the horse would give it signals but there are many cases where this does not apply.

M— All that kept coming to my mind is that this thing is a fantasy. I was not alarmed at any point. It was comical but serious, as the horse kept demanding my full attention. Ruth is back there, I am facing the owner, and the horse is rapid-fire talking to me and demanding that I turn around and look into his eyes. You better believe I looked into his eyes for two reasons. Number one, I was concerned that she couldn't control that horse. and the owner was so concerned, that she wanted to stop us going any further. But once the horse started communicating with me, he was thrashing slightly from side to side, but at the end of that communication it was unbelievable what happened.

I— Did he know that you understood him?

M— Yes because he was getting the feedback from the owner of the horse who was talking to me. We were trying to keep it hushed. We did not want to invade her privacy.

S— If anyone here heard the NBC nightly news this week, I was wondering if you heard that particular report on an experiment done in England with a number of dogs, so you know what I am talking about. This particular experiment was done by a psychologist, by the name of Rupert Shobrake. It seems that what they did was to devise an experiment to see whether certain dogs could know in advance when their masters were coming home, regardless of what the time may be. So what they did was to set up different video cameras to photograph the animals at different times in the day and they found out after experimenting, for two and one half years that certain dogs, about forty eight percent of the dogs that were tested, had the uncanny ability to know just a few minutes ahead of the time when their master was coming home and there was no way they could have known that through sensory cues or other means. This experiment is very significant because it has always been believed that dogs and many animals have a psychic sense. I am sure that you have found animals who find their way home after being lost. There are cases of animals traveling six months to find their way to their home. I just thought that this was very interesting that an experiment has been done which clearly shows that animals do have a psychic ability.

M— And to support that, though I can't document it, but you can't take my word on it. I had a one hundred sixty five pound dog we called Rufus. I lived on the twentieth floor in Brooklyn Heights, which was an elevated building. My husband would have to come through a garage to park his car and come upstairs. My dog did not hear the elevator or my husband. It never failed. The time it took to park a car and get on an elevator my dog was already by the door waiting and drooling for my husband to step in. It was way before I knew about Eileen Garrett and anything about her experiences so that a lot of things that have occurred to me I didn't know until I had read about her. Less then ten hours before my dog was officially declared dead Rufus looked up at me and he said, "I won't see you tomorrow." With that he lay down on the floor, we are talking about a dog the size of a human, and I saw the gray smoke come out from the top of his head. I looked at him, ran over and gave him a kiss and he was dead. When my cat was supposed to die I heard her say, "No, not now, later." So there is constant communication. Everyone here has had it even if you don't verbalize it. All of you have these wonderful connections with animals.

S— Obvious there are scientist who are still very skeptical and always will be but this kind of phenomenon is so outrageous it is difficult for people to accept something that is so different from what our current paradigm is in the field of science. They are so sure that anything we can feel and touch with our many senses and instruments, is all there is to reality and unfortunately it is not. That's the problem. There is a lot more that we don't see, that we can't detect with our instruments. It is a fascinating field and I am sure as time goes on we will develop instruments that will be able to give us more reliable information along these lines.

M— Well, we can now start. I will try to "lose myself" so that Eileen can come through.

I— What do you do to "lose yourself"?

M— That is just an expression.

I— Can I do it?

M— There isn't anything that I can do that everyone here can't do even better.

V— Is there anything to oral listening?

M— Mental hearing. Ruth uses it to write fantastic poetry and she never makes a mistake. Everything she says she hears. When it comes to poetry, does healing, or does certain other things, she hears. I think that is a beautiful gift. I am very happy that there are people who have that ability. I have never heard a voice in my life. She hears like you and I are talking.

S— So she hears an external voice. Ruth, are you in an altered state and what kind of voice is it?

R— No, I am not in an altered state and the voice has no gender. In the poetry mode they give me sentences, stops, and then continue, and that is the way the poetry comes through.

S— But you can't record this voice.

R— I hear everything through the left ear. The right does not hear.

M— I hear the voices in my head. I have never heard anything in my ear. Even when Sam called me into the barn and I ran in a panic, I heard in my head a masculine voice. I can't duplicate the voice but certainly a man could duplicate that kind of growl. I will now go under. Just know that I don't give it a definition. I did not know that Eileen Garrett shared the same feelings that I feel but the onus is on me to make sure what comes out here is legitimate, truthful and as accurate as possible. Now, since my mind disassociates or does something while Eileen comes through, keep in mind that I will have no memory when I awaken. Will I remember a portion? Again, I tell you it is like waking up from a dream. You remember just a little bit and then it fades out and it becomes more difficult and you can't hold any memory at all. Eileen is a fantastic lady. She is not speaking in the voice she spoke when she was mortal. She can only use my voice to the extent that she can and it cannot go any other way. We are trying. Are there any questions of mediumship, per se? And I do feel responsible, but at the same time as I relinquish over to her, I feel that I am working on a connective consciousness level. Somehow, our minds are linked. Why they are linked, I don't know. I didn't want to wake up one day and say, "I want to connect with her." It doesn't happen that way. At least, not for me. I like to think I am not a storefront cheap thrill. I have the highest regard for this work and when it is done well it can be a very beautiful thing.

I— Marlene, is it possible to hypnotize you and raise the voice box?

M— Yes, me you can, but you can't hypnotize Eileen or James.

I— Suppose I hypnotize you one day and say that your voice box will change.

S— We will try that some other day.

M— You have to sing, "When Irish Eyes Are Smiling." To help me relax, and permit Eileen Garrett to enter the group. (We begin to sing as Marlene begins to relax in her chair. (Within a minute her facial expression begins to change and her eyes close Eileen Garrett steps into Marlene's body and speaks with an Irish brogue throughout the entire interview.)

E— That was quite nice. Thank you. (Eileen always hears everything that is taking place)

I— Hello, Jenny. It is nice to be with you again.

E— Why?

I— Because I love you.

E— We know that.

S— Hello, Jenny, how are you?

E— I don't know how I am but I will say that I found it strange that every day you listen to what you have to listen to and you didn't hear me say "hello" to you. I did come to visit you.

S— That is quite possible. We did have many strange things happening.

E— It is very aggravating and frustrating when I put myself in a frame of thought to travel to meet you and you don't even know I am here.

I— How can you make Spenser aware?

E— It is not for me to do that. That is part of his growing.

S— What did you attempt to do?

E— What I attempted to do was tickle your toes.

S— How about knocking?

E— No, I don't like to disturb people that way. I really like the drama of just appearing.

I— I am going to call you Jenny because you like that better. Jenny, when we cross over, how do we recognize our loved ones? Will we know them and will they know us if and when we meet again in the spiritual world or on earth when we are once more in a physical body?

E— (emphatically) You come here with the complete recall of your existence in the lifetime that you first had. If you choose to examine further, then you are aware of different lifetimes. So when you come "here" and you are fully cognizant of this existence you only have to think the thought of who it is you want to belong with. And that is then connected to you and manifested in your thought. You do also project an image of you, as you would like yourself to be. Not necessarily as you truly were. Keep in mind we are perfect "here." We cannot be anything but perfect. Thus you want to create yourself in the image of perfection. Yes, is the answer. You just think it and it comes. That is the bottom line.

I— So the mind is the most important part of it.

E— (in a hushed tone) Yes, the temperature on this female (referring to Marlene) is up to 102. We have to bring it down.

I— Do we have a fan here?

E— That is all right, as long as we understand when we work through her. I am trying to show you that not always, when a medium speaks, does the room have to get very cold. What we have been doing with Marlene is the opposite. We bring the temperature way up and you can see the heat upon her face now. So now I have to work with James and he will do it and bring it down to at least one hundred.

S— Are there any of the changes going on in Marlene's body that are dangerous?

E— (confidently) Yes, the temperature we constantly work with as you can see. It is bad now. But she will not pass out from it. We also work on minor healings, but those that are programmed for existence to learn from, she must take. When she understands about the pain, she then knows to get rid of it.

V— Is Abdul with you Eileen? (Abdul Latif was Eileen's guide when she was in the physical world.

E— Yes, when he is near. It is difficult because he likes it warm.

I— Eileen, what does it feel like to be borrowing the personality of Marlene for a while?

E— I do not borrow her personality. I never have nor will I. We are two separate personalities, though I was much more complicated. All I am borrowing really is the space in the thought processes so I may exemplify who I used to be and along with that I am using the voice. Quite frankly, I can also do it when she is silent (sleeping) but since I was not exactly known for expressing myself artistically with a brush, I could do it all in automatic writing.

I— By the way, there is a breeze coming through here (windows were opened)

E— We know and we are aware and realizing that it will be fine and we thank you. We don't want her body to lose five pounds today.

R— Eileen, would you describe the room upstairs at the Foundation and what furniture you brought with you? When you worked there?

E— No, Ruth. Until the people there are willing to recognize even the remotest possibility that I am party to this female's life, (Marlene), I will not honor that question. This woman (Marlene) here, as you know, not only went upstairs at the Eileen Garrett Foundation, but she was so wonderful and so gracious. She allowed me to touch Eileen's desk. She allowed me to look at the photo of myself and my daughter. Marlene stayed upstairs until I was ready to go and when she came back in the body, her heart was so overwhelmed that she was weeping like a baby. Jo Ann (the foundation secretary) had to go and get a tissue.

R— I know.

I— Can you use the vocal cords of anyone?

E— No, what I can do is to come to your thinking. You think of me and I am then able to go near your mind. I cannot always remember what it was like to touch your thoughts, but in Marlene's mind, I can afford to touch and through her I can feel like you did with the silly picture the artist made of me. (I made a copy of Eileen's picture from the cover of one of her books and brought it to a meeting one time to show it to her.)

I— But that was a picture of you.

E— But that was a silly one.

I— I know it wasn't a good one.

E— I think not. I was beautiful. A little on the exaggerated point but I was a good-looking woman.

I— You looked good on the last picture I just saw that Marlene showed me.

E— I should hope so. I tease, I like to.

I— Can you tell me if any kind of an electrical field will augment psychic perception.

E— The test that was made, that you know about, was the Faraday Cage. That was a wonderful test and I regretted not having to stay with it throughout its entirety. But I had other things to do.

I— I understand you itched in that Faraday Cage. Is that true?

A— Well, not itched. I have to tell you Uvani came through at one point (Uvani was Eileen's spirit protector when she was in the physical world.) He answered by telling them to please close off a light and to do something else. He would not come through and stay but the end result was the same. He spoke anyway. The electric current did make it easier for Uvani to sleep, but it made it more difficult for them to test Uvani. There were two levels working. My telepathic feeling was greater but Uvani's was less.

R— Eileen, does Abdul have any information about the use of magnets that are being used? (Abdul also was Eileen's protector when she was alive.)

E— He finds it interesting but is not ready to comment but experimentation is being done. He feels that anything that promotes exemplifying good health is an absolute trial period.

I— Is there the danger of a medium or psychic just being drained of energy?

E— . (Vehemently) Absolutely not. That is hocus-pocus.

I— I remember one day you said Marlene was drained?

321

E— But it was not from us. We brought her more energy. Her loss of energy was not due to the medium work but due to her way of living.

V— Who is Uvani?

R— Uvani was a wonderful man who spoke through me.

E— I see the scene of a ship and there will be a big crash soon.

I— Where?

E— I would say south.

S— Is this going to be a terrorist attack?

E— No, this not a terrorist attack. More important do you remember that I told you about your future society where you wouldn't have to worry about healing yourself because your biochemists will develop parts of your body to be installed and they won't be rejected. Well, ladies and gentlemen, you are already up to that. (Eileen told us in September 1996 and in 2001 doctors are installing artificial hearts)

I— What parts are you referring to?

E— Bones and actual parts of your organs. They can now reproduce what grows it and you are not that far away from actually growing a new heart, a new limb, not on you, but in the tube, and then have it transplanted in you because it is from your own body.

I— Where are they working on this?

E— You go and find out. I am giving you the information. I told you this would be and I am so happy that this positive thought is now being worked on.

S— We have not heard anything concerning this.

E— Maybe I am sensing it to yet be in your news. Think of it. It is happening. The question was asked whether mankind would have liked immortality and I said no. I said his brain would still get fatal diseases and that is how he will come "home", because your society will invent yet even more wilder viruses to deal with.

I— That ship crash you are talking about. Can you tell me if it is in the Atlantic or Pacific?

E— I would say it is in the Pacific. I still see it. If I am off with the weather, I apologize. I also told you that you will have an earthquake in California. It will not be directly as a result of the San Andreas Fault but it will indeed be coming from the Madrid Fault earthquake, which is way up toward the Oregon area.

I— It still will be in September.

E— . (doubtfully) Uncertain

S— You originally said it would be in January.

E— But I am not upset if I am wrong, Spenser. I cannot focus on a period of time. I have great difficulty. It is only when the time is eminent as it was with Ruth not to take a train (Ruth was told not to take a certain train which crashed the next day.) We know she could not take it.

S— So, it may still happen.

E— We don't know that it is happening in September but we surely will be prepared for it because it is going to happen.

I— You said before the first of the year.

E— Yes, definitely. We feel part of Mexico will be pulled into it.

S— Will there be a loss of life.

E— A great amount and also a great amount of property. But at the same time there will be plenty of fair warning. There will be days and days of after shock from a different quake. So the next quake in two more years are baby quakes.

I— Since you are involved in a large degree with research would you care to comment on what you believe good research to be, and what scientists should be studying?

E— (intently) I will simply say at this point "here", it is easier to say that a lot of the scientists have begun to open up to a difficult task to do this. They are still missing the boat. It is, "how they have to approach it." I am not saying that I have to accept it. A healthy skeptical mind is necessary. But when they find out that one thing is acceptable and it cannot be replicated, they should not be so quick to throw it away. But they should work harder because maybe the type of question they are asking is incorrect. And they have to work on their own minds to open up their thinking towards these. One of the ways they can approach it is to manifest an angel for themselves. When I say an angel, it means that scientists should produce the vision of what an angel is, and make it become active and alive, materialistically speaking for all to see. Mostly it has been talked of but it hasn't really been done. There are delusions of grandeur of some people who have claimed to have done it. There are studies, I understand, in your universities that are now going on. Then think, how does that produce a technique. I answer the question. If you produce a technique to know what to ask and you produce a condition so that you can replicate what you produced, then you will have success. But you are still stuck in how to think. The thinking part is the greater part of doing this work. It also means that the scientists in psychology and psychiatry must work hand in hand. There is so much distaste for each other that you have to get over yourselves, and your jealousy and competitiveness that dwell in nastiness. Another way to approach it is to keep daily records. For every time something happens you must try to replicate it. In the programs that you can give to the process, to condition yourself to replicate it, is one tiny minuscule way of proof. But you want to be in the laboratory and you also want to have freedom so that when you go outside, that you are not going to become a walking telephone book. We understand that. I would have done exactly what I did and added to it the integrate part of intellect, so that I would have learned to examine what atoms are. What do these atoms mean to me "here"? What am I made up of. What is mind? What does it mean when I say the collective, connective unconscious thus is the collective, connective consciousness? What is not universal law, not space-time continuum? I am not talking hypothesis. I am speaking strictly on even terms so that you can comprehend it. Not biblical terms. I leave that to James (He is the other spirit who speaks through Marlene). Open up your mind and you will be hearing what I am saying. I can tell you. I have done it in the classes with the students (Eileen was teaching classes through Marlene using Marlene's voice.) when I have allowed a thought to come through and a normal person would believe it is their thought. I have done it by mental speaking and somebody will say something, and not even be aware that I gave it to them. But I can tell you, I am doing it with the students that come to Marlene's class. Marlene is keeping records on it, and it is exciting. The students don't know it because they are in so much awe of what they are capable of doing that they have yet to lick the iceberg.

S— Eileen, when you were in your physical body, did you also have classes similar to what you are doing with Marlene?

E— No, you know that I could not do that. I was a businesswoman. There was a period of time where I felt that I had to get away from all this because I had to validate it for myself, not really for them. I wanted to make sure I was not crazy. I had to be so detailed and careful. I had to protect my family. I even had to protect my friends, at times. I did not mind them being polite toward me. My ability was much greater than Marlene's ability. Yet, I could not do her kind of mediumship. I do not have the privilege that she has with communication with me and bringing in a whole feeling of them. I only thought I went into my trance and indeed through that, Uvani came and later on Abdul. (Uvani and Abdul were Eileen Garrett's spirit guides.) As you know, these two I had already mentioned. I became suspect in believing that when Uvani is present, is it when I make it happen, or whenever he wants to talk. Well, I can tell you ladies and gentlemen, from this beautiful paradise where I am sitting in, it is when I want to talk, not when Marlene wants to talk. Now, I have to prove that it is going to be a lot of fun, let alone even accepting this dialogue.

I— Jenny, would you comment on so called physical mediumship and psychokinesis?

E— All right. First of all I did psychokinesis in the hospital, during one of the times when I was very ill. I believe this was the time of my appendicitis, my lover died, and my future husband died too. I was so ill that time that it took a trauma in my life to create the great thirst of extraordinary things to occur, and most of you are familiar with that. In this particular time frame I was so alarmed that things started to move in the hospital room. I wanted to be able to control and move objects. The power of the telekinetic thought was a passion of mine and I do recall telling you, that it is also a great passion for Marlene. So we have that link too. In that time frame things were moving and binding and it was wild. Hewitt McKinsey (he tested Eileen's powers) never wanted me, when I worked for the British college, to get involved with that kind of mediumship. He saw no value in it and he thought it could drain or possibly hurt or offend me. So we kind of kept it as a separate part. But I had to know what it was like and it occurred, and I said, "No more."

I— What did you move?

E— I didn't move it. It was just the creative energy of the extreme passion and the bottles of drugs were going crazy and things were falling into the bed. It was terrible. It frightened me because I could not stop it. In working on Marlene's body we were trying to elevate the temperature because she freezes up so badly and is in so much pain. We so love this woman. We thought we would give her an internal 85 degrees in the ambient temperature around her.

I— Are you comfortable now?

E— I have no feeling but when she (Marlene) was greatly perspiring we knew we raised it too high.

S— Eileen, can you tell us something about Kundalini energy.

E— Oh yes. Marlene also knows about it so you will be getting it from the connective connection there. She was wise enough to learn when she was only about fifteen what the zipper effect was. I on the other hand had the benefit of a Mr. Carpenter. I was taught so much about it. Ruth once joined us and all three were in a hotel and there was a wonderful Tai Chi master who explained to us what Kundalini was. It is an energy force which rises up, and you pass all the chakras or what

327

you like to think of as the Eastern philosophy of your chakras, knowing that there are many more chakras. You balance your Kundalini, your energy force, and your life force. It is in perfect harmony. Unfortunately, people who have wicked lives always cannot live in the Kundalini perfect harmony state.

I— Eileen, does Marlene spread open a little door in her subconscious and holds it open so that you can talk?

E— I have nothing to do with Marlene's subconscious. I have more to do with the super conscious. In other words the back of the head I called the subconscious, in the middle of the head I called the conscious, right here (pointing to her forehead), and in the front I called it where paranormal fun took place.

S— Does it often happen that people come to you who are not related to the people who are "there" but wish to speak to a specific person on the "other side."

E— Most times that occurs. They specifically say, "Can my momma come through?" I cannot control who is going to walk through the door. You have to realize that when you have a circle.

S— When you hear the name of a person, do you get other thoughts in addition?

E— I try not to. I like it to be pure. I do not like to know that I am myself telepathic. But then I feel part of the teaching here is to be specific and some are not specific, as some of you know, but some have gotten specific things. If the spirits are not specific as to what they tell me, then as you would say, they have to go back to school. I am not here to teach them. They must grow on their own, as I did on mine.

S— Eileen, is it true that some people are better communicators then others?

E— That is a fact. Some people never want to do it.

I— If a male person shows gentleness, greater sensitivity, patience, joy, inspiration and a sense of humor, can that person develop into a good medium.

E— No, but if he is available I would take him. (Laughing)

R— Eileen, why have you not allowed Marlene to speak to another sensor in Hollywood that I have been asking her to?

E— You are talking about the research center. We don't mind if she writes but it is a bit awkward for her to promote herself. If you want to talk about her, then you can write it.

I— Jenny, is it possible to command the subconscious to transmit only the truth.

E— The subconscious does not know the difference between lies and truth. It has only the endless will of gathering information of what took place. It has no opinion on good or bad or evil. It only knows what took place. And to tap into it is to bring it to the conscious mind to use in a good way and then of course to get beyond that.

S— Would you comment about the subject of multiple personality and how it relates to you?

E— It does not relate to me. First of all, most of Eileen's personality, according to the clinician's point of view, can only come from a person who has been abused when they were younger. That is then the whole psychology behind the person who is either too weak or what have you, and as they grow they have other personalities that dominate them. I was not a multiple personality. I believe that

329

perhaps I have split Marlene's personality. Even though I consciously did not want to do mediumship work, I did not understand. Don't forget I did have clairvoyance, so I was able to hear. I was absolutely amazed when I heard voices with Marlene, we have to literally shake her or put a blank board in front of her eyes so she sees me.

V— Can Marlene's classes work on healing? I have a torn ligament.

E— Yes, Ruth does hands on healing but you are asking for a torn ligament to be healed and Edgar Cayce (he is the psychic who died in 1945 and healed people) is telling me to tell you what liniment to use, and I will tell you that if I can. We have not set up a class where we can teach healing. The degrees are useless because everybody in the class is a healer and has some kind of background in it. Ruth strictly does the hands on healing and James has done two or three healings through Marlene during the course of her lifetime. Again, we can examine that. Abdul is near too. Abdul does agree with Edgar Cayce, Ruth, and he would tell you to use not only the peanut oil but make the castor oil mixture and lay it on the ligament. It will bring great relief but it won't cure the problem.

I— Jenny, if you have Edgar around maybe he can give me the answers to my friend here who has the headaches.

E— Yes. Her equilibrium is off and I am surprised she does not feel dizzy. It is because the stomach is lousy. Madam, (speaking to one of the women in the room) your stomach is lousy and that is why you have the headache. It is collecting in the sinus area, then it goes into the head, and I am surprised you don't have a migraine or two with it. Your toxicity is too high. You need more flushing. You must get more fluids into your system to flush it out.

S— Eileen, what is it you would need in order to give a reading for a person. I know somebody now who certainly could use some kind of a reading or message. Of course, you have not met this person physically although you have spoken to this person. Is there anything that you would need to use in order to help you make contact with that person so you could give that person a reading that would be meaningful?

E— I don't know if it is ever meaningful, that is a very relative thought. After all, we do give readings through this female (Marlene) every Monday. And I can tell you those readings are quite relevant and important to the existence of their lives. We don't like to call it charity or pity work. This was the week we opened up the doors and we helped people who were suicidal and they called us back and they were amazed that they didn't do it.

S— Do you see these people physically?

E— I can see them. I don't like to deal with people who want to throw in the towel. You know how I feel about that. It is a personal feeling and I do come to this life of Marlene with that intact.

S— What are the ramifications of a person committing suicide?

E— Nothing. You are not denied it or anything else. What it is, you reflect upon it and realize that you are going to die anyway. It is part of the map-out. Do you recall the last time we were together that your wife was talking of unconditional love and it was during that conversation that I told her when she said, "How do I reach unconditional love?", what she really meant is, how does anyone reach it? And I had quickly stated that euthanasia is the method. What that meant is that "dear ones" come "home" and then you will have unconditional love.

Enjoy your humanness. You are allowed to have a fire under you. You are allowed to be angry. You are allowed to be sad. You are allowed to be miserable. But don't stay there. It is part of being alive. You are allowed to have opinions but do it with love. Don't kill each other in the process. After all, you created your lives. You prayed to "them" (aliens) for a reason, for lessons to learn not to just go through and say just love, love, love. You begin to look like robots otherwise.

I— Jenny, as an individual begins to suspect that he has some medium mystic talents, what exactly should he look for?

E— It has nothing to do with the mediumship. It has to do with up here. (Pointing to the head). Mediums are born and we accept them. A medium can do channeling work, healing work, anything you want to put in front of them. Channelers cannot always become a medium. But some channelers are better than some of the greatest mediums.

I— Then what is the purpose of going to Marlene and learning if you have to be born with this ability?

E— What Marlene can tell you is that you are a medium or one of the greater minds to deal with telepathic communications. If you fall into that category then you will do excellent channeling work. And if you don't fall into the channeling category you will go into your past life recall. If you don't fall into that, you will overlap into other areas. It is so varied.

I— So she can tell you how much power you have for certain.

E— This is not a thing of power. I prefer to use the term "realize it is love."

S— Eileen, do you know what the meaning of "proxy sitting" is all about?

E— Yes, of course. Ruth does that.

S— What is a proxy sitting?

E— She does it when she does proxy healing. The proxy sitting is, if I can feel somebody near, somebody else is sitting for that person in the presence of me. Then, of course, I am giving the information to them, which will go to the other one.

S— How are you able to link up with the person who is not there?

E— I realize you are on that same level of thought, and then I will try to answer it as uncomplicated as I can. It is called telepathy.

S— Eileen, when you were a medium, did you at any time ever have the feeling of certain physical illnesses for the sitters you gave readings to.

E— (intently) Absolutely. As a female we give out what is called a life line and I have taught her and have showed her that when she speaks of the organs of the body I often go from the toes up to the head and even the inside of your ears. Of course we do. It is important to do that. Who do you think told her about the dog and the cat and the beast?

S— Did you suffer any consequences as a result of doing that type of work.

E— No, I did not become what you are thinking. I have been blessed with understanding that if I felt the nausea of other people that it would come with me for a while. I would meditate and I would learn how to dispense it. Keep in mind Marlene learned that before me, because when she has to feel for the people's lives she would also get their illness and know immediately what it was. But she did not accept it. Again, she has her uncle near her. I had Abdul, and our communication was not the same. Eventually everything goes into the healing aspect of this work.

V— When I spoke to you the last time we met, you hit exactly on two names, which were incredible, and you mentioned them. There were two spirits that were hanging around. I was just wondering, are they still around? (A reading given by Eileen, to a visitor at one of our meetings).

E— If you are talking about Esther, keep in mind that Herb is not always close to you. He really does care for you and he apologizes for making your life miserable. But Esther says, "Thank you"; because she has been with you through your entire life. You know that.

V—- She was the birth mother of my two children.

E— That is right, and Esther says that she really appreciates it. She won't leave you. She will be with you for the rest of your life. She says, "You have done a bang up job." She says she doesn't think she could have gone through some of the excuses, the expressions and garbage that you had to take. She also says there were times when she was telling you, that you should get angry. You should have expressed it more. But you held back a lot for the sake of peace. But you have a good heart, for God sakes, and you were a wonderful mother. She says "Thank You."

S— Eileen, did you at any time while in the physical body ever meet the current secretary of the parapsychology foundation, Joanna, the one Marlene met?

E— I think not. I think it was later that she came. I am trying to remember. We had a chubby girl there. I demanded good-looking people. She was not my secretary.

I— Jenny, would you care to describe the nature of your environment on the other side when you are not speaking through a medium?

E— In planning my future life, I am already actually living one of them although I won't tell you about it. I am involved with speaking to my family, the life of Garrett, and also with other people who have been part of a different existence. So I am busy.

I— Are you learning on the other side?

E— Yes, all the time.

I— Where does Marlene go during this trance?

E— Actually, she can hear me but she will not retain it.

I— Where is Marlene at this moment?

E— I believe she is sleeping or perhaps she is visiting you or perhaps she went to say hello to Rose (my fiancée who died.) She can teleport her thoughts wherever she chooses.

I— But if she is sleeping is she sleeping on a bed?

E— Not like that, Irv. You are talking of a mortal body. When we do this with Marlene, consider this, that the mind is connecting. When the mind connects, it allows the flow of my thoughts so that her thoughts are put to sleep. As like, when Spenser asked the question about Joanna, my sensing was that I had to say things that I didn't know. And I didn't know because I was not seeing it. But then I had to connect it to the time when this female (Marlene) and her friend went there and Joanna did tell them that she knew Garrett.

S— Eileen, did you drink liquor?

E— Not really. There were a few kinds of drinks that I enjoyed when I would party. Occasionally I would have a glass of wine or cup full of brandy.

S— Did you ever get drunk?

E— I do recall I did experience that state but I was not that type of woman. I seldom drank. There was no need to, and I am speaking of hard liquor.

I— Jennie, did the extended periods of pain you suffered through your life on earth make you appreciate the gift of life a good deal better.

E— Well, I could not comprehend why I was the way I was. Yes, I did appreciate life. As most of you know, I greatly worried about human life. I was pretty selective in those I called friend and anybody I allowed to become my friend. You have to understand, he or she had to really earn it. But when I opened up that way I was fierce in my protection of them.

I— I want to know if you appreciated the gift of life.

E— I valued life. I valued everything that was alive, not only of humankind. I loved plants and animals.

R— In the future will we have the same life forms that presently exist on earth?

E— (speaking without hesitation but firmly) Your future life forms will change, after your scientist create new parts for your body, like going for an auto part, and you will be able to live a long, long life. Your heads will begin to get larger, and as it creates the largeness, it will accommodate greater minds to think. With the formation of your body, you won't need your cumbersome clothing, the skin will have a different thing on it, not hair but it will actually grow things to protect it because your earth will be so polluted. What a joyous world I am coming back into sometimes after 2000 years.

V— Will people be much smaller than they are?

E— They won't have to be smaller or taller. That will be a personal choice. It will be like going to a special bank and remaining for a day, "I want to know what it is to be fat. So let me feel what a body felt like to be fat." A lot of the romance of living will be gone.

S— Eileen, most of the people who come into this world suffer a great deal of pain for one reason or another, emotional, psychological or physical pain. Must we endure this every time we come into this life?

E— No.

S— How can we avoid it?

E— It is not a question of a learning lesson if you avoid it because of the problem. Keep in mind that the soul exists in you, and you house the soul strictly for it to grow. Your bodies are to learn, suffer, respond, and rise above that which you give it so that emotionally, mentally, physically, psychologically, technologically, all sorts of things intellectually, will one day be in harmony. But you are a far, far cry from even being near there. You cannot devote ninety hours a week to just studying your Kundalini. That is not what life is for. Nor can you be Mother Teresa.

R— Jenny, why can't you bring all this knowledge back when you are reborn?

E— (matter of factly) Sometimes a glimpse of it can come through. And those scientists who are opened enough to use their thoughts to connect to scientists that are "here" will indeed bring it into the foremost knowledge for people to comprehend. One of the reasons as to why you do that is because you are supposed to be learning a lesson. Think how you would be feeling if this man, Irv had been your father in a different lifetime and he murdered you because you were

337

too wild. I don't think Ruth that you would like that. Do you understand? Now if you came in with this pre-knowledge and you knew all these things and then you had to add to it by learning your karma, it would not be too good. But you can take it in doses. It does level out. Many times people should not be together because they have finished the debts with each other. So very often you realize people who are in divorce situations, do despise each other after a while and they are collecting new debts.

I— I was not thinking that. If you remember, I was a good doctor in 1618. (A past life "reading" was given to me by Eileen).

E— You are talking about how to help mankind. Then you have to speak to those people programmed for that and you will be able to open up and come to it on a telepathic level.

I— But consciously I don't remember anything I did as a doctor.

E— That is to protect the life you are now using. The soul is what does this, just the soul. Your physical body means nothing to the soul other than it is using it for the lesson the body has to learn. You are all part of learning living. There is not one among you, even if one is born with a terrible illness or is physically incapacitated, who did not have to learn. The soul had to learn how to overcome those obstacles. Then it reaches a point where it says, "it is time to leave." So the human body feels devoid of soul and wants to die, to be separated always from emotional problems.

S— How much concern do the people on the other side have for people who are still in the physical body?

E— Great concern. Even though we are involved with many different lifelines going on in this one plain. When you belong to "us" then we gather the wisdom of knowledge of knowing that you played a role. We understand that love merely is abound, then we go to the living family, the people who feel for us and we go near them and we try to tell them to please don't cry at the game you are playing. Open up to it and know the soul just has to experience it. And we know how much pain you are in. Don't be. It is very difficult for us, but I of course can either feel the emotion if I choose to, or rise above the emotion so perhaps I can get through in a telepathic way and instruct them how to make their lives lighter as to what to do.

I— Is James and Edgar Cayce always around you?

E— Always, Yes. Adieu. (Eileen leaves so James can speak. James enters Marlene's body)

I— Hello, James.(Marlene's voice changes into a deep, raspy male voice)

J— I don't think I want to stay. I just want to say hello to you.

I— Would anyone like to ask James any questions.

J— Not on any subject. Only regarding my brother Jeshua.

I— Does anyone want to know about Jesus?

V— Is Jeshua the same as Jesus? Is Jeshua the one that went into Israel when Moses commanded?

J— You are talking about the song with the wall of Jericho. I am not here to discuss the bible. I am here to discuss Jeshua. If you want to call my brother Jeshua you can call him Jeshua. If you want to call him Joshua, you can call him Joshua. The best name is Jessie, how is that? (Laughter in the room).

V— I want to know if it is true that Jessie studied for a while in India?

J— Yes, why not continue the thought and ask at what age?

I— What age?

339

J— He was fourteen on his first trip to India.

V— Until when?

J— It wasn't continuous in India. We shipped him away with a cousin and he was traveling for about three years, traveling to all foreign countries to learn about their cultures and deities.

I— How old was Jeshua when he died?

J— I would have to say your calendar is a bit different and to translate it into years it would be close to fifty-one or fifty-two.

I— How old was he when he was on the cross?

J— He was in his early thirties.

I— So when he came down from the cross he left. Is this correct.

J— Not completely. We did work on him. The "Essenes" were a fantastic healing group.

I— They healed him.

J— Yes, it took a while. And then they ushered him out to India. He already had friends in many different countries. You must realize the world was not that big then. It was a month's journey to go there.

I— How long did he stay in India?

J— I believe he said that trip was about three and a half years.

I— Did he come back to Qumran?

J— Yes.

I— Did he continue to preach in Qumran?

J— Yes. We disguised him.

I— You had to disguise him because they were looking for him?

J— Everyone thought he was dead. And we wanted to keep up the facade.

S— Did Jeshua actually bring Lazarus back to life or was that a misinterpretation.

J— It is not a misinterpretation. Lazarus' heart had stopped momentarily. You have a name for it in your modern times but there have been plenty of you who have been buried alive, because you did not understand that you can go into a condition with the body that will almost put it into a freeze, like on ice.

S— It is called suspended animation.

J— Thank you.

V— So Jeshua really didn't die on the cross.

J— Oh heavens, no.

V— Years ago I had the experience that I saw Joshua inside of my head.

J— As long as you show him as brown, not white, then you are correct.

V— He didn't have any beard?

J— He did have a beard. We did not have instruments to shave our face. It was unholy for us to shave our hair. I can also tell you my brother did not have blond hair and blue eyes. My brother was a nice man. He was not big in the "good look" department.

S— Does your brother ever communicate to a medium?

J— Never, never

S— Why not?

J— Why would he?

S— Why do you?

J— Because I intend to still proselytize the words of my brother.

V— I am Jewish but the moment my father died, I saw somebody whom I loved very much on a cross being crucified. I have often wondered, is there a connection there?

J— Because even though you became a Jewish lady in this life, you were also in other lives a nun and a very devout Roman Catholic, and you were a great Catholic. You were a Russian Orthodox Christian. So that it is still in that part of the mind that you are connected to feel love.

S— There is a book that was written recently called "A Course In Miracles."

J— That is not recent. It has been out in your town for quite a while.

S— It is alleged, to have been written, in part by your brother.

J— I have no comment. I believe the lady was made of gold and what she brought to all of you was pure gold.

I— James, many thanks for coming forth and speaking with us.

J— I am not feeling too kind tonight. I say it because I am aware that there is a part "here" that has a need to say something as excited, as it will be. May I say it.

I— Please

J— When you think of Jeshua, you think of him on a cross. Why not think of my brother as sun. Why not think of him as love. Why not think of him in passions of love and passion for your life. To put him on a suffering cross hurts my feelings. Can you approach it from a way of thinking that my brother was filled with love and the essence of that love was to announce to the world that you are filled with that love too? Adieu, Adieu, Adieu Goodbye.

(Marlene returns)

I— Welcome back, Marlene.

M— Thank you. (End of session).

11/96

EILEEN GARRETT AND JAMES

(MARLENE SLIPS INTO TRANCE AND JAMES COMES IN)

J— Let me just correct a misguided thought as to who I was. I was a Hebrew, son of Miriam and Joseph. I was the next son born in Egypt three years after my brother Jesus was born. We were Hebrew. We were Hebrew always and we died as Hebrew.

V— We call that first, last and always.

J— Thank you for the personal feed. Eileen is powering me to leave. (James gives the group a blessing and then leaves)

E— I did what he asked. That is something that you have to understand. These are the feelings from "here" (the other side). Hello to all of you and welcome. Now get on with your questions.

I— Is it true that an altered state of consciousness means we are perceiving and acting to the universe as if it were run on a different set of laws and principles than those, which we normally seem to be operating?

E— What you are really asking me is when you finish your mortalness, does the exemplification of thought continue intact with that which you were? Clearly the answer is yes.

S— Eileen, during the time you did your work as a medium, did you ever speak in any foreign languages?

E— I myself, as you know, did speak French fluently. I had to as I lived in France for a long time, and I also comprehended some pieces of foreign languages.

S— You said that you spoke French fluently. Where and when did you learn how to speak French?

E— Well, you do know that even though I was raised in Ireland, and part of my ancestry was there, keep in mind that all people in Europe in those days spoke all languages that made up Europe. Because of that type of necessity, for obvious reasons the languages were always comprehended, even if they were not spoken well. During World War II, I did spend my time in France and I became active and you also know I lost my money there too. During that time frame I was very bored with the thinking of the French people. In order to understand them, they had to comprehend me, but I was an English citizen. It was very difficult, to say the least, to leave. Especially, with the Germans marching in.

S— Did you have any formal school training?

E— When I was age twelve, I went to a formal boarding school in Dublin where languages were taught. Languages at first were difficult for me because I romanticized what I wanted to think of in a language. I loved hearing things. But when I had to sit with an instructor, it was rather difficult and stifling.

S— Do you know anybody that can confirm the fact that you were able to speak French fluently?

E— I would think that if you spoke to Marvin Engels, (he was Editor of Eileen's published newsletter) he would tell you and the same with Alan Angolff, (one of Eileen's writers) that I was able to speak enough of it to converse quite well and also to understand it. That is a fact.

S— I spoke to Marvin Engels about that and he said that it is true that you did know French. When you left your physical body, the experience that you had, was it exactly what you expected?

E— Of course it wasn't. When my oldest son died at the age of two and I watched a misty essence rise out of him, I tried and tried through the years of my life to understand what that was. I still see it and I am certain that it is a shape of part of who we are. When I came "here" the feelings I had of what I had done were easily washed away. I was left with, not the visualization of Garrett, but with the essence of what you resort to as soul. That began to create a thinking for me that resorted in praising of me. It is not to be taken as a self-praised attitude, but when you come "here", in fact, what happens is that you are essence of your soul. The teeny life that you had, as to who you are, was just a little bit of the total soul. You then go into the fulfillment of the completion of who you are. Symbols like colors and geometric shapes and others did mean something in my mortal existence as it does for you. Here you no longer need symbols. You simply have total knowledge, mostly of yourself and the other fragments of you that make the completion of soul. We do not deal in the space-time continuum, but in some ways, we have to deal in special thought, which is much, much more than what you call humanness.

V— Eileen, who were some of the people that helped you in the psychic field?

E— Eileen Garrett, essence of mortalness, was trained early on by the people that she drew into her sphere in England. However, many of you have heard that I played with the essence of the "children" I saw at the age of three. You have to understand that there were three children that I played with. The communication was not called anything other than Eileen having imaginary friends to keep her company. Early on, my symbols were my teacher. I saw in color that the earth was my teacher, the yew tree became a major symbol for me because it did not only accept me as me, but it had no emotion to give back and there were other teachers along the way. There were Hewitt Mackenzie and Conan Doyle. There were tons and tons of things interacting with me. My work with Ira Prokoff proved to be very good. We spent four years together. There were other teachers. There was the Uvani factor and the Abdul factor. There was the Rahma factor (these were three spirits who spoke through Eileen). Some people are not aware of the last two. I worked with Howard Carrington. I worked with so many proud names. I did the dream states, and so on and so forth.

I— Does a person with Alzheimer's disease regain his or her memory when they cross over?

E— What you are talking about is humanness. We are not speaking in terms of humanness. We are speaking in terms of intelligent energy. Intelligent energy has no feeling or deformity. We really are viewed "here" with that overused word, Love. The soul of the Alzheimer patient has perfect memory.

V— Eileen, suppose a person is born in this life completely retarded, and then dies retarded. When he goes to his energy level, does he have a memory of this life?

E— (speaking with certainty) Absolutely, because the intelligent aspect of the fragmentation of him is "here" as soul. That "one life" was here for his lesson and for the soul to elevate and learn the lesson when it again takes on mortal form. It is also a lesson for society at large to comprehend, to have the word compassion and comprehension, and also to eliminate this type of deformity for future existences. That little brave soldier that came here with that deformity grew much quicker and much more proudly than the one who sat back and said, "For the next five lives I am going to have it sweeter than sweet." The choice is always yours.

I— Jenny, what do you do for entertainment over "there?"

E— We play with you. (Laughter) and we recall everything in a way that humors us. We have business here. We do not think in terms of work as you do. We connect to the thinking that relates to the power of love.

I— I am thinking of an entertainer like George Burns. When he crosses over, what will he do? What does Sammy Davis Jr. do?

E— I can tell you when George comes, he will be regarded as "God."(laughter, George Burns played God in a motion picture)

S— Eileen, you mentioned before the name of Ira Progoff. He is an interesting person to me. Could you tell me anything about the kind of tests you did with Dr. Progoff? What was the purpose of those tests? (a researcher of Eileen)

E— I wanted to know about Uvani and Abdul who spoke through me. Ira was kind enough to do experimentation with me using hypnosis many times and also allowing them to come through but they could never be hypnotized. But the personality of me could. The experiments were good in the sense that it allowed me to progress so that my mind as Eileen Garrett was able to do most of the connections to the realm of the soul, if you will, in a more conscious state. I did not always afterwards need the hypnosis.

S— Do you know what Dr. Ira Progroff (researcher) was attempting to do in the work that he did with you? What was he trying to prove?

E— I believe he was trying to prove the truth of the Bible and also what we were about.

S— Was he trying to show that your trance controls were separate from you?

E— That was what we tried to do but he was also very completely aware that it could have been part of me, since I did not understand it myself. The experience of testing allowed me, not necessarily examining it from his point of view, an awareness that if this was part of my subconscious, I would then have to work with it as such. It did not negate the good work. It simply allowed us to examine it in a more truth ful and honest way.

I— Jenny, what was accomplished through testing in the Faraday Cage, (a large copper cage that blocked out external energy waves) the experiments with LSD, and experiments with your brain waves?

E— You are aware that the brain waves did show a difference when I was in the trance state and the pharmaceutical industry was very open to it. I was very devoted to this field so I did not take LSD, as you perceive it. Dr. Progoff was giving me tiny amounts to see whether or not, in certain states, with the use of certain drugs, if we could show that it was part of my mind creating this. It would have been wonderful. It also had its qualitative impressions, which were magnified, and I was able to verbalize these impressions. I can also tell you that under these strict laboratory conditions the essence of Uvani and Abdul came through and told Ira Progoff how to accept it. Think about that. He came through and told them how to accept what he was saying under those strict conditions. That is not in my books. Also keep in mind that I did the dream state in Brooklyn at Mammonides Hospital, which was exciting.

S— Who did you work with?

E— I worked with my doctors including Andriya Paharich. Also that was an experiment that would have gone much further. They really didn't need me for that but it was interesting. It did not prove, other than the fact that in a dream state the mind can accept information and also, what we like to think of as the telepathic level.

S— Did you know an Ingo Swann?

E— Swann was involved in searching out things about me and testing me. You have to understand that many years before that I was involved with a Dr. Sole too. Those tests were also in regard to separating the parts of the mind, to prove that disassociation was at play. By using the faculty of disassociation, the conscious and subconscious mind separated so Uvani could speak.

S— Where did you meet Dr. Sole?

E— This was done when early on we were doing experimentation. It was also during the time when, I am not too certain of the year, I was thirsting to understand the connection there. It was, I believe, when I was also involved with Dr. Rhine, (from the university of North Carolina) and it set off that whole program with Dr. Rhine. A lot of the experiments could not be replicated. In England I went to many doctors, but no one could replicate the experiments of Dr. Harrington. I did work with Harrington in a way that was superb and superior to most others. But it got lost to the world when Anita Muhl's home was broken into.

I— Jenny, did you know Carl Jung?

E— I was impressed with his equalness to my thinking on the connected unconscious thought.

I— Did you participate with him in various experiments?

E— Yes.

I— Can you describe some of those various experiments?

E— It was mainly to put me in a trance like state, deepen the hypnosis and show whether or not the impressive personalities that spoke through me was separate or part of me. You understand, there was never one experiment, including the deal with the Faraday case.

S— Do you remember the experiment that was done with you where an attempt was made to enable you through hypnosis to see from a distance as to what was going on in another place?

E— Yes, but it wasn't hypnosis. What that was is teleportation. We were doing it with somebody, and in that light trance state Uvani came through and we were able to describe the furnishings of a room that the professor asked about. We did long distance teleportation where an out of body experience takes place, or astral travel if you will. We also did mind transference. We then used the terminology called teleportation. The experiment was very good, but how is that any different than the experiment with Hincliffe? (Another experimenter) when I was much younger and you think about it. The communication took place. The reasons for them were different, but it occurred.

S— You used the word teleportation in a very unusual way. Usually when they refer to the word teleportation they mean the actual transfer of the physical body from one place to another.

E— Oh, that is absurd. We are talking in "mind" and your scientist of today should get together and create with their thoughts, an essence.

S— When you refer to teleportation what exactly are you talking about?

E— I am talking about my mind being able to teleport myself to the presence of your home and I am able to tell and feed back what you are doing, what you are wearing, the sensing of what you might be saying.

S— We call that remote viewing.

E— The societies are getting so bogged down with terminology that they are forgetting what the most important thing that is here. It is telepathy on different levels.

V— When James comes through he speaks about religion. Is there religion on the "other side?"

E— We don't have religion. That is a presumption from you. We have no religion "here." What James perpetuates is "what was then" for the sake of those that read the bible. He perpetuates that with sincere love in "Him", his brother Jeshua. He also brings about to all of you with love the correct 100% information of what took place then although we could get quite boisterous about it, since I still have not met God.

You as humans created the reality of "God." It was not the other way around. I know, you still don't accept the aliens as your mommies and papas. They are not Gods, but are essence of soul. Do you not realize that your soul is the collective consciousness of all the existences that you have experienced? Think of this as I told you before, if you are all that soul, don't you realize your soul is the same as the alien that you are.

V— Who is in control, you or James? When Marlene is driving a car, can you take over?

E— James is the focal point of the control. Oftentimes I have a remembrance of what it was to drive a car. My daughter and I drove through the countryside in Europe, mainly France and Germany and places like that. No different than other people. So I will oftentimes want to sit upon Marlene's thinking and her feelings and invade her consciousness and enjoy it. Telepathically I whisper in her mind, "It is my turn dear, let me feel for this." She allows it, and yet it is both ways that I allow it. I must clear up a misconception about the mediumship you are born with. It cannot be learned unless you are born with it. Then you will come to someone like Marlene who will push your buttons and then it will bloom. Channeling as you know today is a taught thing. Mediums can do channeling. Some channelers will become mediums, but no channeler can become a medium if they declare that they want to be, for it is not for them to decide.

V— Was Jesus born from the Immaculate Conception?

E— This answer belongs with James. And you know what his answer was. That more than 88% of the present bible is incorrect. That means that you have a few percentage points left. Of that, whatever Paul gave was correct, but not correct when following Jeshua. What was correct was Paul's inventing, so more than 88% of the modern bible was interpreted after the wisdom of Paul. It should be called the "Paulian" Religion, not Christianity, which is a beautiful religion, and Jeshua loved Paul too.

I— While alive in the physical world were you familiar with the writings of Sir Oliver Lodge, Stuart Edward White, and Madam Blavatsky?

E— You know these people were part of my life. Do you think I did not peek into the Nostradamus book that was given to me? Why do you think I published it? It was a good book.

I— How many books did you publish?

E— (speaking modestly) About forty. Even more I think. I had about ninety in my stack. I can't recall the numbers, but I did good work on at least about forty. With my own personal books, I did not have that many. I believe I wrote the book, "Telepathy" in five weeks.

I— How many books did you write for yourself?

E— I wrote a total of about seven or eight. I had two or three papers also that were written.

I— I found three books that you wrote. "Nonsense" was one.

E— Isn't that a bundle of joy.

I— I enjoyed it.

E— I hope everyone here reads that book.

S— It was a great book.

E— Oh, thank you, Spenser. Great, I like that word. I don't suffer from taking praise "here." You have to understand I gave up writing and became a publisher. I knew nothing about the publishing industry, so I learned, and boy, what a joy.

V— Jenny, do you use any other person as a medium?

E— No.

V— You once mentioned that your Abdul Latif would come back as someone else. What does he have to do to prepare?

E— It is simply what you will have to do when you come "here." The preparation really regards what it is you have to grow into, a miserable life or a winning life. When I use the word miserable, keep in mind that no life is miserable. It is all taken as a lesson for a soul journey. I will not divulge Abdul's course, but I will only say that, for me, the enjoyment will be to connect to exactly what I am doing here again. I will come back and connect to "mind thought", but I will have the advantage of advanced computers.

S— When you were in your physical body, did you ever consider the possibility that you would be doing this kind of work in somebody else's body?

E— (responding with nostalgia) I questioned it for me and I was not certain what was occurring. I felt that we go through life only once. I did not buy into reincarnation. I did not buy into the connecting of this kind of feeling. I felt I wanted to do other things. My thought of the life that I believed I saw, the brilliance, the colors, the shapes, the knowing of unusual love, which was the greatest factor involved, was eagerly awaiting me and I would find myself "there" experiencing it. I am also conducting what we call a séance for you.

V— Eileen, can we all look forward to possibly doing that when we pass on?

E— Much more than that. For instance, if you would like to sit among the greatest scientist in creation, you would only have to say, I need to grow from so many thoughts and you would create that reality and you would enjoy it.

V— Jenny, is it possible that if someone suffers pain it is because they did bad things or sinned?

E— That is part of the evilness of the men who interpreted the bible and the bigger shame is that they listened to those words and caused great harm to humankind.

S— Eileen, is there such a thing as soul mates?

E— (reflects for a moment) I know that the great Dr. Bryan Weiss is presently involved with that thinking but I will temper the thought by saying that those of you who are attracted to another being, male or female, or even animals, and you just know that you spent time together, what you are really referring to is the fact that you experienced different lifetimes with that soul. That is all it is. It doesn't necessarily mean that it was a loving or endearing or a productive lifetime. You could have had that same passion with somebody who has been absolutely cruel to you in this lifetime or a past lifetime or a future lifetime. But the interesting thought upon that will be when the people begin to project into that future life or the fragmented part of their mind which is already simultaneously experiencing their future life while they are still who they are. Hypnosis will embark upon that and it will be much more exciting because you will be able to prove it.

S— With regard to predictions, there is a lot of material in the field of parapsychology, especially in the situation where a person has had a dream that appears to be a future event or possible disaster and because they had that dream were able to avoid it. You mentioned that the future from your point of view is fixed.

E— I am not saying you do not have free choice or will. In fact we are saying that you do. I am saying, even that word that we use to describe the "knowing before hand", to prevent the occurrence was predetermined.

S— By whom?

E— (without hesitation) Yourself. If you seek out a sensitive and the sensitive tells you, "Do not walk under this place because a safe is going to crack your head open," obviously, you are going to avoid it. Part of the program, the map-out in you life, was to seek out the sensitive to get the information. If you did not seek out the sensitive to get that information and got hit on the head with the safe, that would have been your undoing, but when you are "here" you would learn that because you were not open enough to comprehend quick cognitive events, you paid the price. Because you will label it as Oh!, it saved my life because if I had not known I would have been dead. Nonsense, it was supposed to happen like that!

I— From the "other side" how are you able to keep up with what is going on in the physical world all the time?

E— Via this female (Marlene), and my family (daughter and grandchild) when I choose to be with them. I don't always want to be there because it becomes a thought really linking it to my sensing of emotions and it is much neater to sense the emotions. But anyone can when they are "here." Most of us are above that feed unless of course you die tragically. Then you are still dwelling in the emotional pool of what occurred and weeping and other things of a sad nature that occurred, including if you are murdered. You will be angry but you will rise above that for your lesson has been grief. Do you understand me. Murder creates the lesson of grief.

V— You know there is a controversy about cremation.

E— That is because of religion. To those of us "here", we do not feel the burning of the body in cremation. Nor do we feel the rodents and cockroaches eating us. But I am being open here and I am tall enough to comprehend it. So if you wish to donate your organs, by all means do. You have no further use for them. And that is an elevation of man's journey. And keep in mind with the elevation of that journey, those of you who freely do that, don't look upon burial cremation as anything other than liquidation of the mortal body. It must go somewhere.

I— In looking into the future, can you see whether mankind will donate their organs automatically?

E— Mankind will eventually. We are going many hundred years into the future, where mankind will be able to rebuild their bodies, but mankind will never be able to regenerate the mind. Anything of matter and the physicality can be regenerated.

S— There are people who feel that it is important for their bodies to be frozen and that sometime in the distant future they could be brought back to life because at that time medical science will be much more advanced. Do you consider this a possibility?

E— (assertively) Absolutely, yes.

S— What is happening to the soul in this period of time?

E— It is busy doing what it has always been doing. It is experiencing its other lifetime.

357

S— But can it reincarnate if there is a possibility of the body coming back to life.

E— Of course it can. You should comprehend the thought here, which stresses simultaneousness. We do not deal in time "here" as you do. The soul of mine in which I am privileged to have had the Garrett life is given that point in time when I was Garrett through this woman called Marlene. Yet, I am also enjoying the lifetime of a different life. Do you understand me even as I speak here? Fragments of a pie. The central part, the nucleus is the core, the soul. The many different parts of that soul, the wheel if you imagine it in your mind's eye are the many different lifetimes that you are existing in as we speak.

V— You say the mind cannot be regenerated. I want to differ with you on that.

E— The brain is different than the mind. We are not talking brain. The mind is that which we call the connective force of living. We are not speaking brain.

V— Are you speaking soul?

E— If you choose that term we accept it.

V— You say our organs will regenerate.

E— Yes, speaking of the physical side of mankind.

V— In other words, if the brain is destroyed by disease, humans, may someday rebuild the brain.

E— Absurd, because the brain will be that part which will always have to deal and connect to mind. Mind will not allow immortality because mind must dwell in soul. Your terms of living will be different and in the future the people will not look like you. You will have bigger heads and more hair. So enjoy your furnishings and your pretty clothes now.

I— Jenny, when are you coming back?

E— I have mentioned that I was going to come back between 2204 or 2208. I am already leading that life which is my passion with my personal feelings.

I— How can you be living that life if you are not back here on earth?

E— Because there is no time for us "here" and this is already that time there. I wish just to say that I am studying the passion of a perfect flower.

I— Jenny, if I live to 2010 and you are back here in 2204, I will not be able to interview you.

E— Why not?

I— Because, you will not be coming through Marlene?

E— Well, I will still be talking "here." But I will not be what your conception of me is and all of us "here." Is it not correct? When the soul reincarnates, it does not mean that its wholeness goes into that one life. It means that the fragmented part of the nucleus of who you are resides in that life to experience its lesson.

I— So how many fragments are there?

E— As many as need be required to exemplify all that man creates, so that in each society you create many additional thoughts.

I— Could I come back as Chinese or Russian?

E— Of course, you have already had these feelings.

I— Do I make up my own mind as to what I want to be?

E— Certainly, down to the very, very fine-tuning of who your mom will be.

I— Who set that up, I don't remember that.

E— Well, because your conscious mind now cannot adapt to that way of thinking and it would not be too happy to dwell on that, otherwise you would not be living your life to it's potential.

I— If I go into hypnosis can someone find out these things about where I am going to be in the future?

E— (excitedly) It is possible, why not. Do it. Did I not say earlier that the wonderful experiments that will be done will take place by using the technique of hypnosis to project into future lifetimes that are concurrent with you present life. Think of it, wow!

I— As it pertains to Marlene, can I take her into the future as to when she will meet you again.

E— Marlene is already in that life and she is already using me to speak through and I am speaking to her.

I— (puzzled) I mean when Marlene passes over.

E— That is what I am talking about.

I— Very interesting.

E— No, you are confused.

V— You say we are living this life and also living a future life.

E— As many as you must crave to learn from.

V— Will there ever be a time when you no longer have to be incarnated.

E— Yes.

V— How will you know when that time comes?

E— You will know because you will no longer need mortalness. When you learn everything there is to know, you will then go back to the oneness of creation.

S— And there is no need to reincarnate.

E— Correct.

V— What happens then?

E— You are the sun then you are your universe. You are the sky, you are everything.

V— Will we still have a mind?

E— Absolutely, Yes.

I— Who has reached that state already?

E— You have. That part of you is already in that perfection.

S— Eileen, you know that the universe is tremendously vast. You know, it is much vaster than it was 300 years ago when our conception of the universe was limited.

E— No, it was only limited by man's thinking. It has always been the same size.

S— Do you have any idea where the nearest area in our universe exists where life and intelligence is similar to ours?

E— Not in human form. You have Uranus and you have Saturn. (Alvin Leary as Noran in the front of this book mentions that he came to earth from the planet Uranus)

S— What kind of life would be there?

E— A little bit better than Mars, but not in human form. The capability of connecting to it is greater. Adieu everyone.

(End of tape.)

12/96

CONTACT WITH MY DECEASED GIRL FRIEND

AND

A PICTURE OF THE FUTURE

S— (Speaking to Marlene who is not in trance.) When you do this type of work, are you aware of losing consciousness?

M— (without boasting) First of all when I do this kind of work I am not aware of losing consciousness and when I go to sleep I am not aware of losing consciousness. One refers to just being tired enough to go to sleep, the other refers to doing this work where I am absolutely, positively surrendering, all thoughts or as much as possible in my creative conscious mind to allow something else to take place. You are hearing what that other is. And it happens sometimes spontaneously. Oftentimes, I joke around and I tell you I feel her driving my car with me and I know I can't do that left turn and before I know it we are around where we have to be. There are many things I personally have witnessed, have participated in, have experimented with and have come up with. Using a positive and negative thought, they have come up only positive. But I am a skeptic. I am probably my worst enemy when it comes to this work. I am not eager to throw all my marbles in but I do believe that something exists beyond us. What that is, is undefined.

I— Marlene, how do you answer the fact that when I spoke to you on the phone, Eileen came through and told me something that I alone knew? (A personal item that only my dead fiancée and I knew about)

M— That is correct. I answered that and it still is in a questionable state. That does not prove survival. It does not prove survival if one of your dearly departed comes through and gives you accurate information or a shade closer to accurate information. All that says to me is that something is working on a high telepathic level and connecting and giving answers. I cannot yet give a definitive answer. I don't know. I know that something takes place. Everybody is eager to say, "This is who it is." I cannot honestly do that. I can only hear the occurrence.

V— What has to happen to make you believe that this is all real? What evidence are you seeking that will convince you.

M— There is probably no evidence known to mankind that I can think of currently that would make me believe that. I do have little presentings and big presentings once or twice a month that I know is not of me. I have evidence of knowing things like that, but I am still not eager to say, "This is what is occurring." And I have seen channelers and so called mediums and I have walked away ad nauseum wanting to say, "Oh God, protect me from my brother." And this is the truth. I do not like to feel that I am part and party to the charlatans out there and I am very steadfast and very straightforward. I want you all to be happy. I want you all to have a good experience. I cannot explain the occurrence other than knowing that something has happened. That's where I'm at. I may change. Sometimes I have full belief and there are days where I say, "Oh yes this is such bull."

S— How do you explain some of the experiences you've had where you have seen apparitions, so called ghosts?

M— I call that second sight. I was born that way. It is a freak of nature, an oddity.

S— What are these oddities?

M— They are ghosts. They look like you and then they fade out. Is there a portion of ones mind that can hallucinate? Of course there is. How do I know whether or not it is hallucination? I am used to door knobs turning, smoke clouds occurring and other people sharing this kind of phenomena with me. But I still say something exists after us. What is it? I don't know. I am calling it an intelligent energy form. But I don't like to use the word "dead." It is not a dead thing. That is why I phrased it that way. It is not a death that we are talking about. I think this is work that belongs in a laboratory and I am honored to know that I am an oddity that should be in a laboratory.

I— How were you able to talk to animals?

M— I have no idea. And how do I know that the conversation was right? Because the owner of the animals verified it. There again, is not telepathy in play? How many times have you sensed or said something to people who own animals, that the animal feels this way and the animal says this or that.

V— That is true.

M— Don't be too quick to rush to judgment. Be positive. Keep an open mind.

(The group begins to sing "Irish Eyes Are Smiling" to help Marlene slip into trance so that Eileen Garrett can come through.)

E— (Eileen enters) Hello, everybody (speaking in her Irish lilting voice.) I realize that plenty of thoughts, are created by thinking a thought and I won't be giving you tongue twisters today but I want you to know there are presents for you in the openness of your thinking. There are feelings here about authenticity. That is fine. Remain heightened by your thinking and even though you may be accountable for what you think, you are actualizing the thinking and presenting it as a word. I am telling you that you have to relate to your thinking. If you do you will clearly open up to who it is that I am. If you don't you will allow yourself to go off and think silly thoughts that I am neither here nor there. I am energy with the connective collected conscious thinking. That is what we are. Do you understand and comprehend what I just said. I am intelligent energy with connected collective thinking. That is no mystery "here." Now, if you ask me to rephrase it I would simply say, "Existence of what you call mortal self exists." We do not deal in your space-time continuum. We do deal in spacial time to bring a thought connection to you. But it is not other than your spacial time.

I— I believe Eileen is Eileen who she says she is and is coming from the "other side."

E— That is good because I am who I say I am.

I— I believe that James is there.

E— Oh thank you, he says thank you too.

I— I believe that your time is different than ours.

E— We don't deal in time. There is no space continuum here.

I— What makes your side different from ours?

E— We don't have a clock. Everything is spontaneous. When we create a thought it exists.

I— If this is all true, is my fiancée Rose who died a month ago over "there"?

E— We did speak with her.

I— She is over "there"?

E— Yes, she is.

I— Is it possible since I never said good-bye to her to be able to talk with her?

E— You did say good-bye to her.

I— Then she never said good-bye to me

E— She did say good-bye to you.

I— I did not hear it.

E— That is because you are a bit thick. But she said good-bye.

(The day Rose slipped into a coma, and taken to the hospital, I sat by her bed, held her hand and spoke to her the entire evening even though she could not answer. Before I left, I said goodbye to her.)

I— Is there any way you can bring her through that I can speak with her.

E— Rose is with you right now. She has not been away from you. The memories that you have of the female have created an even greater bond between you. She is not ready to rescind her hold on you and she said that you better remember that she was the best. She said, "Don't go harping around with a bunch of females because she can still pick up a frying pan."

I— But she said to me to go out and find another woman.

E— She also said to you, while the two of you were hot, that if you ever looked at another woman she would kill you. And dump you in the garbage can. She was very particular as to where your eyes went.

I— Can you tell me whether I can ask her a question?

E— I cannot guarantee that she is capable of conversation.

I— Why not?

E— Because she is still not sure of doing this, she was sure of this in living her mortal life. She sure is not open to it "here." Because we are together she is very ambivalent in her thinking and she does not yet understand that all she has to do is release it and say, "Tell him." But she is not ready to do it and I did tell you that the last time we spoke.

I— Is Rose angry, because she was taken away from me?

E— No, in fact she says that she is not taken away. She is actually a very good spy now.

I— Spy on whom?

E— You. She is teasing. You must understand the humor "here". And it comes out dry but the chocolate now and then is appreciated. The only thing Rose says is please don't fabricate a tale about her. Think of her as a feeling of light and think of her in terms of connecting to God for she says she is sensing something sweet near her. That is now where she's at. I can also tell you, from my knowing, that when she lets go from the Rose aspect of her life, she will indeed communicate freely.

I— Do you have any idea when?

E— I cannot give a time. I have no understanding of the time that she is referencing and seeing.

R— (who is a healer) When did you take part in the mediumship circle in England?

E— I did not take part in it like that. I was not what you would call anything other than being trained early on and the things that were available then were not really mediumship circles. It was like a group of people who got together to get messages. But it is good that you think that, because it has references to the spiritualist thought that you and many friends are participants in. And I will say that a lesson will soon come to you and to others who do participate in your chapels metaphysically or otherwise. I cannot give you the lesson but I will say, open up your hearts and understand that when you are ready to separate the chaff from the wheat you will have the answers you need, but don't be fooled because someone is on a pulpit. Especially, don't be fooled by the whole metaphysical movement that you have in your shoppers today, because that is without a doubt sometimes the biggest hurt going to mankind. I alone had hopefully protected myself all my life from helping the coo-coos out there, and if you bring coo-coos to you, you will be associated with them. I suggest, most respectfully, take your wisdom and your talent to where it can be recognized for what you do, which is healing, and it is wonderful what you do. Don't give in to the swine, as you say, when they scorn you. Give it to people who love you, respect you and have great admiration for you. You do not have to prove your worthiness Ruth. You are among the greatest hands on healers. And I am telling you that.

S— Eileen, how do you feel about the prospect of speaking to Marvin Engels (worked 12 years as Eileen's editor in her publishing business) in the near future?

E— We enjoy that prospect because he will be able to have a conversation with me that will recollect the time when I gave him a job.

S— Do you feel you remember sufficiently?

E— No, I think I recall some things. What it is I have to do is to go back into that time frame and I don't want to feel the emotions of the time for there were times when I myself was in such doubt doing this work that I have no way of assuming things. Marvin is a beautiful man with a kind heart and I certainly would regard his feelings first and I do assume that he will not reject me as to who I say I am. That is a normal, natural assumption to make. I further feel because of the discrepancies that we have put forth, some beliefs you can understand and some to stir your minds; you would become more fierce in your questioning of me. I do feel that until the proper approaches are made, I can no longer feed into curious things. Oh, I have shocked you. Marvin is a treat for my existence but I do feel until he opens up to knowing that, I have to consider my speaking in this way. I have dropped most of the Irish accent. (Eileen had been trying for years to speak the way she did when in physical form) And I am trying to manifest the real Garrett's visions so that those things that he shared with me will just be between us. I hope to bring forth some information that was completed personally between us, and I can also tell you that the man is a very worthy man. He doesn't need me. I know what his thoughts are and the subject matter, and he was often telling me to rest a bit. And I still am not resting, am I?

S— What kind of work would be valuable in furthering the cause of parapsychology and psychical research? What do you think needs to be done?

E— My feelings haven't really changed too much. If science, religion, and psychologists work hand in hand to create the unison that is needed, then we would have a subject matter, for instance, like Ruth or people who are gifted, and we would learn about them from all three aspects. We would allow the scientists to probe hand in hand to comprehend the analysis that would be produced, which you understand I was trained to do. Along with that, we would find out why they feel for God, the creator of man. So it would be the three shields in unison through a fusing of thoughts that will lead to comprehension and thus create an environment that is conducive for greater research and findings coming from the research.

I— Eileen, can you remove the pain and suffering of an individual?

E— We "here" cannot interfere with the many steps that you take to have the enjoyment and suffering in your lives. Remember, the understanding and knowledge to make a healthier you comes from the sorrows and the suffering you must endure. For you are then blessed with joys and happiness.

R— Eileen, did Annie Benant (deceased psychic) have the same idea on thought as you?

E— No, Ann Benant had her own way of dealing with her ability, and so did Mrs. Piper (deceased psychic) and others. They were involved in a manner that was conducive to the environment that they had to live in. And I can guarantee you Ruth, that many of the ideas that they have formed since they are "here", are created by what they didn't know then.

I— Don't you need a full name to determine who the spirits are?

E— (deliberately conversational) No, I prefer no name at all. Let them learn and grow and reach a level of comprehension that they can tell me who they are. As I was a teacher of this in thought, in my physical life, I am still that way "here." When I am presenting myself to you in the Garrett thought, I can thus create the environment for it. But I want you understanding it in your thinking. You must raise your thinking to comprehend that I was used as a telephone wire, but for Marlene it is difficult. She is not as perceptive as I was.

I— Are you teaching "over there"?

E— I am teaching Marlene's class here.

I— I mean do you teach anyone on "that side."

E— We have measured thought that is called teaching. We don't piddle "here". We are quite busy.

S— Do you have any sense of touch.

E— Through Marlene I can touch.

S— On the other side?

E— No, we don't have anything related to your mortalness.

S— How do you recognize one another?

E— With thought. It is annoying. Ask a sensitive and they will tell you the same. It is a knowing. It is even better "here" because we don't need what the visions of your eyes need to see, but it is simply of the mind seeing. So the mind is connecting to the thinking of this personality or that personality. We do recall what you have as memories but it is on a level that is complicated for you to comprehend.

V— Eileen, when someone passes over, do they have some kind of orientation on your side?

E— (burst of laughter) Oh, wouldn't that be delightful. Orientation is not how you perceive it, but it is a wonderful idea. I will put in a good word for thinking for orientation to the universe so when all of you come "here" you will be oriented. It is a wonderful thought. Some one "here" just said "Dankeshein." I will also tell you that the people "here", if I may use that concept of the collected connective consciousness for a brief moment and call "us" people, the people "here" are not saying that they didn't exist as a human being. They are saying that it is sometimes hard to seek. They are saying they never knew they could talk. They are saying, I didn't even know I was "here." Imagine that. You've been fed and read books that whenever you pass over, that all of a sudden you are brilliant. It doesn't happen like that. Orientation! We are going to have that. I think I will invent a giant thought called Orientation and hang it over the universe, for comprehension must take place.

R— Eileen, you had said previously that things occur in cycles.

E— No, what I told you Ruth, if you read my work, is that it was my mortal thoughts. That many things came in cycles and all human beings know that they feel they do, and often the cycle is finished. Then you go into another level of perhaps a better way of life for personal reasons and of course to the connection with the Universe. "Here" we do not think of that in those terms. In fact when you say cycles, I am immediately thinking of my spindle so that cycle or cyclonic has a different meaning for me "here." It only refers to a time period that I shared in the Garrett life and was able to connect to the spindle effect and how it opened up a broader and broader understanding along with the symbols that were part of my existence.

For each one "here" it is difficult at a level of comprehension to expand a thought about giving more than what you are supposed to have, for we understand we can only give that which you are able to comprehend. Oftentimes I give you a bit more and you do not comprehend what I am telling you. It is never wasted but it is put into your subconscious and then when it is time for you to remember, you like feed it slowly to your thought., similar to planting a seed in ones mind. We haven't yet gotten to subliminal thinking. The art of giving is very, very impolite and we apologize for that. But keep in mind we cannot stick to your accurate thoughts sometimes.

S— Do you think that automatic writing is a better way to communicate?

E— In the early part of the thirties, I worked with Dr. Anita Muhl and Herewood Carrington, When I worked with Dr. Muhl I was able to do the automatic writing. I certainly was aware of its existence. I felt that what it did achieve for me was to understand things that perhaps were in my own subconscious mind, that were brought forth to a conscious level. Perhaps when I thought about a pre-destined thinking, I had to realize that I was indeed giving information that was part of a connected consciousness from Dr. Muhl. From where I am now, that is something I did think about. Remember I was always analyzing. I was always open to research and always experimenting with the thoughts connected to the subconscious.

S— The reason I bring this up is that there is a book out in the market that I heard about. It is called "Conversations With God" and presumably God is speaking through the Automatic writing of the individual who is asking the questions.

E— (chuckles) Isn't that interesting, to have an individual pipeline to God. I think that is superb, and all of you have it too.

The power there based upon whether it is truth or not, let us grant that it is true, has to be beautiful and correct, so it is accepted as an act of beauty. Ladies and gentlemen, life continues, not how you think we are, but we do continue. And one day we will show you how much we care for you by showing you your own life "here."

I— In relationship to earth where is this place you call home?

E— That is an excellent thought. "Home" is where my thoughts are. Right now my thoughts are in here, in this female I am presenting myself through. Being in this home is where my presence is. Thus, I would say for an accurate answer this is me. I am her. I am Jennette Garrett. I am her. I am never out of the connection of the mind that we had to plant in her. I can no longer be away from her existence. But, even if she is not even thinking of me, I have my world of thought here. Energy formed matter cannot be created nor destroyed. We continue as an intellectual thought that recalls everything if we are open to remembering. Including in that thought is that thinking is paradise. We are perfection "here." There is no illness "here." No family squabble. We are of one thought, that created thinking connects to you. That is how it is done.

I— That is perfection?

E— Of course, we can only be perfect.

I— Then why would someone want to reincarnate to suffer again?

E— Because the gentle thinking on a mortal life is an actual presentation to the soul. When the presentation is to the soul, which I call the connected consciousness, what occurs is, it is understood that only through these simple journeys of life where you are able to have sensing and heartache and joy that the soul can elevate itself to even greater perfection.

I— You said we are perfect already.

E— (vigorously) Absolutely, but for that one soul to have it's perfection it has to occur almost simultaneously, because we did exist in your time space continuum, almost simultaneously As souls, we are already perfect because we have already had every life there is to have and will be. Understand it as a simplistic thought. I, Garrett have already had all lives guaranteed to be perfect but I am speaking to you only from my life as Jeanette Garrett. Did you get it right? You knew exactly where I was coming from. I would sit where you are and I'd say, "Well if that were so, then why bother living." The reason why you bother to have a life and I can tell you from "here" is because even though you are perfection "here", I am coming to you not from that one perfect soul but from a fragmented part of it's many lives it had to have. As a human being you come back to your existence for the soul benefit of having the perfection. You have young souls "here." You have ancient souls "here." The ancient souls return to what you think of as God connection, total oneness. But I guarantee you, it takes many journeys for your mortalness before you relinquish completely any attachment with humanness. I, Garrett, loved and valued human life as I did the planet I lived upon. I, Garrett, guarantee you that you will open up to what I just told you. I guarantee it. So relax your mind and for those of you who are stuck in thinking of me as an elevated light, I thank you. I accept it. And for those of you who do not, I cannot tell you how you are to obey your thinking, but I offer you the thought of thinking about how it is for me to connect to you. And it is just the same way for you. So connect to me.

V— I have a question from somebody else. This person wants to know why is it that time goes so fast?

E— I can't answer that. That is the person's own feeling. I cannot answer as to what that person feels about their life. I can offer educated guesses but I cannot assume the answer is correct.

V— How about an educated guess?

E— An educated guess is that when one is having a fulfilled life, whether it is part suffering or joy, then every day is measured as not being enough because you want more and you have to go more into it. If you are of the nature of giving you do not have enough time in the day to accomplish your thinking about what to do next. Usually those who are suffering are internalizing or they are in a situation where they are depressed. They don't even have the concept of time. But many others who tend to feel hedonistic and have too much time on their hands don't know what to do with it. They don't know where to put their creative thinking to enhance their life or other peoples lives, and those people usually say, "What am I going to do now and how am I going to kill a day, instead of saying, "How may I make this day perfect."

I— Eileen can you go into the future to 2005 and tell me if passenger aircraft have changed and in what way?

E— Electric cars will definitely be a thing of the future. There will also be hovercrafts which travel over land. Aircraft's will remain pretty solid the way they are but will find another kind of fuel to use.

I— Will there be an increase in the number of people on board the plane.

E— In 25 years there will be a definition of what is constituted as a flying bird. It will change.

V— I read about that in time magazine. They mentioned the new type of cars that are coming out, electric steered cars, which will be programmed to take you where you want to go on separate types of highway. The Japanese are a little ahead of us in that type of car. What the world has not opened up to is conflict and jealousy.

E— In the future, jealousy is something that will be disappearing according to the journey of what has to be learned by each person. Conflict is something that will exist out of creative thoughts because man is unwilling to relinquish what he has gained. He is not too eager to share.

I— Will religion ever disappear?

E— (with emphasis) Going way into your future, definitely, of course. Everyone understands eventually that the religious clubs will be called only clubs. Let us not get into agnostic versus anti-agnostic issues.

I— I am just thinking of all the religions that kill each other for no reason like the Irish Catholics and Protestants.

E— They don't call the Irish other than wonderful little darlings.

I— Aren't they fighting the Catholics over there?

E— It is more political than religious. They have always used the religion as the excuse. It is politics over territory.

I— But they still are killing each other.

E— Of course, and it won't last too much longer. It is not beyond grandparents to do it. It is for mankind to grow, connect to it

377

collectively. Do not deny the sensing of soul "here" to connect to a greater awareness of growing. Suffering is part of the accepted form of growing. The connected collective consciousness of man thus becomes elevated so that they no longer need the pain that they had to endure. Think of a futuristic society in which the pain of man will exist no more.

I— And no more wars will exist. Is that coming in the future?

E— Your wars will be only a thought and how to adjust to a greater power. The mind will equal out a thought and the brain capacity of thinking will increase. I also told you that your physiology, you physicality will change. You will not look the way you do. Your heads will be greater and your bodies will have more hair on it. Enjoy the fashions that you create today for in your future, future, future, future and then some, there will be no need for what you call clothing.

S— Why is that?

E— Because you will not need garments to protect you from the harshness of your universe. Your earth will go through multitudes of climatic change and a new star is coming to your land. And this will create problems that you have never existed under, although you have, because you are all "here" with me too, as we speak. The new star will be called a planet and the human eye will be able to see it, but it will not come about without major shifting in the poles. But I will save that for another discussion.

I— Who was Anita Muhl?

E— Anita Muhl was such a good teacher, a patient doctor. (She did experimenting with Eileen.) She was working with the emotionally disturbed in California and the one feature about her was gentleness and patience. I still feel that anyone who came into her path had to benefit. Some of the work with her that I started to tell you about was in regard to allowing the thinking from the subconscious to come forth. What it did for me on a personal level was to bind my work on a conscious level and it also prepared me to combine the major understanding of me as a human being. There was a lot of analysis going into these things. so it was not the act of automatic writing. I am also speaking of Hereward Carrington. For it is a story that combines feeling of the psychoanalytical point of view of what the old conscious stored and it was discussed through automatic writing. One can help themselves through automatic writing, especially those who are mentally unstable or diseased.

S— If someone was to say to you that what I am hearing is not Eileen Garret.

E— I agree 100%. I would not even doubt it.

S— So if a person says that this was nothing more than a secondary type personality, you would agree with him.

E— No

S— Tell me why?

E— I have no way here of opening up Marlene to the real Garrett personality. I can only come through because James allows me to speak here. James is the control, if you will, and I am here because I am still of the thought of Garrett's thinking in the work. I can tell you the difference and a second personality is definitely not part of her existence. I am who I am;,separate from her, which is something I just recently tried to prove to myself in my life. There were many journeys to take, disciplines to follow, and many tests to complete before I came to any conclusion, and as you know, in my physical life, I had many. But I will say that Marlene here has no other personality involved with her thought. I intend to work through her and to exemplify the work that I was doing when in the physical. Not the test to prove whether or not dates or people I knew or this person's life or that person's life is too much to talk about but mainly because, the only way to show it, is to also have the electro magnetic field test. When I had it tested I was delighted and when she has it tested, she will be delighted. She does not have, what I commonly call the split-off personality. I, for many years believed that the entity speaking through me was nothing more than some part of my subconscious mind. I guarantee you that I sense you and you sense me. If you say a secondary personality is mine that I am presenting to you, I can only tell you that when I have my correct way of talking, then you will appreciate some of my wit. I hate to say it but it is difficult, at best, speaking through sickness.

S— You had a very good sense of humor. (He knew Eileen from having met her personally when she was physical.)

E— (wistfully) I certainly did. I thought I did and my sense of humor was always there. When I cared for someone, I cared 100%. If I believed in you, I was with you 100%, but when I didn't like you I always stayed away 100%. I was not so much opinionated. I had no time for nonsense. Oftentimes, it led, on quest, to simply examine myself even deeper. So you understand that those feelings are part of Marlene's feelings too, for it is not an easy thing to be compounded by my personal feelings.

V— Can you give us a thought or idea and an easy way to open the seven houses or glands to pass our energy through to reach a higher consciousness?

E— I believe you are already there. You put into motion your belief system to produce something that will allow it. You know when you think of yourself out of yourself, present a double of yourself to look at, and when you present a vision of which you would love to look like, you are faced with reality when you look in the mirror. So when you look back in the mirror and you see your own proud reflection, feel for that which your soul chose to learn with. You are already on what you deem a higher consciousness level. You could not be talking to me if you weren't open to your chakras and if you feel you have to do it that way and examine your kundalini and unclog the piping, then do so.

V— Has the energy in the earth changed in the past 10 years, and if the earth is a magnet and we, as human beings, are also attracted to the earth, when the energy in the earth changes will the energy in the human body change?

E— (a long pause) That's a good question. I don't think human beings will be affected greatly because everything will be changing together but it will be equal to what it is now. Of course you will have to deal with the scientists and talk about gravity. The heat that is given off will be enough for you to live with. It will not be bad. I am going to give you a clue and maybe in some greater way you will understand me. If you do not understand then it would definitely be my thinking that is limited here. I am not a scientist nor do I think on those terms. I can only offer you a suggestion about turning in to what your belief system is and the answers will come. That is not a cop-out. That is to make you aware and now here is the hint. As you create the feeling about your humanness, thus your earth will be created to accommodate it. And that goes for everyone. But as a hint, I cannot go further because that is where you have to accept it. I cannot say, "Fear not" because certainly if I heard this I would say, "I fear plenty." but not to be alarmed, and I never was an alarmist, I would resent it if someone left here thinking that I gave information that would offend you.

V— How is it that on the "other side", since you don't have a body, you can tell the difference between man, woman, and animal?

E— Each one of us has a vibration in us, not to be used in the terms that you call vibe but literally an energy vibration that continues and it is an intellectual understanding, a thought.

E— The message that is universal for those of you who wanted a message and didn't get it from your so called relative "here" or enemies, is that only one word exists here for us and we do live by it, and it's called love. And the love has the emotion of every emotion we ever exemplified in our humanness.

Ladies and Gentlemen, I thank you for your patience and time. Remember, you are in a working light and that means you have to give back to your life a big hug and hope. Think about it.

Open up the brilliance of your thinking and allow the wisdom to pour in. Adieu.

(Eileen leaves and Marlene returns)

EPILOGUE

There are many skeptical people who have read this book. Because of their belief, they do not permit themselves to open their minds to the possibility of life after death. My research challenges most conventional beliefs that are based upon rigid ideas and close-minded thinking. However, I find that when an incident is verified in the present-life or in a past life in which only that person and the deceased party were familiar with, then the close-minded thinking seems to disappear. For example: If someone close to you has died and a psychic medium tells you of an incident that only you and the deceased person did or acted upon when he or she was alive, the set idea of death that you possessed seems to disappear. Or you may have a belief that you will never be able to ride on roller skates, but you will know that you can do it by putting on a pair of skates, wobble and fall a few times and suddenly find that you can balance yourself and you are able to skate. Once you have experienced roller-skating, you will never believe again that it is impossible.

Another study that is related to reincarnation is a phenomenon known as xenoglossy, the speaking and writing in foreign languages. Some regresses, who are reliving previous lives, seem to be able to speak and write in languages that they do not know in their present life. Ian Stevenson, Professor at the University of Virginia, who made a life-long study of reincarnation, mentions the fact that responsive xenoglossy, in which the speaker is able to converse spontaneously in a foreign language with another is a skill that cannot be transmitted either normally or para-normally from one person to another. It must be learned the hard way through practice. Alvin Leary spoke and wrote in sixteen different languages, yet quit school, in the tenth grade.

I believe, based on my research, that the soul is immortal, but we will never know until man creates the machine that will make the soul visible. We are born to be reincarnated again and again depending on your enlightenment and moral purification. Sherwood Eddy, author of "You Will Survive After Death" writes that he frankly admits that there is not only triviality and contradiction, but fraud and trickery in the psychic field. In this book, I have based my belief on my personal experiences. Everything you have ever learned is like this. It comes from life's experiences, but when it happens to you, THEN YOU BELIEVE. "YOU WILL NEVER DIE", is it fact or fiction?

About the Author

Irvin Mordes is a very provocative, knowledgeable, compassionate and thoroughly trained certified hypnotherapist. He studied at four schools of hypnosis in the United States and one school in Montreal, Canada. He graduated in psychology from the University of Baltimore.

Mr. Mordes is an expert in the field of past life regression and also helping clients eliminate their problems of smoking, weight, anxieties, fears, improving in sports and every day problems.

He is a lecturer and has appeared on TV and radio. His book "You Will Never Die" is the result of extensive research into the field of reincarnation for the past forty years.

Printed in the United States
72332LV00003B/14

9 781410 766137